Thomas Allin

**Universalism Asserted as the Hope of the Gospel**

On the Authority of Reason, the Fathers, and Holy Scripture. Sixth Edition

Thomas Allin

**Universalism Asserted as the Hope of the Gospel**
*On the Authority of Reason, the Fathers, and Holy Scripture. Sixth Edition*

ISBN/EAN: 9783337091347

Printed in Europe, USA, Canada, Australia, Japan

Cover: Foto ©Lupo / pixelio.de

More available books at **www.hansebooks.com**

# UNIVERSALISM ASSERTED

AS THE

## HOPE OF THE GOSPEL

ON THE AUTHORITY OF

Reason, the Fathers, and Holy Scripture.

BY THE

*REV. THOMAS ALLIN.*

"*A threefold cord is not quickly broken.*"—ECCLES. iv. 12.

SIXTH EDITION, ENLARGED AND REVISED,

WITH A PREFACE BY EDNA LYALL
AND A LETTER FROM CANON WILBERFORCE.

LAWRENCE BROS.,
WESTON-SUPER-MARE.

WILLIAMS AND NORGATE,
14, HENRIETTA STREET, COVENT GARDEN, LONDON;
20, SOUTH FREDERICK STREET, EDINBURGH;
AND 7, BROAD STREET, OXFORD.

1895

WESTON-SUPER-MARE:

PRINTED BY LAWRENCE BROS., THE PUBLIC LIBRARY.

# CONTENTS.

|  | PAGE. |
|---|---|
| NOTE | iv. |
| PREFACE | v. & vi. |
| CANON WILBERFORCE'S LETTER | viii. |

CHAPTER I. THE QUESTION STATED . . . 1
  „   II. THE POPULAR CREED WHOLLY UNTENABLE 13
  „  III. THE POPULAR CREED WHOLLY UNTENABLE 52
  „   IV. WHAT THE CHURCH TEACHES . . 80
  „    V. WHAT THE CHURCH TEACHES . . 127
  „   VI. UNIVERSALISM AND CREATION, &C. . 172
  „  VII. WHAT THE OLD TESTAMENT TEACHES . 210
  „ VIII. WHAT THE NEW TESTAMENT TEACHES . 220
  „   IX. WHAT THE NEW TESTAMENT TEACHES . 251
  „    X  SUMMARY AND CONCLUSION . . . 285
ERRATA . . . . . . . . . 322
INDEX . . . . . 323

BY THE SAME AUTHOR,

## REDEMPTION, Price 4d.,
AND
## LARGER HOPE LEAFLETS.

- No. 1. THE DEVIL'S VICTORY.
- ,, 2. THE BIBLE v. ENDLESS EVIL.
- ,, 3. THE POPULAR HEAVEN.
- ,, 4. THE LARGER HOPE AND SIN.
- ,, 5. THE UNCHANGING GOD.
- ,, 6. CAUSES OF UNBELIEF.
- ,, 7. THE POPULAR HELL.
- ,, 8. THE ATONEMENT AND THE LARGER HOPE.

1s. per 100.   LAWRENCE BROS., Weston-super-Mare.

---

NOTE.—In this issue the references to authors quoted have been given more fully, and the edition used has been stated when making the first quotation. In quotations from the Psalter, the Fathers, as a rule, follow the Septuagint, which numbers differently from the Hebrew, uniting *Ps.* ix. and x., and also cxiv. and cxv. into one, and dividing cxvi. and cxvii. each into two, thus, *e.g.*, the Psalm quoted as cxix. appears in Patristic writings as cxviii. and so in other cases.

# PREFACE.

UNIVERSALISM ASSERTED seems to me to fill a great want of the day; a book was needed which should face fairly and thoroughly, the subject of future Punishment, for although there are many works on the subject, they either face one aspect of the matter only, or they are written for scholars only, not for the multitude. Mr. ALLIN's writing is emphatically writing which can be "understanded of the people," and surely his book must kill the false accusation so often made that, those who believe in the ultimate triumph of Christ, and in the Redemption of the world, make light of sin.

Far from being a weak sentimentalist who shrinks from the thought of suffering, the Universalist, as Mr. ALLIN shews very conclusively in his second and third chapters, is convinced that every sin meets with its just and remedial punishment; he points out, too, how very injurious is the moral tendency of the popular belief in the everlasting existence of evil,—in a purposeless suffering, in an unjust and revolting system of torture. And all this is written calmly and thoughtfully, with a view to meeting the difficulties of those who are in doubt on the subject.

Perhaps the most interesting part of the book is that which shews how throughout the entire history of the Church the belief in universal salvation has been held by many of the best and truest of Christ's followers. And to my mind one of the finest touches is the description given in chapter i., pp. 10-2, of the position of those who, shrinking from the current notions of hell, and dissatisfied with that most unsatisfying theory—Conditional Immortality, take refuge in saying, that nothing can be definitely known, and that they are content to wait in uncertainty.

The sympathetic way in which the writer meets their position, and his fearless exposure of the dangerous vagueness which lurks beneath its apparent humility is beyond praise.

How is it possible that those who know the depths of sin and ignorance, those who hear the character of God slandered by believers and unbelievers, those who *love* the ones who pass unrepentant into the Unseen—how is it possible that they should rest satisfied, while retaining in their hearts even a shadow of a doubt that, "as in Adam all die, so in Christ shall all be made alive?"

The old merciless teaching is still taught; there yet remains in many a nursery, as well, alas! as in many a missionary school abroad, a well-known book called "Peep of Day." In this, little children are allowed to read such doggrel as the following :—

> "Now if I fight, or scratch, or bite,
> In passion fall, or bad names call,
> Full well I know where I shall go.
> Satan is glad when I am bad,
> And hopes that I with him shall lie,
> In fire and chains, and dreadful pains.
> All liars dwell with him in hell,
> And many more, who cursed and swore,
> And all who did what God forbid."

Surely it is time that everyone who believes that the Everlasting Father lovingly, eternally, educates all His children should speak out plainly, and not be ashamed to confess with the Psalmist, "My trust is in the tender mercy of God for ever and ever."

EDNA LYALL.

Eastbourne,
    10th December, 1890.

# PRESS NOTICES.

The following are some of the most recent Press Notices :—

"By all odds the ablest Universalist book of English authorship."—CHRISTIAN LEADER (Boston, U.S.A.)

"Its points are well and freshly put, and its matter admirably arranged."—DOVER MERCURY.

"In "Universalism Asserted" Mr. Allin has written the most valuable book thus far produced on this side of the Atlantic in defence of the ancient faith of the Christian Church . . . Several years ago the UNIVERSALIST called attention to its remarkable array of evidence in favour of our faith, and its peculiar and unique value to all who would understand the faith of the early centuries. The last edition shows that the author has continued his studies with great advantage to the Church and the original work."—THE UNIVERSALIST (Chicago, U.S.A.)

"Mr. Allin's Book is the ablest and most convincing assertion of Universalism we have yet met with, it is also valuable as furnishing a thorough digest of the teachings of the Fathers on this subject, . . . it is equally strong in the Scriptural argument. It bristles all through with pointed texts . . . and all that is necessary to give them weight is to assume that when the Bible says 'all' it means all."—WORDS OF RECONCILIATION.

"A masterly compendium of facts and arguments . a most valuable book."—ETERNAL PUNISHMENT (C. F. AKED.)

"Advocates of the larger hope must welcome this book, closely argued and written in a true christian spirit."—NOTTINGHAM DAILY EXPRESS.

"It is certainly a very full, interesting, and vigorous book . . . we commend it warmly to those who want to know the pith and marrow of what has been advanced by many writers; and also for the earnest and cogent words of one who has himself thought long and deeply about these great questions."—LITERARY WORLD.

"In this author the doctrine of eternal hope has found no common champion."—THE STAR (London).

*Letter from Canon Wilberforce to the Author.*

THE DEANERY,

SOUTHAMPTON,

August 6, 1890.

MY DEAR SIR,

"I am deeply grateful to you for your NOBLE book, 'Universalism Asserted.' I am *greatly* indebted to it, not only for the inspiration, but even for the very thoughts in some instances, of the two Sermons enclosed. It is the very best compendium of the glorious truth of modern times.

"May Our Father continue to send you forth to vindicate His character against the slander of Atheists on the one hand, and Conventionalists on the other.

I am, faithfully, &c.,

BASIL WILBERFORCE."

# CHAPTER I.

## *THE QUESTION STATED.*

"Shall not the judge of all the earth do right?"—GEN. xviii. 25.

THE following pages are written under the pressure of a deep conviction that the views generally held, as to the future punishment of the ungodly, wholly fail to satisfy the plain statements of Holy Scripture. All forms of partial salvation are but so many different ways of saying, that evil is in the long run too strong for God. The popular creed has maintained itself on a Scriptural basis solely, I believe, by hardening into dogma mere figures of oriental imagery; by mistranslations and misconceptions of the sense of the original (to which our authorised Version largely contributes); and finally, by completely ignoring a vast body of evidence in favour of the salvation of all men, furnished, as will be shewn, by very numerous passages of the New Testament, no less than by the great principles that pervade the teaching of all Revelation. Again, I write, because persuaded, that however loudly asserted and widely held, the popular belief is at best a tradition—is not an Article of Faith in the catholic Church—is accepted by no general Council, nay, is distinctly opposed to the views of not a few of the holiest and wisest Fathers of the Church in primitive times; who, in so teaching, expressed the belief of very many, if not the majority, of christians in their days.

Further, I write, because deeply and painfully convinced of the very serious mischief which has been, and is being, produced by the views generally held. They in fact tend, as nothing else ever has, to cause, I had almost said, to justify, the scepticism now so widely spread; they effect this because they so utterly conflict with any conception we can form of common justice and equity.

Therefore of mercy I shall say little in these pages: it is enough to appeal, when speaking of moral considerations, to that sense of right and wrong which is God's voice speaking within us. Indeed, among the many misconceptions with which all higher views of the Gospel are assailed, few are more unfounded than that, which asserts that thus God's justice is forgotten in the prominence assigned to His mercy. This objection merely shews a complete misapprehension of the views here advocated. For these views do in fact appeal to, and by this appeal recognise, first of all, the justice of God. It is precisely the sense of natural equity which God has planted within us, that the popular belief in endless evil and pain most deeply wounds.

And these considerations are in fact a complete answer to some other objections often heard. "Why disturb men's minds," it is said, "why unsettle their faith; why not let well alone?" By all means, I reply, let well alone, but never let ill alone. Men's minds are already disturbed: it is because they are already disturbed that we would calm them, and would restore the doubters to faith, by pointing them to a larger hope, to a truer christianity. A graver objection arises, but, like the former, wholly without foundation in fact. It is said, "By this larger hope you, in fact, either weaken or wholly remove all belief in future punishment. You explain away the guilt of sin." The very opposite is surely the truth, for you establish future punishment, and with it that sense of the reality of sin (to which conscience testifies) on a firm basis, only when you teach a plan of retribution, which is itself reasonable and credible. A penalty which to our reason and moral sense seems shocking, and monstrous, loses all force as a threat. It has ever been thus in the case of human punishments. And so in the case of hell. Outwardly believed, it has ceased to touch the conscience, or greatly to influence the life of christians. To the mass of men it has become a name and little more (not seldom a jest); to the sceptic it has furnished the choicest of his weapons; to the man of science, and to the more thoughtful of all ranks, a mark for loathing and scorn: while, alas, to many a sad and drooping heart, which longs to follow Christ more closely, it is the chief woe and burden of life. But the conscience, when no longer wounded by extravagant dogmas, is most ready to acquiesce in any measure of retribution (how sharp soever it be) which yet does not shock the moral sense, and conflict with its deepest convictions. And so the larger hope most fully recognises at once the guilt of sin, and the need of fitting retribution: nay, it may be claimed for it, *that it alone places both on a firm and solid basis,* by bringing them into harmony with the verdict of reason, of conscience and of Holy Scripture.

It is better now for clearness sake, to define that popular view of future punishment, of which I shall often speak. It is briefly this: That the ungodly finally pass into a state of endless evil, of endless torments; that from this suffering there is no hope of escape; that of this evil there is no possible alleviation. That when imagination has called up a series of ages, in apparently endless succession, all these ages of sin and of agony, undergone by the lost, have diminished their cup of suffering by not so much as one single drop; their pain is then no nearer ending than before. Those who hold this terrible doctrine to be a part of the "glad tidings of great joy" to men from their Father in heaven, differ indeed as to the number of the finally lost: some make them to be a majority of mankind, some a minority, even a very small minority. This division of views is instructive, as illustrating the ceaseless revolt of the human heart and conscience against a cruel dogma.

For the Bible is clearly against any such alleviation when read *from their own standpoint*. The texts on which they rely, if they teach the popular creed at all, teach, *just as clearly*, that the lost shall be the majority of men. "Many are called but *few* are chosen." "Fear not, *little* flock." "Narrow is the way that leadeth to life and *few there be that find it*." These are our Lord's own words. They present no difficulty to those who grasp the true meaning of "life," and "death," and "election," the true working of the purpose of Redemption throughout the ages to come.

But they present an insuperable difficulty to that very common form of the traditional creed, which seeks to lighten the horror of endless evil by narrowing its range. Indeed, it seems perfectly clear that the popular view requires us to believe in the final loss of the vast majority of our race. For it is only the truly converted in this life (as it asserts), who reach heaven; and it is beyond all fair question, that of professing christians only a small portion are truly converted; to say nothing of the myriads and myriads of those who have died in Paganism. But even waiving this point, the objections to the popular creed are in no way really lightened by our belief as to the relative numbers of the lost and the saved. The real difficulty consists in the infliction of any such penalty, and not in the number who are doomed to it. Nor need we forget how inconceivably vast must be that number, on the most lenient hypothesis. Take the lowest estimate; and when you remember the innumerable myriads of our race who have passed away —those now living—and those yet unborn—it becomes clear that the number of the lost must be something in its vastness defying all calculation; and of these, all, be it remembered, children of the great Parent—all made in His image—all redeemed by the life blood of His Son; and all shut up for ever and ever (words, of whose awful meaning no man has, or can have, the very faintest conception) in blackness of darkness, in despair, and in the company of devils.

Let me next shew what this hell of the popular creed really means, so far as human words can dimly convey its horrors, and for this purpose I subjoin the following extracts—" Little child, if you go to hell there will be a devil at your side to strike you. He will *go on striking* you every minute *for ever and ever* without stopping. The first stroke will make your body as bad as the body of Job, covered, from head to foot, with sores and ulcers. The second stroke will make your body twice as bad as the body of Job. The third stroke will make your body three times as bad as the body of Job. The fourth stroke will make your body four times as bad as the body of Job. How, then, will your body be after the devil has been striking it every moment for a hundred million of years without stopping? Perhaps at this moment, seven o'clock in the evening, a child is just going into hell. To-morrow evening, at seven o'clock, go and knock at the gates of hell and ask what the child is doing. The devils will go and look. They will come back again and say, *the child is burning.* Go in a week and ask what the child is doing ; you will get the same answer, *it is burning.* Go in a year and ask, the same anwer comes—*it is burning.* Go in a million of years and ask the same question, the answer is just the same—*it is burning.* So, if you go for ever and ever, you will always get the same answer—*it is burning in the fire."—The Sight of Hell.* Rev. J. FURNISS, C.S.S.R. "The fifth dungeon is the red hot oven. The little child is in the red hot oven. Hear how *it screams to come out ;* see how *it turns and twists itself about in the fire. It beats its head against the roof of the oven. It stamps its little feet on the floor."—ib.* "Gather in one, in your mind, an assembly of all those men or women, from whom, whether in history or in fiction, your memory most shrinks, gather in mind all that is most loathsome, most revolting * * * conceive the fierce, fiery eyes of hate, spite, frenzied rage, ever fixed on thee, looking thee through and through with hate * * hear those yells of blaspheming, concentrated hate, as they echo along the lurid vault of hell ; everyone hating everyone * * * Yet a fixedness in that state in which the hardened malignant sinner dies, involves, without any further retribution of God, this endless misery."—*Sermon* by the Rev. E. B. PUSEY, D.D. "When thou diest thy soul will be tormented alone ; that will be a hell for it: but at the day of judgment thy body will join thy soul, and then thou wilt have twin hells, thy soul sweating drops of blood, and thy body suffused with agony. In fire, exactly like that we have on earth, thy body will lie, asbestos like, for ever unconsumed, all thy veins roads for the feet of pain to travel on, every nerve a string, on which the devil shall for ever play his diabolical tune of hell's unutterable lament."—*Sermon* on the *Resurrection of the Dead.* Rev. C. H. SPURGEON. Awful as are these quotations, I must repeat that they give no adequate idea at all of the horrors of hell; for that which is the very sting of its terrors—their unendingness—is beyond our power really to conceive, even approximately: so totally incommensurable are the ideas of time and of endless duration.

But it will be said, "we no longer believe in a material hell—no longer teach a lake of real fire." I might well ask, on your theory of interpreting Scripture, what right have you so to teach? But let me rather welcome this change of creed, so far as it is a sign of an awakening moral sense. Yet this plea, in mitigation of the horror your doctrines inspire, cannot be admitted; for when you offer for acceptance a spiritual, rather than a material flame, who is there that cannot see that the real difficulty is the same, in either case. If evil in any form is perpetuated then the central difficulty of the traditional creed remains.

Merely to state the traditional doctrine in any form, is to refute it for very many minds. So deeply does it wound what is best and holiest in us; indeed, as I shall try to shew further on, it is, for all practical purposes, found incredible, even by those who honestly profess to believe it. This terrible difficulty, felt and acknowledged in all ages, has been largely met for the Roman Catholic, by the doctrine of Purgatory, which became developed as the belief in endless torment gradually supplanted that earlier and better faith, which *alone* finds expression in the two really catholic and ancient creeds, faith in *Everlasting Life.* How immense must have been the relief thus afforded, is evident, when we remember that the least sorrow, however imperfect, the very slightest desire for reconciliation with God, though deferred to the last moment of existence, was believed to free the dying sinner from the pains of hell, no matter how aggravated his sins may have been. Among the Reformed Communions this difficulty was met, no doubt, by a silent incredulity—often unconscious—yet ever increasing, on the part of the great majority: indeed, some divines, have at all times, both in England and on the Continent, openly avowed their disbelief in endless torments. This growing incredulity has found, in our day, open expression, in a remarkable theory, that of conditional immortality (itself a revival of an earlier belief). This doctrine, briefly stated, teaches that man is naturally mortal, that only in Jesus Christ is immortality conferred on the righteous—that the ungodly shall be judged, and, after due punishment, annihilated.

Of this dogma* I shall at once say, that, while it degrades man, it fails to vindicate God. "It is that most wretched and cowardly of all theories, which supposes the soul to be naturally mortal, and that God will resuscitate the wicked to torment them for a time, and then finally extinguish them. I can see no ground for this view in Scripture but in mistaken interpretations; and it does not meet the real difficulty at all, for it supposes that evil has in such cases finally triumphed, and that God had no resource but to punish and extinguish it: which is essentially the very difficulty felt by the sceptical mind. I have called it cowardly, for it surrenders the true nobility of man, his natural immortality, in a panic at an objection; and like all cowardice, fails in securing safety."—*Donellan Lectures*, QUARRY.

---

* Is annihilation possible? "Nulla enim natura potest corrumpi ut penitus non sit, et ad nihilum redigatur."—*Erig. De div. nat. lib.* v.

Further, let me reply thus; (I.)—"I believe in one God the Father Almighty, who willeth not the death of a sinner." If, then, even one sinner die finally, God's will is not done, *i.e.*, God is so far defeated and evil victorious. Annihilation is the triumph of death over life: it is the very antithesis to the Gospel, which asserts the triumph of Christ over every form of death. It is strange indeed that able men, who write elaborate treatises advocating this view, should overlook the fact, that all schemes of partial salvation involve a compromise with evil on God's part. (II.)—No less strange is the assertion that the moral sense is not shocked by God, who is absolutely free, yet forcing the gift of life on those whom He knows to be in fact destined to become the prey of evil so completely, that they either rot away of sheer wickedness; or, being hopelessly corrupt, are extinguished by their Father. (III.)—Death nowhere in Holy Scripture implies annihilation, for earthly destruction is, especially in the case of the Old Testament, that which is denoted by the term, death: but as a rule this term has a wider significance, and one far deeper. Nay, as I hope to point out, (ch. vi. on death,) there is in Scriptural usage, especially in the New Testament, a deep spiritual connection between death and life; death becomes the path to, and the very condition of, life. (IV.)—Further, this theory wholly breaks down in practice. So far from "perishing" implying final ruin, Christ came specially to *save* that which has "perished," —*to apololos*, the "lost," "ruined," "destroyed;" the original term is the same which is often translated "destroy," and on which the theory of annihilation is so largely built. The same word occurs in *S. Luke* xv., and there is applied to the Sheep, the Coin, the Prodigal Son—all of which are thus 'destroyed," "lost," and yet finally saved. In *S. Matt.*

x. 39, xvi. 25, to "lose" (destroy) one's life is stated as the condition of finding it. So Christ is sent to save the "lost" (destroyed) sheep of Israel. So Sodom and Gomorrha are destroyed, and yet have a special promise of restoration. —*Ez.* xv. 53-5. Take the Antediluvians. After they had "died" in their sins they were evangelised by Christ in person.—1 *S. Pet.* iii. 19. Hence the unanswerable dilemma, either all these are annihilated, or you must give up that sense of " perishing " on which the theory is based. (V.)—Probably I have said enough, but yet a very grave difficulty remains. This theory stands in hopeless conflict with the promises to restore all things, to reconcile all things through Christ, which abound in Scripture; nay, which form the very essence of its teaching when describing Christ's empire. It seems amazing that able men are found capable of maintaining that a reconciliation which is described as co-extensive with all creation, *Col.* i. 15-20, can be equivalent to restoring some (or many) things, only after annihilating, as hopelessly evil, all the rest.

Another view adopted by a number, probably extremely large, and increasing, differs altogether from that last stated. Those who hold it have had their eyes opened to the fact, that the New Testament contains very many, long neglected, texts which teach the salvation of all men. They have also learned enough to have their faith gravely shaken in the popular interpretation of the texts usually quoted in proof of endless pain. The theory of conditional immortality fails to satisfy such men. They see that it is altogether unsuccessful in meeting the real difficulty of the popular creed, *i.e.*, the triumph of evil over good, of satan over the Saviour of man, and therefore over God. They perceive, too, the narrow and arbitrary basis on which it rests in appealing to Holy Scripture. And so they decline to entertain it as any solution of the question, and say, "We are not able definitely to accept any theory of the future of man, because we do not see that anything has been clearly revealed. Enough has been disclosed to shew to us that God is love, and we are content to believe that, happen what will, all will ultimately be shewn to be the result of love divine."

It is impossible to avoid sympathy with much of this view at first sight, but only then; for when closely examined it is seen to be open to the charge of grave ambiguity, or far worse. It may mean that in the future God will act as a loving human parent would, and then, I reply, this is precisely the larger hope. Again, it may mean a very different and very dangerous thing. It may mean that at the last my ideas of right and wrong will undergo a complete change—that the things which I now pronounce with the fullest conviction to be cruel and vile, will at that day seem to be righteous and just, and that thus God will be fully justified though He inflict endless torment. But take this statement to pieces and see what it really means. It means, in effect, practical Scepticism. It means blank Agnosticism. This is easily shewn. For what this view really tells me is that my deepest moral convictions are wholly worthless, because that which they declare to be cruel and revolting, is right and holy, and will so appear at the last. But if this be so, then I have lost my sole measure of right and wrong. What is truth or goodness, I know not. They cease to be realities; they are, for aught I know, mere phantoms. Religion, therefore, is impossible. Conscience ceases to be a reliable guide. Revelation is a mere blank, for all revelation presupposes the *trustworthiness* of that moral sense to which it is addressed. Thus the above plea, plausible as it seems, is wholly ambiguous, and does in fact lead either to the larger hope, or to mere unbelief.

In opposition to both these theories stand the views here advocated, which have been always held by some in the catholic Church; nay, which represent, I believe, most nearly its primitive teaching. These views are, I know, now widely held by the learned, the devout, and the thoughtful in our own and in other communions. Briefly stated, they amount to this:—That we have ample warrant, alike from reason—from the observed facts and analogies of human life—from our best and truest moral instincts—from a great body of primitive teaching—and from Holy Scripture itself, to entertain a firm hope that God our Father's design and purpose is, and has ever been, to save every child of Adam's race.

Therefore I have called this book, "*Universalism Asserted.*" But let there be no mistake. I assert this not as a dogma, but AS A HOPE: as that which after many years of thought and study seems to me to be the true meaning of Holy Scripture, as it is certainly in harmony with our moral sense, and has been taught by so many saints in the early Church. The term, "Universalism," may not, indeed, commend itself to some, but I retain it advisedly. It seems to convey an essential truth. "The kingdom of Christ * * * is in the fullest sense * * * universal."—*Lightfoot.* It is an universal remedy to meet an universal evil. While sin is universal, and sorrow and pain universal, shall not our hope be universal too? Shall not life be as universal as death, and salvation as universal as sin?

Can we even think of a divine life and a divine love as other than in their very essence universal?

## CHAPTER II.

## *THE POPULAR CREED WHOLLY UNTENABLE.*

"These questions * * * educated men and women of all classes and denominations are asking, and will ask more and more till they receive an answer. And if we of the clergy cannot give them an answer, which accords with their conscience and reason * * * then evil times will come, both for the clergy and the christian religion, for many a year henceforth."—Canon KINGSLEY.—*Water of Life.*

"The answer which the popular theology has been tendering for centuries past will not be accepted much longer * * * I disclaim any desire to uphold that theology which I have never aided in propagating."—Rev. Dr. LITTLEDALE.—*Contemporary Review.*

AT the outset let me protest against the common and ignorant prejudice that connects universalism with lax views of sin or of dogma. As to the first, I shall have occasion bye and bye to point out, that no system so effectually affirms God's hatred of sin, as that which teaches that He cannot tolerate its existence for ever. Again, as to the second, I shall largely base my argument for universalism on the fullest acceptance of the great catholic verities. A narrow catholicism is a contradiction in terms. To this point I shall return, confining myself here to the remark that a partial salvation aims a blow at both the Incarnation and the Atonement. For a vital part of the Incarnation is the taking of the race of man, *as an organic whole*, into God through Jesus Christ, the second Adam. But with this fundamental idea, a partial salvation is in hopeless contradiction. No less vital is the blow aimed by the popular creed at the Atonement. First it dishonours the Cross by limiting its power to save, to the brief moments of earthly life. Further, it virtually teaches that the Cross is a stupendous failure. This is easily shewn. For plainly that which misses its end is a failure. And if the end aimed at be noble, then in proportion is the failure greater and vital. But the scriptural evidence is overwhelming, that the object of Christ's death was to save the *world*. "The Father sent the Son to be the Saviour of the world." He came that the world through Him might be saved; *i.e.*, the world in all its extent, not a part of it, however large. If, then, this end be not gained, if the world be not in fact saved, the Atonement is so far a failure. Disguise the fact as men may, the dilemma is inevitable. Answer, or evasion, there is none.

The next step will be to state more in detail the various considerations that render it impossible to accept the traditional view of future punishment; or any modification of it which teaches the endless duration of evil, moral or physical, in even a solitary instance; a fact essential to bear in mind, when I refer to the traditional creed, or the popular creed anywhere in this book. My first appeal shall be to that primary revelation of Himself which God has implanted in the heart and conscience of man. I am merely expressing the deepest and most mature, though often unspoken, convictions of millions of earnest christian men and women, when I assert, that to reconcile the popular creed, or any similar belief in endless evil and pain, with the most elementary ideas of justice, equity, and goodness (not even to mention mercy), is wholly and absolutely impossible. Thus this belief destroys the *only ground* on which it is possible to erect any religion at all, for it sets aside the primary convictions of the moral sense; and thus paralyses that by which alone we are capable of religion. If human reason be incompetent to decide positively that certain acts assigned to God are evil and cruel, then it is equally incompetent to decide that certain acts of His are just and merciful. Therefore if God be not good, just, and true, in the *human acceptation of these terms*, then the whole basis of revelation vanishes. For if God be not good in our human sense of the word, I have no guarantee that He is true in our sense of truth. If that which the Bible calls goodness in God should prove to be that which we call badness in man, then how can I be assured that, what is called truth in God, may not really be that which in man is called falsehood? Thus no valid communication—no revelation—from God to man is possible; for no reliance can, on this view, be placed on His veracity.

"We dare not," says the Bishop of London, "let go the truth, that the holiness, the goodness, the justice, the righteousness, which the eternal moral law imposes on us as a supreme command, are identical in essential substance, in our minds and in His."—*Bampt. Lect.* "*We dare not?*" Why? Precisely because, if we do, the foundations of religion collapse—perishing as the moral order perishes. We are worshipping once more the unknown God. Mere scepticism is our sole refuge. We have lost our standard of right and wrong, and are wandering in a pathless desert, creedless, homeless, hopeless, mocked all the while by phantoms of virtues that are probably vices, and of vices that are probably virtues. For let me repeat that if goodness in becoming infinite turns into evil—if infinite love may be consistent with what we call cruelty—then, for aught we know, truth may turn into fasehood, justice into flagrant wrong, light into darkness. Therefore, we *dare not* let go the truth that in our moral nature we have a true revelation of the divine mind, *i.e.*, that the ideas of right and wrong are in their essence *the same* in our minds and in God's— that they are true *universally ;* as true beyond the grave as here and now. But if so, then that which so flatly contradicts all our deepest moral convictions, as does the dogma of endless sin (a dogma which, however modified, no imaginable hypothesis can reconcile with either justice or mercy) must be absolutely *false,* and in teaching it we are but libelling God.

Further, if endless evil may be defended, in even a solitary case, it may be defended logically in every case. This follows strictly from the ground taken by advocates of the traditional creed. " They say we cannot judge what is cruel or the reverse on God's part." Be it so, for argument's sake. Then it follows, that if every human being fall under the sway of evil for ever, and God be thus left face to face with an universal Pandemonium, then we should have no right even to murmur, for we have right to judge, having no faculties adequate to the task. But in fact we are not alone justified in arguing from our own minds to God's ; we are *forced* to do so, or to remain agnostics. It is from our minds that we gain a knowledge of the divine mind, from the working of our intelligence and will that we gain a knowledge of God's will and intelligence. This is the pathway God has traced, the foundation He has laid. And there is no other possible. " Ils ont beau me crier ' soumets ta raison.' *Il me faut des raisons pour soumettre ma raison.*"—*Emile.*

We smile at the ignorant savage who mutilates his body, thinking thereby to please his God. Are not we far worse who think to please our God by mutilating our noblest part, and to *hear Him better by silencing His voice in us?* But our opponents do not forbid the argument from our nature to God: they only forbid the argument from what is best in our nature to His. They are ready to ascribe certain base qualities of humanity to God. Because we delight in vengeance, so does God. Because we are cruel, God must be so. But eighteen hundred years have not taught the mass of christians to credit their heavenly Father with even so much love for His children, as a frail woman can feel for her offspring.

The mode in which the ordinary creed does its hateful work of hardening the sceptic, and saddening the most devout, may be shewn by two brief extracts. "All the attempts yet made," says a stern moralist, "to reconcile this doctrine with divine justice and mercy, are calculated to make us blush, alike for the human heart that can strive to justify such a creed, and for the human intellect that can delude itself into a belief that it has succeeded in such justification." "Nothing," says the late General GORDON, "can be more abject and miserable than the usual conception of God \* \* \* Imagine to yourself what pleasure it would be to Him to burn us, or to torture us. Can we believe any human being capable of creating us for such a purpose? We credit God with attributes which are utterly hateful to the meanest of men \* \* \* I say that christian Pharisees deny Christ \* \* \* A hard, cruel set they are, from high to low. When one thinks of the real agony one has gone through in consequence of false teaching, it makes human nature angry with the teachers who have added to the bitterness of life."

The popular view is familiar, and most men do not realise its true bearing, or the light in which it really presents the *character* of God. But consider how this dogma of endless evil must strike an enquirer after God, one outside the pale of christianity, but sincerely desirous of learning the truth. There are such men—there are many such. You tell this enquirer that God is not Almighty only, but all good; that God is indeed love; that God is his Father. But these terms are words *without any justification at all*, if they have not their common ordinary sense when applied to God. Such a man will say, you tell me God is good, but what acts are these you assign to Him? He is a father; but He brings into being myriads of hapless creatures, knowing that there is in store for them a doom unutterably awful. He calls into existence these creatures, whether they will or no; though the bottomless pit is yawning to receive them, and the flames ready to devour them. The question is not, whether they might have escaped; the real questions are, *do they in fact escape?* and *does He know* that they will not escape? and, knowing this, does He, *acting freely, yet create* them? And you assure me that this Great Being is Almighty, is Love essential, is the Parent or the Creator (here the terms are practically equivalent) of every one of these creatures, who are doomed and damned. What fair answer do you propose to give to these questions if addressed to you? I may put the enquiry in the words of a well-known poet. A lost soul asks—

> "Father of mercies, why from silent earth
> Didst Thou awake, and *curse me into birth?*"
> 
> —*Night Thoughts.*

Pressed by the irresistable weight of these arguments, many take refuge in ambiguous and evasive phrases, *e.g.*,

"Be sure God will do the best He can for every man." Ambiguous and evasive words, I repeat, as used by the advocates of endless torment and evil. For if they really mean that the *best* an Almighty Being can do for countless myriads of His children is to bestow on them,—practically to force on them—whether they will or not, an existence, stained with sin from the womb, knowing that in fact this sin will ripen into endless misery—then such phrases as the above are but so much dust thrown in our eyes, they are as argument beneath refutation. And if they do not mean this, such pleas are worthless as a defence of the ordinary creed. If endless misery is the certain result, known and foreseen, of calling me into existence, then to force on me the gift of life, is to do for me not the best, but the worst possible.

Others take refuge in the vain assertion that the larger hope implies the escape of the wicked from all punishment, and places the sinner on a level with the saint. Let me once for all reply that no statement can be more unfounded. For the very method of healing the finally impenitent, as taught by the larger hope, is the severity of the divine judgment, is that consuming fire, which must burn up all iniquity. Thus the larger hope is especially *bound to teach* for the obstinate sinner the certainty of retribution, for in God's judgments it sees the mode of cure (see chap. vi.), the mode in which the grace of the Atonement often reaches the touched heart. Thus, unrepented sin leads to awful future penalty, to penalty proportioned to the guilt of the sinner and continued till he repent. The larger hope—so falsely called "sentimental"—thus not merely accepts, but *emphasises* for the ungodly the dread warning of wrath to come—of the fires of Gehenna—for in these it sees not a wanton revenge, but at once a just retribution ; and a discipline that heals the obstinate sinner.

Again, it is said, that perhaps the flames of hell may be needed to terrorize some far distant sinful orb; that rebels against God in some other planet may read, by the light of hell-fire, the dangers of sin. Yes, it has been gravely alleged that a Being, Whose name is Love, will light, and keep alight through unending ages, a ghastly living torch for such a purpose as this—a torch—each atom of which is composed of a lost soul, once His child, once made in His image, once redeemed by the Cross of His dear Son ! You know this has been taught, and yet you actually complain that men are sceptical, and that thoughtful artizans reject such a creed with scorn. Many, too, but in vain, seek to mitigate the just horror and loathing which the popular creed inspires, by saying that the torments of hell are not material but spiritual ; and by asserting further (contrary to the plainest teachings of experience) that somehow the majority do really turn to God in this life, or at the last moment of half conscious existence. I say nothing of the bribe thus offered to the selfish instincts of the majority, by the assurance that somehow they will shuffle into heaven, and that only a worthless few perish. But this shabby plea is (1) false from the standpoint of those who teach it (p. 4), and (2) does not, if true, even touch the central difficulty of the popular creed. For whether our Father *permits* (to use the softest term) the endless misery and evil of countless myriads upon myriads of His own children, or of thousands only ; whether hell receives fifty, or five, or only one per cent. of the sons of God, of the brothers of Christ Jesus : and again, whether its torments are applied to their bodies, or to their spirits, all these are points that, however decided, do not even *touch* the central question, *i.e.*, can evil be stronger than God, ever, under any circumstances?—can a Father permit the endless, hopeless, sin and woe of even one of His children, and look on calmly for ever and ever unmoved and unsympathising—can the Bible be mocking us when it teaches a restitution of *all things*, and that a time is coming when God shall be " All in All."

Some will, no doubt, say that we have no right to measure God's ways by our private judgments, no right to seem to dictate what He will or will not, can or cannot do. I reply that this objection rests on a complete misapprehension. We do not presume to discuss what God, in the abstract, can or cannot do, still less to dictate to Him. The argument employed in these pages is open to no such objection as the above, for it is simply this—that God has both in His primary revelation of Himself to our moral sense, and in His written word, distinctly and emphatically declared against the doctrine of endless evil. Because God has so spoken, we therefore speak. Others again assert that endless misery is sufficiently accounted for by saying that it comes as the natural result of sin, and not as arbitrarily decreed. I am wholly unable to see how this in the very least alters the divine promise to restore all things, or annuls the work of Christ, which is to "put away sin by the sacrifice of Himself." Surely the more *natural* the tie between sin and misery, the more assured is the destruction of both; for the closer the bond, the more certain it becomes that to put away, *i.e.*, to abolish (Heb. ix. 26) the one is to abolish the other.

But the law of continuity, it is said, forbids universalism. Those who go on to the close of life impenitent must be presumed to continue impenitent hereafter. But why? They will continue so only if the forces working for impenitence hereafter are stronger than the forces making for good. And the conditions under which these forces will work in a future state, will certainly be very unlike those now obtaining, and very much more favourable to conversion. "In that other life there will be no room for unbelief, when Christ has been seen. Then that great source of evil which is in the flesh, will be at an end; no inner lust will remain: no external food for vice: no temptation to concupiscence, to ambition, to avarice, will survive. How then the lost can for ever cling to sin, unless divinely hardened, I fail to see."—BURNET *De statu mort.*

I may add that beyond the grave illusions will cease. Here men are blinded; and most often, if not always, follow evil not as being evil, but as a fancied good. "*Had they known, they would not have crucified the Lord of Glory,*" —1 *Cor.* ii. 8—pregnant words. In fact, this objection seems but a roundabout way of saying that the devil is stronger in the long run than God. Surely the presumption, even apart from a revealed promise of the restoration of all things is, that evil being an intruder and an alien, and the world being under divine government, this government can never cease working, till order and right wholly replace disorder and wrong. Why are we to assume that God means to share His throne for ever with the powers of evil, or that He has, in any case, exhausted His means of cure in the present brief life?

In fact, we totally err in our estimate of the relative strength of good and evil when we treat the latter as though it were on a par with the former in fibre, in duration, or in essence. For this there is no shadow of excuse: it is dualism thinly disguised. It is this degrading heresy to which the traditional creed is ever tending. I deny, then, any presumption that because evil has gone on for years it will go on always. The logical and moral presumption is precisely the other way, viz., that the weaker will in the long run yield to the stronger: the usurper to the lawful owner: the evil one to God. Further, the facts of the physical and spiritual worlds are alike fatal to any such narrow theory of continuity. What is the Creation but a striking breach of continuity? So, too, was the Deluge; so is every earthquake, &c., &c. And it is worth careful noting that the only appeal in Scripture to the laws of physical continuity comes from the unbeliever, and is made *in the interests of scepticism.*— 2 Pet. iii. 4. I admit that there probably is a higher continuity than any we can at present trace. The very breaks in the established order may be but parts of a higher order, and may thus range themselves on the side of and not against a true continuity. But it is impossible to argue that, merely because a certain order of things continues for long unbroken, it will therefore go on for ever. If so, there could be no Creation, no Resurrection, no final Judgment. It is merely suicidal for a christian to argue as the objection requires.

I turn to consider a further objection frequently alleged against the larger hope. It is said that probation in order to be real involves the possibility of some utterly failing. Note first, the ambiguity of this plausible plea. It speaks only of a possibility of failure; I ask, then, *must* some be lost finally, if all are put to a real trial? Unless this be so, the objection does not help the traditional creed; for if 1,000 persons can be tested without a single failure, why not 10,000 or 100,000? Why not all? But if a real probation of all involves endless evil in some cases, then I reply such probation is an immoral thing. For probation is but a means to an end, viz., the promotion of a higher standard of virtue than if men were not tested. Now it is immoral to use an instrument that brings to some men a higher standard at the cost of the endless ruin of others. A higher type of virtue in the saved would be an evil, if gained practically at such a price as the hopeless degradation of the lost, and the perpetuation of evil in the universe. Meantime, all the difficulty arises from men's believing *probation* to be an adequate description of our position under God's moral government—an assumption *absolutely groundless.* Such conceptions imply a radical and most mischievous error, viz., that God's relation to us is like that of a Head Engineer testing his works, or a Police Inspector on a vast scale. But God is "Our Father," and if so the central fact is, and must be, His *education* of His children. True, we are being tested, but only as a part of our *education*—which is the real conception of our position as God's children. Realise this truth, and how absurd becomes the objection we are discussing: how truly absurd it becomes to say "God's education *cannot be real unless some of His pupils go the devil for ever;*" or, there cannot be a second probation—which really means that God cannot continue and complete His work of education.

Some again say—"Why try to solve a question which is probably insoluble, viz., the problem of man's destiny?" In reply we ask what the objection really means? Are we to give up every great question because we can only partly solve it? To do so would be to give up all questions, to bid farewell to all knowledge. For every great question contains an insoluble element. Take, *e.g.*, the problems of Life, of Matter, &c. Take such questions as the Trinity, or the Incarnation. Are we to give them all up? All human knowledge is in fact the knowledge of things partly known, partly insoluble at present. To act as the objection requires would simply land us in agnosticism, scientific and religious. Lastly, the objection lies equally against the traditional creed, for that decides this so-called insoluble question quite as much as does universalism—a fact which the objectors quietly ignore.

A further plausible argument against universalism is the alleged danger of teaching the larger hope. Those who so argue surely forget what their words involve if true. They involve a serious reflection on the Creator (*a*) who permits His children, made in His Image, to descend to such an abyss of degradation that only an endless hell can restrain them from sin; and Who, (*b*) knowing this, yet conceals, or permits to be concealed, from the vast majority of men this necessary antidote to sin; and Who, (*c*) in the Old Testament, gave a special revelation of Himself, and said nothing or almost nothing of it. And this cry of danger has been used against every improvement, moral, social, or scientific.

Having premised this I meet the objection frankly by saying—look at the verdict of history. Its answer is decisive. Never did lust and vice in every guise so rage and riot as when in the middle ages this dogma was most firmly held. Hell-fire bred a veritable hell on earth. Those who talk of universalism as antinomian do not face the facts of history. Better were it if they did so, and then were to look at home, and remember the awful danger of teaching a creed whose fruits are so often those well described in the following striking words, in which a Roman Catholic Priest states twenty years' experience in the Confessional: "The dogma of hell, except in the rarest cases, did no moral good. It never affected the right persons. It tortured innocent young women, and virtuous boys. It appealed to the lowest motives, and the lowest characters. *It never, except in the rarest instances, deterred from the commission of sin.* It caused unceasing mental and moral difficulties. \* \* \* It always influenced the wrong people, and in a wrong way. It caused infidelity to some, temptations to others, and misery without virtue to most."—*R. Suffield.* What, I ask, has the dogma of endless pain and sin really effected? Has it checked the growth of heathenism in our cities? Has it kept the artizan in the fold of Christ? Can a single sin be named which it has banished from our midst? Has the Gospel of fear evangelised thoroughly a solitary English family?

Hell-fire is preached inside the Church, while outside the baptised harlot plies her trade, and the burglar weaves his plot. What wonder, so long as we preach to the fallen a God, nominally loving, but in fact a God Whose acts towards myriads of His children would excite horror even amid the outcast, and the lost. Ineffective always, such teaching is more than ever so in these days, because the intelligent are by it forced into open revolt; and because experience clearly teaches that gigantic penalties go hand in hand with gigantic crimes, and penalties diminished to a reasonable amount with diminished sin. Such has been the result in our penal code. Such has been the result in Norfolk Island, in Western Australia, in Germany, in Spain, &c. Excessive terrorism provokes not alone incredulity but mirth. Even in days far more credulous than ours, satan, in the religious dramas, soon subsided into a clown; his appearance provoked shouts of laughter.

But true universalism deters from sin, because it preaches

a righteous retribution with unequalled force and certainty: on this its creed largely hinges. Restoration is taught *because* of retribution, a fact on which too much stress cannot be laid. "*Thou, Lord, art merciful, for Thou renderest to every man according to his work.*"—*Ps.* lxii. 12.

But probably the way in which most people satisfy their own minds, when doubts arise as to the endless nature of future torment is this: "Endless pain and torment is but the result of sin freely chosen and finally persisted in by the sinner.

First, before discussing this, let me ask—*why* all this stress is laid on man's will to ruin himself, rather than on God's will to save? Is man the pivot on which all hinges? To me it seems bad philosophy, and worse theology, not to recognise God as centre, and His will and purpose as supreme. But to resume, (I.)—I would point out one consequence of defending endless evil and misery, on the plea of man's free choice, viz., that, if this plea avail in any one case to excuse endless evil, it would avail, logically, in every case: and it would justify an universe in which every reasonable being should choose evil finally, and God should remain presiding over an universal hell. (II.)—Again, if endless sin be repugnant to every true conception of God, if it be repugnant to morality, for God freely to create any being, for whom such a doom is reserved, then you do not alter this fact by any possible theory as to the power of the human will. That which is incapable of defence morally, remains indefensible still. (III.)—Next, you cannot fairly oppose a mere theory to a revealed assurance of the reconciliation of all things to God finally. Your theory indeed proves a *possibility* of the final choice of evil: you cannot reasonably oppose a possibility, to a direct statement of Him

*Who made the human will.* (IV.)—Next let me add, that the very term, "free will," is ambiguous; it may mean a will partly, or a will wholly, free. If it mean the former, I am most willing to admit man's freedom. But if the latter be meant, then let me remind my readers that the acts of a will wholly free, *i.e.*, undetermined by motive, *would have no moral value whatever.* (V.)—Doubtless the problems of freedom and necessity contain an insoluble element. But we can look at them practically. You insist that everything depends on human choice. I reply, see how on the contrary man's choice is limited at every hand. First, man is born in sin; that is, certainly not wholly free. Take, next, the facts of life. In the first place man can exercise no choice at all as to the time and place of his birth—facts all important in deciding his religious belief, and through that his character; no choice as to the very many and very complex hereditary influences moulding his entire life, though most often he knows it not; affecting for good or for evil every thought, every word, every act of his; no choice at all as to the original weakness of his nature, and its inherent tendency to evil. More, still, man can exercise no choice at all on this *vital* question, whether he will or will not have laid on Him the awful perils, in which, on the popular view, the mere fact of life involves him. Further, man can exercise no choice at all as to the strength of that will he receives; no choice at all as to the circumstances that surround him in infancy and childhood, and which colour his whole life; man has no choice as to the moral atmosphere he must imbibe in those early years of training, which colour almost of necessity, the whole after life. "But a creature cannot," you reply, " choose these things, from the very nature of the case." That, I answer, only proves my point, that a creature cannot be wholly free, from the very nature of the case. What the facts point to, is that God grants a limited freedom, intending to train man, His child, for the enjoyment hereafter of perfect freedom. (VI.)—The vast extent of human ignorance also confirms the view that the final destinies of the universe are not placed in man's keeping. We know nothing absolutely, we know but appearances—phenomena. We are acquainted with the outsides of things at most, with the insides never. We talk of Life, of Matter, but these and all other things, are in themselves to us unknown, and unknowable. Every thing we do, every object we see, every natural operation is to us incomprehensible.

Are these the hands to which a wise Creator is likely to commit absolutely the awful issues of endless sin, the ruin of creation?

(VII.)—But it is said, that if man be not wholly free, his goodness is but a mechanical thing. If so, I reply, better ten thousand fold a mechanical goodness that keeps one at the side of God for ever, than a wholly unrestrained freedom which leads to the devil. But the assertion is in fact as hollow as it is plausible. Man is not a machine because the power of defying God finally is not granted to him. Freedom enough is granted to resist God for ages; freedom to suffer, and to struggle; to reap what has been sown, till, taught by experience, the will of the creature is bent to the will of the Creator. If all this does not involve a freedom that is real, though limited, then human words are vain as a vehicle for human thought. (VIII.)—A reasonable theory of human free will is in perfect accord with universalism: so true is this, that the greatest advocates of the larger hope have been the most earnest champions of free will, *and often base on it their teachings ;* while the advocates of endless sin and hell, like Augustine and Calvin, have been enemies to free will. Indeed, man's rescue depends on his freedom. (IX.)—Further, this pleading for endless sin in hell on the ground that it is freely chosen by man, would, if true, but enhance the great difficulty of the popular creed—the victory of evil; for plainly, the more free on man's part, the more wilful his choice of sin, so much the more complete is the triumph of evil, so much the more absolute is the failure of the Cross. What is this plea but in fact seeking to vindicate the Almighty by laying stress on His defeat, seeking to justify Omnipotence by emphasising His Impotence? (X.)—This plea contradicts itself; for to assert that because of man's freedom he can go on for ever choosing evil, is, in fact, to plead not for human freedom, but for servitude, the basest, the most degrading. Take the assertion to pieces, and it comes to this. To preserve man's dignity he must be permitted to become the slave of evil if he will, the associate of devils for ever—to secure his prerogative of freedom he must be allowed to sink into hopeless servitude to sin. What would you say were an earthly father to reason thus?—I will permit my child to become a hopeless drunkard for the sake of preserving his sobriety; I will permit my daughter to sink into vice for the sake of preserving her chastity. Under these circumstances, it is mere rhetoric to talk of "forcing" the will. The will yields, because it is free, and because good is finally the strongest force in an universe ruled by God. (XI.)—Nay, the only condition of true freedom for man is the divine control. The seeming paradox is true—constraint of man's will, because it is weak and evil, is his emancipation. "If the Son make you free, then shall ye be free indeed."—"*Deo servire est libertas.*" To plead against this constraint of the divine grace, as annulling human freedom, is as unreasonable as it would be, on the part of the friends of some fever-stricken patient, to object to the restraints of the sick room and the physician. A lunatic is to be restrained; a criminal to be imprisoned; an incendiary to be arrested; but the moral criminal, the spiritual incendiary, these are not to be constrained even by grace divine! They are to gravitate slowly to perpetual *bondage*— in the name, I repeat, of LIBERTY? God's will is to be set at naught permanently, in order that the devil's will may be done. (XII.)—Next, is it not strange that this claim to be independent of God, to defy His control finally, is made for man, in one direction only, *i.e.*, precisely when and where it may do to him irreparable mischief? We cannot add so much as a cubit to our stature, cannot determine so much as the length of an eyelash. We cannot of ourselves take a single step heavenwards. But we can, on this theory, take as many steps hellwards as we please. We cannot save ourselves, but we can damn ourselves. (XIII.)—But again, it obviously follows that if man is in this sense free, *i e.*, is free to defy God finally, then either (*a*) God does not in any real sense will the salvation of all men, but does will man's absolute freedom, at the cost of his salvation (if the two conflict), or (*b*) He does will it, but is unable to accomplish it. And, if so, then He is not free. He wills, but His will is useless to save; it is fettered and bound. And what is this but a virtual denial of the true God? Whoever such a being may be, He is not the God of the Bible. To the *very essence* of God it pertains to be sovereign and supreme over all wills and all things whatsoever. "I appeal to the tribunal of a sovereign judge," says Canon WESTCOTT, "Whose will is right, and Whose *will must prevail.*"—*Hist. Faith.* And again, "It is enough for us to acknowledge the supreme triumph of divine love from first to last—one will of one God reconciling the world to Himself in Jesus Christ His only Son."—*Ib.* (XIV.)—It is impossible to quote more than a fraction of the passages in which Scripture, while *recognising in man a power of choice*, so that no one is saved against his will, but by God's working in Him a good will, yet points distinctly to God's will as supreme, as certain finally to prevail. " My counsel shall stand, and I will do all my pleasure."—*Is.* xlvi. 10. "Whatever the Lord pleased, that did He, in heaven and on earth."—*Ps.* cxxxv. 6. "He doeth according to His will, in the armies of heaven and among the inhabitants of earth."—*Dan.* iv. 35; v. 21; iv. 3, 17; vii. 14. *Prov.* xix. 21; xxi. 1. *Ps.* lxix. 13; xcix. 1; ciii. 19; x. 16; xxix. 10, &c., &c. Nay, Scripture goes farther still. It tells us plainly that the creature (creation) has been made "subject to vanity (sin and imperfection), *not willingly*, but by reason of Him who hath subjected the same in hope."—*Rom.* viii. 20. Again, "*God hath shut up all* unto disobedience that He might have mercy upon all."—*Rom.* xi. 32. And so of salvation we are plainly told that it is "NOT OF HIM WHO WILLETH, BUT OF GOD Who sheweth mercy."—*Rom.* ix. 16. "Ye are saved *not of yourselves,*" says St. PAUL.—*Eph.* ii. 8. And S. JOHN assures us that the sons of God are born *not of the will of man, but of God.*—*S. John* i. 13. "Ye," says a greater than S. JOHN, "have *not* chosen Me, but *I have chosen* you."—*Ib.* xv. 16. So the Gospel is the proclamation of His kingdom. "Thy kingdom come," not Thy Salvation, but Thy *Rule*. We are to work (and so far are free), but behind and above and beneath our work, there rules and works the will of God. "Work out your own Salvation," says the Apostle; but *why?* not because here is a sphere outside the divine will, but, precisely because here too God rules, "*for* it is *He* Who works in you both to will, and to do." It is "*not* according to our works" that He calls and saves,—2 *Tim.* i. 9., but "according to His own purpose;" "according to the counsel of His own will."—*Eph.* i. 11. This divine supremacy is ever in S. Paul's thoughts in passages too numerous to quote. And so our Lord does not hesitate to say "compel"—literally *necessitate*—"them to come in."—*S. Luke* xiv. 23. For "the Lord God omnipotent reigneth."—*Rev.* xix. 6. Men fear the reproach of Calvinism, which is quite another creed from this; and so have lost all true conception of a divine sovereignty, which is universal love. Nor is man a machine, because God is and must be, Master in His own house. Man *can resist*, but God's grace is stronger. Perhaps the strongest assertion the New Testament contains of human free-will is *S. Matt.* xxiii. 37, "Ye would not;" but, reading on, we learn that even they, who would not, are one day to say, "Blessed is He that cometh in the name of the Lord."

The exigencies of controversy must be great to induce men to teach, on the authority of the New Testament, that the clay can absolutely defy the great Potter. May I remind our opponents that, when controversy is forgotten, we all in fact admit this divine supremacy. So the Prayer Book tells us that God can "*order the unruly wills of sinful men*," evidently teaching that He will do this. It states that He disposes the hearts of kings (and if so, of all,) as it seemeth best—not to human free-will—but to His will and governance. (XV.)—And that which Scripture so plainly affirms, the very idea of Redemption implies. For Redemption is either an empty sound, or it implies setting free the will of man, *i.e.*, bringing it into harmony with God's will. "The bondage I groan under is a bondage of the will, and that has led me to acknowledge God as *emphatically the redeemer of the will;* \* \* \* but if of my will then of all wills."— F. D. MAURICE. I have stated my glad acquiescence in human freedom, only preserving God's freedom and sovereignty. For if consciousness assure me of a freedom very real in its own sphere, yet there is another side—a Divinity that "shapes our ends, rough hew them how we will,"— words that may fitly sum up this controversy.

In resuming, let me draw an argument from the fact of creation, a subject to which I shall return in a future chapter. "Nothing," says Bishop NEWTON, "is more contrariant to the divine nature and attributes than for God to bestow existence on any being, whose destiny He foreknows must terminate in wretchedness without recovery."—*Final State of Man.* Let us take an illustration that we may see this more clearly. "A frail and narrow bridge swings across a gulf, fearful and fathomless. On this, as it rocks wildly in the winds, a father places his young child. Beyond, on the other side of the gulf, he has placed a prize beyond estimate, which he promises to the child if he passes the bridge safely, and then compels him to go, commanding him to look neither to the right nor left. \* \* \* The boy, heedless and disobedient, hesitates, reels, the bridge quivers for a moment, swings from under him, and hurled into the gulf, he is caught and impaled on a sharp rock down the abyss. There he hangs for long and weary years, agonizing and writhing in torture, and crying to his father for help and deliverance. But his father turns a deaf year to all his entreaties, wholly indifferent to the horrible sufferings of his child, and justifies himself by saying, 'The boy might have passed the bridge safely, he was warned, and he suffers justly.' Admitting the possibility of passing safely, yet all men would pronounce this father a monster and a fiend. And shall God place me on the frail and narrow bridge of life, stretched over the awful and flaming abyss of endless perdition, with the possibility of a heaven beyond, and then leave me there to cross it, swinging fearfully in the winds of temptation, knowing that as a matter of fact I shall, in crossing, be precipitated into the horrible pit, there to lie for ever in hopeless agony?" Who would not cry out with the poet already quoted—

> "And canst Thou then look down from perfect bliss
> And see me plunging in this dark abyss,
> *Calling Thee Father in a sea of fire,*
> *Or pouring blasphemies at Thy desire?*"

Yes, the question is essentially this, and no argument can evade this enquiry :—Is God good, and is He a just God, as men use these terms, or is He not? Indeed, if the God we worship be not good, as we call goodness, it were better for us not to worship Him at all; better for us to worship nothing at all, than to worship an evil deity. But the popular view represents God as doing that which the most degraded human being would not do. "This view," says the Rev. Dr. LITTLEDALE, "puts God on a moral level with the devisers of the most savagely malignant revenge known to history."—*Cont Review*—words that fall far short of the truth.

To this in fact it comes, that the popular view, while admitting God's power and goodness to be infinite, yet teaches that evil shall ultimately prevail—a position obviously untenable, and indeed absurd. "Order and right *cannot but prevail* finally in an universe under His government."— BUTLER's *Analogy*. For argue as you please, refine, explain away, it continues still an *insuperable* difficulty, on the popular view, or any mere modification of it, that the devil is victor, and triumphs over God and goodness. It is nothing at all to the purpose to allege, either that those who perish finally have chosen evil of their own will, or that all evil beings are shut up in chains and torment: it is the very permanence of evil in any shape: its continued presence— *no matter from what cause*—that constitutes the triumph of the evil one. "To suppose," says Canon WESTCOTT, "that evil once introduced into the world is for ever, appears to be at variance with the essential conception of God as revealed to us."—*Hist. Faith.* I repeat that if evil be as strong as God, as enduring as God himself, there is no escape from the conclusion that you proclaim in so teaching the triumph of the evil one. You are proclaiming, not the catholic faith, but a dualism. You blot from the faith of christendom its fundamental article, "I believe in *one* God the Father *Almighty.*" What are all heresies, all errors, that have stained the Church of God, compared with this supreme heresy, this dualism, which seats evil on the throne of the universe, a power enduring as God Himself? The torments, physical and mental, of the popular hell, awful as they are, recede into almost nothing as compared with the far more awful spectacle of God vanquished, of God trying to save but failing, and watching His children as they slowly sink beneath the endless sway of evil; of God's Son returning, not in triumph, but in defeat; of the Cross so far prostrate, paralysed, vanquished.

Again, so revolting to our moral nature is the popular creed, that it more than any other cause, as has been said, produces the most wide-spreading unbelief. "Compared with this," remarks J. S. MILL, "all objections to christianity sink into insignificance." Let me speak plainly. Too

## THE POPULAR CREED WHOLLY UNTENABLE.

long—far too long—have the clergy been silent; content to complain of a scepticism, of which a main cause is a doctrine they continue to teach (without, I believe in many cases, more than a languid and merely traditional acceptance of it). And as this doctrine is the parent of unbelief at home, so abroad in the mission field it is a grievous hindrance to the spread of the Gospel. The very heathen are shocked by a dogma more cruel and horrible than anything of which they have ever heard; the more so when they are asked to receive this awful teaching as part of the message of good news. There is certainly a chapter of missionary work yet unwritten, which would, if frankly told, surprise the friends of the traditional creed. This is a chapter which any thoughtful person can construct, if he will try to place himself in the position of an intelligent heathen, when he learns that the *good news* of the missionary contains a revelation often more ghastly and cruel than any that has crossed his mind. A cruel Gospel produces a scanty harvest. I repeat that no thoughtful man can believe a doctrine condemned by the conscience; and so men will seek a refuge in scepticism, when they hear the clergy teaching these evil traditions (for they are no more) as part of the revelation of that God, Whose blessed Son tasted death for every man. Yes, the peculiar horror of the popular creed is, that it sets up evil as an object of worship —of reverence—of love.

Nor let us forget the insult offered to God by the traditional creed. Amid the crowd of sins there stands out one in sad pre-eminence because it has not forgiveness "for the age," *eis ton aiona*, its forgiveness demands ages—demands a period indefinitely long. Now, from our Lord's own words we may understand in what lay the essence of this awful sin.

It lay in confounding the good and evil Spirit, in ascribing to the one the works of the other. If, then, any one whose conscience whispers that endless misery can only be inflicted by an evil being on his own children, still persists in ascribing its infliction to God, does not such an one incur sad and awful risk of committing this greatest of all sins? I invite your earnest attention to this. Does your conscience say I cannot reconcile this awful doctrine with any idea I can form of love, of justice, or of goodness; and yet I believe it? If so, then beware lest in ascribing such things to God, you come perilously near to, if indeed you are not guilty of, this sin, which is of all sins the greatest (known in the popular creed as the unpardonable sin.)

Yes, the question of all questions is, is God indeed love, is the Gospel really good news, not possible but *actual* glad tidings to all? All around us thoughtful men are more than ever reflecting on these points; what answer do you propose to give? They are thus enquiring—pondering—of themselves, of their lot, of their hopes and fears in the future:— "I find myself in this world;" (so run the thoughts of each enquirer) "on me are laid, *whether I will or no*, the awful responsibilities of time and of eternity. Sin has from the very womb crippled me, before any power of choice was possible for me. For this calamity, too often, I receive blame and not pity. Is it fair or just to bestow sympathy on a body naturally crooked, and to have no pity, but wrath, for a spirit naturally crooked? At my entrance on life I received a nature already fallen; and that for no fault of mine; stained, and that with no sin of mine. And to this nature so weak, so fallen, come, in every variety, temptations, wiles, and allurements such that no man has wholly withstood, or can withstand, their subtle power. Now, if this be a part of my training, if it be a path to better things, I can in submission—nay, in gladness even—bend to my Creator's will: I can take courage, and though faint, still pursue the narrow path that leads to life. But how can I believe that a loving Father—all powerful as He is all good, and absolutely free, does so arrange, does so permit, that for any one soul, this sad and fallen estate of human nature shall prove but the portal to endless woe; that the gift of life—which Providence has forced on me—shall ripen to endless woe and sin?" So men reason. I do not wonder, I rejoice, that they have ceased to believe, that a divine parent can do that which an earthly parent could not do without eternal infamy. For imagine any possible degree of folly and sin that can stain human nature, to be accumulated on the head of some sinful child of man; and I ask, can you believe that any human father, any mother, that once loved that child, could bring herself calmly to sentence her offspring to an endless hell; nay, herself to keep that child there in evil that never shall terminate?

Take next a clear exposure of the traditional creed from another point of view. Christ, we know from the Bible, is the Saviour of the world. He is, therefore, on the popular view, the Saviour of those whom in fact He does not save. This evidently follows. But this principle once admitted, it is wholly immaterial, as a matter of reasoning, what the percentage of the lost may be. Although out of the countless myriads of our race but a few hundreds were saved, God would still *save every man*. Indeed, though *not even one solitary soul* were saved, God would still, on the principle popularly held, save *every* man. For that principle is this, that to offer salvation, though the offer come to nothing, is to save. Hence it undoubtedly follows that God might be the Saviour of the whole race of men, *though not one soul were in fact saved*. All might be *saved* on this principle, though all were in fact *damned!* But there is a further difficulty in the way of the popular creed. Who are those whom it represents as finally unsaved?—the finally impenitent, the most obstinate sinners. And what is that but to say, in so many words, that those precisely whose case furnished the strongest reason for the Saviour's mission, are unsaved? Admit their guilt, recognise as we do to the very utmost the need and the certainty of retribution; still, when all this has been said, it remains true that Christ came to save the "lost," and if so, the more "lost" any are, the more Christ came to seek and to save them, and if He fails, the more marked His failure. Thus on the ordinary view, precisely those for whom Christ especially came receive no salvation; those whose claims are strongest perish, those whose claims on a Saviour are weakest, are rescued. For the fullest admission of the guilt of sin, must not blind us to the sinner's claim on our sympathy. Sin abounding calls out grace much more abounding; such is the great principle enunciated by S. PAUL. Are we to say with the traditional creed, sin abounding beyond certain limits (obstinate sin) ceases to call out grace?

Let us apply this consideration to a plea often used to disguise, if that may be, the awful fact of endless torment by teaching that but few, comparatively, will share this horrible lot. Elsewhere I have shewn the futility of this plea, on other grounds—but here I desire to press this aspect of the case, that these few are precisely those, whose case appeals most of all to a Saviour. Hence, so to argue, implies a misconception of the very essence of the Gospel. Am I to say the Good Physician can heal all except those who need Him most? He came to save *sinners* (emphatically sinners).

Am I to read the passage thus : He came to save all sinners *except the greatest?* And let us not forget how much the traditional creed has fostered in man a spirit of cruelty. It is sad, but true, to recollect how much of the suffering inflicted by man on his brother man, has been due, directly or indirectly, to the belief in an endless hell. It gave to torture an apparent divine sanction—"In every prison the crucifix and the rack stood side by side." Mediæval torments have a character peculiar to themselves "They represent a condition of thought, in which men had pondered long and carefully on all the forms of suffering; had combined, and compared, the different forms of torture, till they had become the most consummate masters of their art."— LECKY; *Hist. of Ration.* i. 330. For if men believed that God would light up the gloomy fires of hell and keep them blazing to all eternity, it was an easy and a natural step, to set up in His name a little copy of His justice, and thus, as it were, to anticipate God's sentence. "As the souls of heretics are hereafter to be eternally burning in hell," such was the reasoning of Queen MARY in defence of her awful persecution, "there can be nothing more proper than for me to imitate the divine vengeance, by burning them here on earth." I say, that however familiar this may be, it is necessary to ponder well the sad facts, for, by awaking a righteous horror and indignation, we may often most effectually combat such dogmas. And more must be said, not alone have the popular doctrines done all this, but they have greatly influenced for evil the general course of human legislation, and human thought. Many pages might be filled in enumerating the horrors, and anguish, added to human life by these doctrines. Let me only add that they have poisoned the very fount of pity and love, by representing Him, Whose we are, and before Whom we bow, as calmly looking on during the endless cycles of eternity, at the sin and agony of myriads upon myriads of His creatures.

Thus it is that by this shocking creed the moral tone is lowered all round, wherever it is accepted. Men are familiarized with the idea of suffering and sin as permanent facts. They have even in some sort learned to consider heaven as dependent upon the belief in an endless hell. The very holiest men believing the popular creed are unconsciously depraved, morally and spiritually. You will find for instance, even one like KEBLE, pleading (see hymn for second Sunday in Lent), for endless torment, on the ground that if this were not true, then endless bliss in heaven would also not be true. To put it plainly, he would, as I understand his words, purchase heaven's unending bliss at the terrible cost of the endless, hopeless, torture of the lost! Here I will only say, that I know not whether his logic, or his moral tone be more unsound. Compare the spirit of KEBLE with, I will not say the spirit of Christ, but with that of S. PAUL, who wished himself accursed from Christ, if thereby he could save his brethren. As to KEBLE's argument, that will be, I trust, fully answered in considering, in a later chapter, *S. Matt.* xxv. 46. Meantime, as a further illustration, I copy the the following from a periodical lying before me: "I was talking the other day with a very learned Catholic ecclesiastic, who told me that he had been called on to give the last sacraments to a poor Irishman. He found his penitent with some free-thinking friend, who was arguing that there was no hell. The dying Celt raised himself up with much indignation; 'no hell,' he exclaimed, 'then where is the poor man's *consolation?*'"—*Church Reformer.*

And this difficulty goes further still; for we cannot

suppose that the saints in heaven are without any memory of the past. Even DIVES, in the flames of hades, remembers with pity his brethren. But unless you make the impossible supposition, that the blessed lose all memory in heaven, then they must either suffer keenly at the thoughts of the torments of their dear ones lost in hell, and tormented for ever and ever; or they must be on a *lower level*, morally and spiritually, than was even DIVES—choose which alternative you please. To this dilemma no answer has ever been given, for no answer is possible. If hades kindle the sympathy of the lost, shall heaven kill the sympathy of the blessed? If the blessed sympathise with the torments of the lost, can they enjoy even a momentary happiness? If they fail to sympathise, are they not sunk in selfishness and debased? Or shall we say that God actually maims His redeemed, depriving them of knowledge and memory, lest they should miss their lost ones? On this view God's ways are so awful that if known they would wither up the very joys of heaven, and so He shuts out pity, and wraps the blessed in a mantle of selfish ignorance. I know nothing more degrading, or revolting in the traditional creed than the baseness of its heavenly state. Fancy a mother thrilled through with bliss while (near, or far off, it matters not) her child is in the grip of devils; a wife joining in the angelic harmonies, while her husband for ever blasphemes!

Such is the heaven of the ordinary creed; if it be not something worse still, an exulting over the torments of the lost. To shew that this is no mere figure of speech, I append a few extracts. They are from sources so widely apart as a mediæval schoolman, and a modern puritan. "That the saints may *enjoy* their beatitude more thoroughly, and give more abundant thanks for it to God, *a perfect sight* of the punishment of the damned is granted them."—*S. Thomas —Summa* iii. Take another instance from PETER LOMBARD, "Therefore the elect shall go forth to see the torments of the impious, seeing which they will not be grieved, but will be *satiated with joy* \* \* \* at the sight of the *unutterable* calamity of the impious."—*Senten.* iv. 50. Again, hear another from a modern divine, "The *view of the misery of the damned* will *double* the ardour of the love and gratitude of the saints in heaven." This is the opinion of the once famous JONATHAN EDWARDS. Another American divine uses even stronger language. "This display of the divine character," said S. HOPKINS, " will be most *entertaining* to all who love God— will give them the *highest and most ineffable pleasure. Should the fire of this eternal punishment cease, it would in a great measure obscure the light of heaven, and put an end to a great part of the happiness and glory of the blessed.*"—*Works,* vol. iv. *Serm.* xiii. To this the popular creed has degraded the ministers of Christ, to penning passages like the above (easily to be multiplied)—passages, than which all literature does not contain anything more revolting. It is easy to be shocked at all this, and to repudiate it, but *how is it possible* for the friends of God to be otherwise than *pleased with His judgments?* I must ask you, as a relief, to read the following touching picture :—

> What if a soul redeemed, a spirit that loved
> While yet on earth, and was beloved in turn,
> And still remembered every look and tone
> Of that dear earthly sister, who was left
> Among the unwise virgins at the gate :
> Itself admitted with the bridegroom's train—
> What if this spirit redeemed, amid the host
> Of chanting angels, in some transient lull
> Of the eternal anthem, heard the cry
> Of its lost darling, whom in evil hour
> Some wilder pulse of nature led astray,
> And left an outcast in a world of fire,

> Condemned to be the sport of cruel fiends,
> Sleepless, unpitying, masters of the skill
> To wring the maddest ecstasies of pain,
> From worn-out souls that only ask to die—
> *Would it not long to leave the bliss of heaven,*
> *Bearing a little water in its hand,*
> *To moisten those poor lips that plead in vain;*
> *With Him we call our Father?*
>
> O. W. HOLMES.—*The Poet at the Breakfast Table.*

I say next that the popular creed does in fact teach men to think lightly of sin. This seems a paradox, and no doubt you wonder: but consider for a moment what the fact is. Tell me that God will permit an eternal hell, with its miserable population of the lost, to go on sinning to all eternity; and what idea is it you really convey to me? It is, I reply, the *toleration of sin*. Have you ever thought of this? "Nothing so effectually teaches men to bear with sin as the popular creed, because we profess to believe that God will bear with it for ever." Further, I say that the practical effect of the ordinary creed is to teach men to think lightly of sin in a very large class of cases, *e.g.*, where a careless and ungodly life has been lived, and no apparent repentance has marked the closing scene. For to those who believe that the few days or moments remaining of life on a sick bed, are the sole period in which salvation is possible, how irresistible must be the temptation to patch up a hollow peace, to accept anything in lieu of a genuine repentance. And so not the thoughtless, but teachers grave and holy—*e.g.*, Dr. PUSEY—do in fact, as they endeavour to escape the awful difficulties of the ordinary creed, lay stress on the possibility or probability of men leading a wicked life, up to the very last moment of existence, and in that last moment receiving the divine grace. Can any teaching be at once more repugnant to all experience, more contrary to all reason, and more likely to cause the young and the careless to make light of sin?

Indeed, it is often precisely those who most deeply feel the taint and evil of sin who reject most completely the popular creed; for in proportion to their horror at sin, is the depth of their conviction that sin cannot go on for ever. There is, too, this further question, if sin is to endure for ever in hell, must it not increase and go on increasing for ever and ever? Think to what point of horror the accumulated sin of the myriads of the lost will have reached, when even a few of the cycles of eternity are over: and this vast and inconceivable horror and taint is to go *on*, and *on*, and *on*, for *ever*, and *ever*, and *ever increasing*, under the rule of Him Who is of purer eyes than to behold iniquity. Think of endless blasphemy and rottenness: of moral foulness tainting God's universe: the leprosy of undying evil poisoning all around: cries of endless agony blending with the angelic choir. God knows how painful such thoughts are to write down. But it is a duty to try and bring home to men's minds what the traditional creed really means. "Think, too, how grotesque a parody of the divine justice it is to say, as the popular creed does, that God requires obedience and righteousness here, but if He cannot have these, He will be satisfied with endless disobedience and sin hereafter as a substitute. We are gravely told that if the wrong be not righted within a specified time, justice will be satisfied to increase the wrong infinitely, and perpetuate it to all eternity." I repeat, that the powers of imagination, if taxed to the utmost, could hardly conceive any more ludicrous parody of justice than the above.

But there is this further difficulty. For we must ask—How is this perpetuation of evil possible? Can a literal fire for ever prey on the hapless limbs, and never consume them? Can nature support this for ever? Are we to return to the hideous conception (of some early writers) of the "intelligent fire," which renews, as it consumes, in order to make the agony endless? Or if we take a more spiritual view of future punishment, can degradation be perpetual? Must not such a process end at some time from its very nature?

Further, all sin, be it never so black (and God forbid that I should even seem to weaken its blackness), is but finite. Yet, for these finite sins, I am told, an infinite punishment is the due penalty. But finite and infinite are wholly incommensurable terms. Have you ever set yourself seriously to realise what punishment, protracted *for ever and ever* indeed means? In fact the idea of illimitable time mocks our utmost efforts to grasp it. "The imagination can come to a stand nowhere or ever. On the mind goes, heaping up its millions and billions and quadrillions of millions. It is to no purpose—time, without a beginning—without an end —still confronts it. As thus thought of, the mind recoils from the contemplation, horrified, paralysed with terror." If we grasp never so faintly the idea of what an *infinite* punishment means, it becomes clear that no proposition more revolting to the idea of justice can be stated than this, that finite sins deserve an infinite penalty. Expand the finite as you will, and it still falls infinitely short of infinity. Hence, it is but the sober statement of sober fact, to assert that a single sentence of unending torment would outweigh the *whole sins of the whole human race*. To prove this I need but assume that, to which every conscience responds, that what is finite can in justice receive only a finite punishment. But any possible number of finite sins put together will still fall short (nay, infinitely short) of infinity—of infinite guilt.* Add

---

\*If it is said, that there may be some infinite evil in sin, that, even if true (which nobody knows and Scripture nowhere teaches), does

together all sins ever committed, be their blackness what it may, be their horrors never so great; still the sum of all, because the guilt of finite mortals is but finite, and unless all justice is to be outraged, would deserve a sentence that, however awful, would be finite. Hence it follows that a single sentence of *infinite misery* would undoubtedly outweigh, if there be such a thing as justice, the sins of all men who have ever lived, and who shall ever live.

There is again, a difficulty—an impossibility rather—in reconciling endless penalties with the view, which either Holy Scripture or reason give of punishment—its object and nature. This most important topic, with the kindred question of the scriptural doctrine of forgiveness, needs our best attention. Let us briefly consider the latter first. Doubtless God always accepted the penitent. But a wholly novel duty of forgiving has emerged since Christ said, "Love your *enemies*, do good to them which hate (are hating, keep hating) you."—*S. Luke* vi. 27. No doubt in this novel view we have a distinct revelation of the divine character. But if so, is it possible to suppose that the Gospel presents us with two contradictory pictures of God, *e.g*, a God Who does good to His enemies only for the few years they spend on earth, and then proceeds to do them all possible evil in hell? If God's attitude towards His worst foes is love, that attitude is permanent, is eternal; nay, must be so. Whatever be the sin of His enemies, He must be to them the same unchanging God of love, and never more so than when He most

---

not make human guilt infinite. For on any just principle, guilt is determined by the capacities and powers of the agent, and all these are in man strictly finite. Nay, the Bible, so far from taking this view, tells us that Israel has received of the Lord's hand *double* for all her sins, which involves a direct contradiction of any such theory of infinite guilt.—*Is*. xl. 2; *Jer*. xvi. 18. Besides, does not endless punishment prove, if true, that the judge never obtains satisfaction?

inexorably punishes. Note the emphatic " BUT I SAY unto you, love your enemies." Here is the very heart of God disclosed; here is the dividing line; here the spiritual watershed between a true and a false theology.

Next I say, that endless penalties contradict the true end of punishment. Apart from all question of its justice—apart, too, from the horror it excites—endless torment, is an useless, and therefore a wanton, infliction: it is a mere barbarity, because it is only vindictive, and in no sense remedial. There is something positively sickening in the thought of the cruelty, combined with the uselessness, of penalty prolonged, when all hope of amendment is over, and when retribution has been fully exacted. To go on punishing for ever, simply for punishment sake, shocks every sentiment of justice. And the case is so much the worse when, as remarked, the punishment is really the prolongation of evil, when it is but making evil endless. But the true view of punishment is not to oppose, but to combine its retributive and remedial aspects, for through retribution it aims at amendment. Our day has seen a complete revolution in the ideas men form of punishment and its end: in few things has the advance been more marked over the past than in our recognition of the true object of penalty. But let me ask, to whom is due this marked change for the better in our ideas of punishment? Surely to that Great Being Who guides and orders by His providence all human things. This being so, it is wholly incredible to assign to the divine punishments this very character of mere vindictiveness, which men have in all enlightened systems abandoned. This is, I repeat, impossible to believe, for when God chastises it is *for our profit*, as the Bible says. He punishes, as an old Father puts it, medicinally. Yes, it is impossible to believe the ordinary dogma;

for if God does indeed by His providence—by His Spirit—direct and enlighten men's minds, leading them to higher and truer thoughts on this subject (as on all others), then to suppose that His own punishments are regulated on the very system, which He has taught us to abandon, is truly impossible. Nor can I discuss this subject without remarking that there is a highly significant expression found in that very passage, most often on the lips of the defenders of endless pain, which yet, curiously enough, furnishes the material for an answer to their creed, I speak of S. *Matthew* xxv. 46. The term there applied to the punishment of the ungodly is not the ordinary Greek word to denote penalty or vengeance (*timoria*), but it is a term (*kolasis*) denoting, literally, *pruning*, *i.e.*, a corrective chastisement—an age-long (but reformatory) punishment.

It is most important to gain clear conceptions as to the true function of punishment. Three stages may be clearly distinguished—though united by a period of transition—through which men's minds have passed in their treatment of crime. At first all penalties are purely vindictive and personal; in the rudest stage of society we have the wild justice of revenge, an eye for an eye, a tooth for a tooth. This idea lingers yet in some semi-barbarous districts, *e.g.*, the Corsican vendetta. Next comes a higher conception, in which the wrong done to the state replaces the wrong done to the individual. Society exacts the penalty; the tribunal takes the place of the knife. In this stage our ideas have rested for centuries. But this stage we now see to be, at least, wholly imperfect. It repeats the wrong, and thus tends to perpetuate it: it thinks little of the criminal's amendment, content to rest mainly on the vindictive idea; differing from the rudest stage in this chiefly, that the revenge is exacted in the name, not of the individual, but of the state.

At length we are on the verge of a truer conception of penalty : we are beginning to dwell most of all on the amendment of the criminal. The main idea is not the wrong done to the injured person, as in the first stage ; nor the wrong done to society, as in the second ; but it is rather the wrong done to the criminal himself by his crime. This is the reformatory age on which we are now entering with steady, if slow, steps. Need I add that the relation of all this to theology is the closest possible ? When we seize on—as perhaps the central idea of sin—the wrong done by the sinner to himself, and not merely the offence against God, *true as that is*, we can better estimate the true function of punishment as retributive indeed, but in its essence remedial. Nor does any sentimentality lurk here, for we recognise the need of stern retribution, and enforce the penalty : but our aim is different. Through suffering we would always heal. The end aimed at is the extinction of sin, and the restoration of the sinner ; for no other end is worthy of God, and of man made in His image and likeness.

## CHAPTER III.

### *THE POPULAR CREED WHOLLY UNTENABLE.*

" Far be it from me to make light of the demerit of sin. But endless punishment—I admit my inability (I would say it reverently) to admit this belief together with a belief in the divine goodness—the belief that God is Love, that His tender mercies are over all His works."—JOHN FOSTER on *Future Punishment.*

THE considerations just stated illustrate well the growth of morality. In fact we have still vast arrears to make up, for the growth of our moral conceptions has been at once very slow, and very one-sided. In the fierce struggle for success the intellectual faculties have been sharpened, while the sympathetic tendencies have been dwarfed. Even yet we have hardly begun to realise what that saying means, "Thou shalt love thy neighbour *as thyself.*" Take an illustration. All christendom is a vast camp : all Europe is armed to the teeth. What does all this mean?—this at any rate, that our whole life is still permeated with a spirit of revenge. These armaments preach the gospel of hatred of our enemies. They are schools ever open, in which the obvious lessons are a formal contradiction of the Sermon on the mount. Whatever reasonable excuses may be offered, certain it is that all this re-acts on our opinions. It blinds us to the idea of Love as supreme, and of humanity as one family. It sets up resentment as an ideal of duty. And if this be so still, how much more was it the case in those ages in which war was the chief occupation, and the chief glory of civilised (?) human beings? Men living in such a state were wholly incapable of rising to true christian teaching. They held half, or more than half, their neighbours in bondage as mere chattels. They tortured their criminals: they burned them, or boiled them alive, their foes they massacred. Now precisely through such channels as these very much of current theology has filtered down: it is, in fact, an anachronism. We are still drinking largely from poisoned wells. But if our awakening be slow it is sure. A cruel Deity watching unmoved to all eternity the agonies, moral or physical, of His creatures, will seem to our children but an evil dream. Is it credible that, when torture has been banished from human justice, divine justice shall stand alone in consigning offenders to torture without any end?

Pursuing our remarks, I must also remind you of another feature of the popular belief, which seems to present a great difficulty; it is what I must call its paltriness, its unworthiness of God. Let us for the moment not think of God as a good, loving, and righteous Being. Let us now simply regard Him as great, as irresistible, as almighty. Viewed thus, how difficult is it to accept that account which the ordinary creed gives us of this Being's attempt at the rescue of His fallen creature man. An Almighty Being puts forth every effort to gain a certain end; sends inspired men to teach others; works miracles, signs, wonders in heaven and on earth, all for this end of man's safety; nay, at the last, sends forth His own Son—very God—Himself Almighty. The Almighty Son stoops not alone to take our nature on

Him, but lower still—far lower—stoops to degradation; meekly accepts insults and scourging, bends to the bitter cross even, and all this to gain a certain end. And yet, we are told, this end is not gained after all, man is not saved, for countless myriads are in fact left to hopeless, endless misery; and that, though for every one of these lost ones, so to speak, has been shed the life blood of God's own Son. Now, if I may be permitted to speak freely, it is wholly inconceivable that the definite plan of an Almighty Being should end in failure—that this should be the result of the agony of the eternal Son. God has, in the face of angels and of men, before the universe and its gaze of wonder, entered Himself into the arena, become Himself a combatant, has wrestled with the foe, and has been defeated. I can bring myself to imagine those, who reject the Deity of Christ, as believing in His defeat; but it is passing strange that those who believe Him to be "very God Almighty," are loudest in asserting His failure.

And continue this thought. If we think of God at all worthily, we cannot help thinking of Him as working for high and worthy ends. Therefore we cannot help thinking of Him, as in creation, working for some end worthy of Himself. But what end does the popular creed assign to Him? A creation mutilated, ruined, and that for ever. A creation ending in misery and endless sin to infinite numbers of the created; and all this misery and horror brought into sharper relief by a vain and fruitless attempt to save all: by a purpose of love declared to all, and yet not in fact reaching all: a creation which is but the portal to hell for so many of the created. And you gravely ask thoughtful enquirers to believe this; to believe that, contemplating these horrors destined never to cease, the morning stars are described as singing together, and all the sons of God shouting for joy on the morning of creation.

The sons of God shouted for joy, as they contemplated creation; but they should have wept had the popular creed been true. For that creed represents the present life as darkened by the prospect of evil triumphant; our present sorrows made keener by the prospect of a future life, which will be, not to the wicked merely, but to the whole race of man, an evil and a curse—a life which every good man would, if he could, bring to an instant end. To prove this, I will take a definite example. Further, I will concede to the advocates of the popular creed one point of very considerable importance (to which they have no right), *e.g.*, that the number of the saved greatly exceeds the lost. "Suppose it were offered to the father of three children to take his choice whether two should be received into heaven and one condemned to hell, or the whole should be annihilated in death. What would a parent say? Where is the father who would dare to secure the bliss of two children at the cost of the endless misery of one? Which of the family would he select as the victim, whose undying pain should secure his brother's immortal joy? Is there any one living who would not suffer himself and his children to sink back again into nothingness, rather than purchase heaven at such a price? Now, if so, if we should so act in the case of our own children, *we are bound morally* to make the same choice with respect to every one. No moral being would consent to purchase eternal happiness at the price of another's eternal woe. Hence it follows that a future life, on the popular view, is an evil to the human race, *not to the wicked, but to all.* For if annihilation of the whole race should be tendered as the alternative, no moral being could, as has been shewn, refuse to accept it."—BARLOW, *Eternal Punishment*. Thus, there is, I repeat, if the popular creed be true, no alternative, no escape from the conclusion that creation is an evil thing, and a future life a curse to the whole human family. What is to be our answer to the scorn of the sceptic, to the challenge of the atheist? So long as we cling to an immoral creed there is none—absolutely none. What awful mockery is a gospel whose message is, in fact, damnation to countless myriads, whose issue is endless sin—sin ever ripening, ever progressing. And I am to accept such a gospel as good news, as glad tidings of great joy—glad tidings of never ending pain and curse and sin.

But again, there comes this very serious obstacle to accepting the popular creed. I shall state it thus, either this creed is true or false. If false—the question is ended. If true, can this strange fact be explained—that *nobody acts as if he believed it?* I say this, for any man who so believed, and who possessed but a spark of common humanity—to say nothing of charity—could not rest, day or night, so long as one sinner remained who might be saved. To this all would give place—pleasure, learning, business, art, literature; nay, life itself would be too short for the terrible warnings, the burning entreaties, the earnest pleadings, that would be needed to rouse sinners from their apathy, and to pluck them from endless tortures. Ask me what you will, but do not ask me to believe that any human being, who is convinced that perhaps his own child, his wife, his friend, his neighbour, even his enemy, is in danger of endless torment, could, if *really* persuaded of this, live as men now live, even the best men: who can avoid the inevitable conclusion that its warmest adherents really, though unconsciously, find their dogmas absolutely incredible? In fact these men (and it is the best thing to be said for them) teach their creed without real conviction. Their best eulogy is that they are self-deceivers.

These remarks also explain an obvious difficulty, viz., it has been shewn how the popular creed cuts at the root of all religion, poisoning the very fountains whence we draw our conceptions of love, of righteousness, of truth. But if so, it may be fairly asked, how is it that society subsists, that morality is not extinct? Because, I reply unhesitatingly, because no society, no individual, can possibly act, or has in fact acted, on such a creed, in the real business of life. It is simply impossible: who would dare so much as to smile, if he really believed endless torments were certain to be the portion of some member of his household—it may be of himself? Marriage would be a crime; each birth the occasion of an awful dread. The shadow of a possible hell would darken every home, sadden every family hearth. All this becomes evident when we reflect, that to perpetuate the race would be to help on the perpetuation of moral evil. For if this creed be true, out of all the yearly births a steady current is flowing on to help to fill the abyss of hell, to make larger and vaster the total of moral evil which is to endure for ever. "The world would be *one vast madhouse*," says the American scholar HALLSTED, "if a realising and continued pressure of such a doctrine was present." Remark again how this doctrine breaks down the moment it is really put to the test. Take a common case: a man dies—active, benevolent, useful in life, but not a religious man, not devout. By the popular creed, such a man has gone to hell for ever. But who really believes that? nay, instinctively our words grow softer when we speak of the dead in all cases. Do even the clergy really believe what they profess? I cannot refrain from most serious doubt on this point. If they believe, why are they so often silent? Habitual silence would be impossible to any one believing the traditional creed in earnest. The awful future would dwarf all other topics, would compel incessant appeals. But what do we find? Everything, I reply, that marks a declining faith in endless evil—silence; excuses; modifications; evasions of the true issue.

Take next a grave difficulty which arises on the popular view. How can you on any such principle deal equitably with the mass of men? Let us speak plainly: do tell me who and what are the great, nay, the *overwhelming* majority of the baptised? They are assuredly neither wholly bad, nor wholly good; they are neither bad enough for hell, nor good enough for heaven. Now how can you adapt your theory to this state of things, which is, I think, quite impossible to deny? Look around you, survey the mass of mankind: of how few, how very few, can you affirm that they are truly devout, converted, Christ-like; take which term you please. Can you affirm this of one in ten, in twenty, in a hundred even, of those baptized into Jesus Christ? Take as an illustration any English parish you please. Take any village, or select some one of our English towns, muster its whole population in imagination, how many true, holy servants of Jesus Christ will you find there? The *mass*—what are they? Let us meet this question, and look the facts straight in the face. What is to be the doom of the mass of baptized christians; they are not holy, but are they bad? Nobody out of the pulpit—and seldom there in these days—ventures to assert any such thing. For in truth there is abundant good in this crowd of human beings; and still more, there is almost infinite capacity for goodness amid the evil. Everywhere you will find unselfish parents, hard workers, loving sisters, true friends; everywhere traces, distinct enough amid all the sin, nay, traces in abundance of goodness, patience, self-sacrifice, sometimes carried even to great lengths. Let an emergency arise, let sickness come, what devotion does it not call forth, what love unstinted, what self-forgetfulness? Now your system, that which you call the good news brought from heaven by Jesus Christ, forces you to believe that God will consign all these hapless children of His, because unconverted in this life, to a doom, which in its lightest form is awful beyond all powers of imagination, to the company of devils for ever and ever. Permit me one question more, would not any creed, or no creed, be a positive relief from such *a gospel* as this of yours? Can there be a mockery more solemn, more emphatic, than to call this any part of the glad tidings of great joy? Is it not time for the clergy, not merely in private to ponder these things, convinced or half convinced of their truth, but to speak out as in God's name—as God's ministers?

And while I am speaking of men as they are, and of the life they lead, let me add here a statement of another very grave difficulty in the way of accepting an endless hell as the doom of any man, the issue of any life. Wherever human beings exist, in what form of community it matters not, in what climate or under what conditions of life soever, there is found everywhere a deep spontaneous belief, call it feeling, instinct, what you please, that connects the marriage tie and the birthday with joyful associations, with mirth and gladness. Now why is this—has it no meaning? So deep an instinct, one so truly natural and spontaneous as this, comes surely from the Creator of all. His voice it is that bids the bridegroom rejoice over the bride, that bids the heart of the mother overflow with tenderness towards her babe. This being so, again let me put the question, and ask, *why* has this been so ordered? It is God who has so ordered; do you think He has had no purpose in so doing, no message to convey to those who have ears to hear? Is it possible that our Heavenly Father should bid His creatures everywhere to rejoice with a special joy at the marriage feast, at the natal hour, if these births were in fact destined to add largely to the ranks of hell, to the hosts of evil? Do think over the matter calmly, and ask yourself if that is possible, if you can believe any such thing? And as you think it over, take with you these words of Jesus Christ (that hint so much). They remind us how the mother, in the " perilous birth" hath sorrow; but add, that all that sorrow is swallowed up in joy—" joy that a man is born into the world." Dwell on these words, that you may grasp all they convey. Indeed, it may almost be said that in this lies the whole matter. It is a *joy* that a man—any man—should be born into the world. See how wide the words are. If you tell me that this joy is but a blind instinct of the mother: yes, I reply, it is this very blindness, as you call it, of the instinct that constitutes its force, for it thus betrays its origin; it is implanted, and by whom? by the Great Parent, for it is spontaneous and betrays His hand. Do you ask me to believe that He has done this without a meaning, without a certain purpose of good? Can I believe that our Father bids any mother's heart to stir with joy at the sight of her infant, while He knows that this infant is destined to be, will be, in fact, shut up into endless torment and sin?

And again, can you reconcile the theory of endless evil awaiting so large a portion of our race with that natural thirst for joy, that longing for happiness each one finds within? It matters not whether this has been slowly developed or created at one stroke, all that matters to this argument is its *naturalness*, its *universality*. This longing for happiness cannot then have been accidental, there must be in it a design on the Creator's part. Now, what was that design? To delude us,—is that possible? " If the popular theory of future endless torment were true, what sublime mockery would there be in placing poor wretches first upon earth, where are heard the merry shouts of careless children, the joyous song of birds, where above our heads "with constant kindly smile, the sleepless stars keep everlasting watch," where beneath our feet the delicate beauty of flowers of every tint gladdens the eye. What would have been thought of the propriety of placing a hundred bright and cheerful objects, suggestive of peace and happiness, in the ante-room to the torture chamber of the inquisition? It deserves, too, to be noted that man, the only animal that laughs, has of all animals, according to the popular theory, least cause to laugh."—*Errors and Terrors of Blind Guides.*

But there is much to be said beyond remarking on our natural thirst for joy and happiness, and the difficulty of explaining why it was ever implanted in man, except with a design that it should one day be gratified, fully and freely. There is this to be said, there is stored in every man a vast possibility of growth, of expansion, mental and intellectual, no less than spiritual. There are almost infinite germs in man, so to speak, latent as yet, but capable of a development perhaps practically boundless: they are probably unsuspected by the majority, and it is only at intervals, and as it were by chance, that we gain a passing glance at them. But undoubtedly they exist, and their existence, like that of all other natural facts, requires an explanation. *Why* do they exist— who planted within us these powers, and for what end? And they have been given to all, not to the good merely, but to man as man. I cannot but see in the very fact of their existence a silent prophecy, an intimation that the spark shall not be quenched in any case. Are they not a very message to man from God, a *hint*, eloquent by its very silence, eloquent, and instinct with hope?

Consider next how strongly the analogy of nature, which is, after all, a very real revelation of God, bears against the popular view, which limits to the few moments of our present life all our chances of discipline, amendment, and probation; and that though "all reason, all experience, all Scripture unite in this, that the divine work of teaching goes on behind, as well as before, the veil." To teach that the mere fact of dying is the signal for a total change from all that has gone before, is to contradict all that we know of God's ways from analogy. Consider this, and say whether any view which interposes so wide a gulf, as that commonly held does, between our present and our future life can be true. In all God's dealings with us no sharp break intervenes, between the successive stages of life: each condition of being is developed out of a prior, and closely related stage. Now this being so, can I believe that in another age all this is reversed, and that men, with capacities for good still existing, are to be at one bound consigned to hopeless sin, to endless torture? And the difficulty (surely an enormous one) of believing that our Father will deliberately crush out all the lingering tendencies to good in His own children, is increased by the following consideration, viz.:—that the whole of our human life here is so manifestly incomplete, so momentary, that in very many cases it has not afforded a satisfactory time of training, and in not a few cases no training at all.

This thought may be pursued further thus: An old proverb says very wisely, "the mills of God grind *slowly*," and this divine slowness, or long suffering, is very conspicuous in God's ways. How very slowly has He been fitting this earth for man's habitation, and by what a long continued succession of stages, age succeeding age. At length man steps on the earth. Now, is all the divine slowness to be at once changed —and why should it be? Man is to live for ever and ever: we are apt to forget what this means, and how altogether impossible it is to assign any proportion between the fleeting moments of earthly life, and the life that stretches away for ever and ever. If we compare a human life of average duration to one second of time, and compare endless duration to the aggregate of all the seconds that have passed since time was, and that shall pass while time endures, still we assign to human life a proportionate duration infinitely too long. Am I then to believe that the same God Who expends millions of years in slowly fitting this earth for man's habitation, will only allow to man himself a few fleeting years, or months, or hours, as it may be, as his sole preparation time for eternity? To settle questions so unspeakably great in their issue—questions stretching away to a horizon so far distant that no power of thought can follow them— in such hot haste, does seem quite at variance with our heavenly Father's ways. Is God's action outside man so slow, and within man so hurried? Is the husk of far more value than the seed? Are millions of years allotted to fashioning man's earthly home, while for man's spiritual training for eternity, but a few brief years are given, and these so largely broken up by sleep, by work, by disease, by ignorance? What should we say—to take a homely illustration— of an arrangement allotting 10,000 years to fashioning a man's coat, or building his house, while assigning to his whole education but a few hours?

Besides, if we look around, a mass of facts point to the same conclusion,—that the present life is rather the initial stage of human training, than its conclusion. The *vast majority* of men have not so much as heard of Christ. In christian countries very many die in infancy: some are lunatic, or half witted; many wholly uneducated; very many grow up in virtual heathenism, from no fault of their own; or are born in a state where evil surroundings aggravate evil tendencies, inherited and innate. Are they—these untold myriads of myriads of hapless creatures—first to hear of Christ at the day of judgment? Perhaps I should speak soberly in asserting, that not one in a thousand of the total mass of humanity is at this moment living in the true fear and love of God.

Next let us pass to Holy Scripture for a moment only, reserving a full examination of its testimony to later chapters. Here we are at once confronted by a difficulty so grave, that I confess it seems to me quite decisive against the popular view. This difficulty is, that you are thus forced absolutely to *suppress* a very large part of the Bible—a very numerous class of passages which clearly hold out a promise of universal restitution, or at least imply a distinct hope for all men. The view generally held is, in short, one-sided, and therefore wholly unfair; it is as though a judge should base a decision of the most weighty importance on one set of witnesses merely, neglecting the others who testify in a directly opposite sense. "Only imagine the book of nature being studied in this way, with one class of facts systematically ignored; with one law, say of gravitation, fully laid down, while the opposite law of centrifugal motion was altogether overlooked, what results in science could follow from such a method? Yet this is the way in which not a few yet read the Scriptures, taking their first partial sense readings for the truth, and *shutting their eyes* to all that the same Scripture testifies on the other side,"—a most weighty charge, made with absolute truth, as I believe. (*see* ch. vii.-viii.)—JUKES.

An interesting illustration of the fact that the New Testament is full of passages teaching the larger hope, is furnished by the undoubted, but often unperceived, occurrence over and over again, in the works of those who hold the popular creed, of language which, if fairly understood, involves the salvation of all men. This no doubt arises from the fact that phrases are used freely, while a traditional creed does, as so often, blind men to the real force of the expressions they employ—blind them in fact to everything outside the line of thought which they are taught to believe constitutes the truth. Perhaps the best illustration that can be given of what I mean will be gained by quoting from some collection of popular hymns. I take, then, the well-known Hymns, *Ancient and Modern*, and quote a few passages as instances of my meaning. Hymn 45 has this verse :—

> "Thou, sorrowing at the helpless cry,
> Of all creation doomed to die,
> Did'st save our lost and guilty race."

But this is universal salvation : *the race* of man saved, if words have any meaning. And this thought—the race saved—finds frequent expression elsewhere in these hymns ; nor let any man who regards honesty of speech, and common truthfulness, say that to offer salvation merely, is, or can be, the same thing as to save. See hymns 56, v. 3, 4, 5, 6 ; 57, v. 3 ; 81, v. 3 ; 200, v. 6, &c. Again, listen to these solemn words and tell me what they mean: hymn 97, Part 2, v. 2:—

> "Precious flood which all creation
> From the stain of sin hath freed."

And again, v. 5:—

> "That a shipwrecked race for ever
> Might a port of refuge gain."

And hymn 103, v. 5:—

> "So a ransomed world shall ever,
> Praise Thee, its redeeming Lord."

Can it be right to talk of a ransomed world for ever praising its Redeemer, and yet to mean that all the time the world is not actually ransomed, and perhaps half, perhaps more, of its population are groaning in endless pain? Is this consistent with truth? Again, other hymns call on all creation to sing God's praise. Shall this praise then echo from hell? I might well quote, in proof of this address to all creation to praise God, the familiar doxology, but I will only notice here a well-known hymn:—

> "O day for which creation
> And all its tribes were made;
> O joy for all its former woes,
> A thousand times repaid."

I will simply ask what these words mean: all creation is to have all its woes a thousand times repaid: if this is not universalism, what is universalism? The same lips, that assure us from the pulpit that half creation goes to the devil, bid us sing that all creation has been freed from sin! Again, over and over, Christ is said to have vanquished sin, death, and satan:—hymns 147, v. 2; 148, v. 2; 196, v. 3, &c. But how can this be true on the traditional creed? To say that sin is vanquished, and death and satan too, while hell receives its myriads of the lost, is worse than absurd; *e.g.*, take this line from hymn No. 196:—

> "Death of death, and hell's destruction,"

and say if the universalist's creed could be more distinctly stated: his utmost hopes have never gone beyond a vision of death abolished, and hell destroyed? To pursue this further is needless, though it would be easy, and indeed full of interest, to add quotation to quotation: but I may point out how significant it is to find the very opponents of the larger hope *forced*, unconsciously, to employ language directly teaching universal salvation. The explanation is simply that they have been using the words and ideas of Scripture, while the fair, honest meaning of their own words is obscured for them by the spell of a narrow traditional creed.

Before passing on, let me remark once more on the injurious moral tendency of the popular creed. Not merely has it fostered in man a spirit of cruelty (p. 41-4)—not alone does it promise a heaven which is one of utter selfishness (p. 43)—not merely does it point to evil as finally triumphant (p. 36), but it scatters broadcast lessons of equivocation and untruth. For if to say one thing, while meaning something totally different, be falsehood, then with falsehood is the popular religious literature honey-combed from end to end. Everywhere it repeats that the race of man is saved, that Christ is the Saviour of mankind, while it really means that half mankind is damned. It tells us, I quote the *Record* (Easter, 1885)—how "satan is utterly subdued," "his empire completely demolished," "his power for ever fallen." This teaching it repeats in a thousand forms, in countless hymns, in sermons, tracts, books; but it really means that satan is triumphant, and his empire as enduring as God Himself. Well may the sceptic exult, and the thoughtful christian mourn at this duplicity, which stains our religious literature: this terrible perversion, in the holiest matters, of those words by which we shall be judged.

Again, there are, apart from all direct promises, certain tendencies in the Gospel, whose drift and character are impossible to mistake. That these tendencies exist, I am far more certain than I can be of the meaning of any number of highly figurative texts, alleged to prove endless evil. Now these tendencies are too clear, too distinct, to be considered accidental. So far from being a product of the age in which the New Testament was written, they are in conflict with the spirit of that age, and in advance of it. They must therefore represent something inherent in the Author of christianity, and something essential to His design. I put the case very moderately in saying, how extremely difficult it is to reconcile the popular creed with these undoubted tendencies of the New Testament. Can I reasonably believe that a system which, beyond all other creeds, has been distinguished by promoting mercy, goodness, love, tenderness for body and soul; a system of which these qualities are the very essence, does indeed teach a doctrine of punishment so shocking, so horrible, that if really believed, it would turn this earth into a charnel-house, and spread over all nature lamentation, mourning, and woe? Who can believe, that a creed which has banished every form of cruelty, so far as its influence is felt, in the present life, yet contains a special revelation of terrible cruelty in the life to come?

Let me next shew that certain great principles of Revelation conflict with the popular creed. "I am sure," says a thoughtful writer, "these are the two fundamental features of the christian Revelation, of which all its utterances are the manifold expression, viz. :—(1.)—The parental love of the Father. (2.)—The solidarity of mankind to be conformed to the image of His Son."—*Letters from a Mystic.*
(1.)—No one can deny that the New Testament contains a

special revelation of the parental tie uniting us to God. When we pray and say, "our Father," these two words convey the spirit of the whole Gospel. Now, it is not too much to assert that the view generally held is an absolute negation of all that the parental tie implies. It robs the relation of all meaning. We have the very spirit of popular christianity conveyed in the well-known line which tells us that we are "ever in the great Taskmaster's eye." *The great Taskmaster!* note the term, for it reduces to a mockery the divine Fatherhood, though that is of the very essence of christianity. What, for instance, shall we say of such a Father's appeal to those who, as He knows, will never hear? To Him there is no future—all is present; the "lost" are lost, and yet He calls them; they are, on the traditional creed, virtually damned; and He knows it, and yet invites them to come and be saved. But all this difficulty comes from uniting two things absolutely irreconcilable—endless love and power, and yet endless evil. If we want to retain endless sin, let us return to the God of Calvin: nowhere else shall we find solid footing. This God at least is Lord and Master. He issues no invitations, knowing them to be in fact futile. He saves all whom He wants to save. His will must prevail. His Son sheds no drop of blood in vain, All for whom He dies are in fact saved, while the rest go to the devil. All this is hard—nay, cruel; but it is at least logical, intelligible. Contrast with this system the flabby creed of our pseudo-orthodoxy. Long ago it was shrewdly said by an old Calvinist, "universal salvation is credible, if universal Redemption be true." For it shocks the reason to be told of an univeral Redemption, when all that is meant is *an attempt* at the redemption of all the race, which fails; it shocks the reason no less to be told of an unchanging love which wholly ceases the moment the last breath leaves the frail body.

I repeat, the essence of christianity perishes in the virtual denial of any true Fatherhood of our race on God's part. Follow out this thought, for it is of primary importance. We lose sight of the value of the individual soul, when dealing with the countless millions who have peopled this earth and passed away. What is one among so many? we are tempted to say, forgetting that the value of each human being is not in the least thereby altered. Each soul is of infinite value, as if it stood alone, in the eyes of God its Father. And more than this, we are altogether apt to forget another *vital* point, to forget whose the loss is, if any one soul perishes? it is the man's own loss, says our popular creed  But is this all? No, a thousand times no. It is God's loss: it is the Father Who loses His child. The straying sheep of the parable is the Great Shepherd's loss: the missing coin is the Owner's loss. In this very fact lies the pledge that He will seek on and on till He find it. For only think of the value He sets on each soul. He has stamped each in His own image: has conferred on each a share of His own immortality—of Himself: do but realise these things; put them into plain words till you come thoroughly to believe them; and you must see how impossible it becomes to credit that unworthy theology, which tells you that such a Father can ever permit the work of His own fingers, His own offspring, to perish finally. One step further to make this clearer: how has He shewn His sense of the value of the human spirit? The Incarnation must say. It is human life taken into closest alliance with the divine—man and God meeting in the God-man. And then follows the Atonement, proof on proof of the same truth, when He tasted death for every man, He in Whose death all died. Such is the chain, whose golden links I have been endeavouring to follow and trace, whose links bind to the Father above every human soul; *every human soul*, be it distinctly affirmed. Or stay, is there not yet wanting the final link to complete this chain? That link is to be found in the great truth, which completes what I have been saying, the truth of the oneness of the human race, its organic unity. Let us consider this.

(2.)—The principle of the organic unity of our race is that which underlies the whole divine work, alike in Creation, and in the Incarnation. It is the divine idea, so to speak, to regard humanity *as one organic whole*, one body summed up in Adam, summed up anew in the second Adam—a whole which must stand or fall together. All this, too, is very legible in the divinely-given symbolism of the old law, and is reflected in the Gospel with perfect clearness. What but this is the teaching of the "firstfruits," and the "firstborn" in Scripture? These imply and include, the one, the whole harvest; the other, the whole family, and not less. Now Christ is the "firstfruits."—1 *Cor.* xv. 23, and Christ is the "firstborn."—*Col.* i. 18. And what follows let S. Paul say, "If the 'first fruits' be holy, the 'lump' is also holy," the whole race. Thus this principle is affirmed in the great central doctrine of the Incarnation. For in Christ, Who is the "firstfruits," mankind, *i.e.*, the aggregate of humanity, is taken into God. And so in His death all died, as the New Testament assures us, and in His resurrection all rise, nay, are risen. In other words, Christ's relation, as the last Adam, is not to individuals but to the race. Further, it is an actual, not a possible or a potential relation; an actual relation giving salvation to all, in a sense as real as the first Adam gave death and ruin to all. "Once introduce the belief in Christ's divine nature, and His death and resurrection are no longer of the individual but of the race. It was on this belief the Church was founded and built up. The belief was not indeed drawn out with exact precision, yet it was always implied in the relation, which the believer was supposed to hold toward God. The formula of Baptism, which has never changed, is unintelligible without it. The Eucharist is emptied of the blessing which every age has sought in that holy Sacrament, if it be taken away. If Christ took our nature upon Him, as we believe, by an act of love, it was not that of one, but of all. He was not one man only among men, but in Him *all humanity are gathered up:* and thus now as at all time, *mankind* are, so to speak, *organically united with Him."*—WESTCOTT, *Gospel of the Resurrection.* And this union of the race of man with Himself, it is that Jesus Christ would teach in one of His many pregnant hints, by always speaking of Himself in His redeeming work as the Son, not of the Jew, not of the Gentile, not of Mary, not of the carpenter, but the Son of Man.

Yes, the organic unity of mankind is a principle that, from the Fall to the story of the Incarnation, runs through the texture of Holy Scripture. Have you ever quietly thought over the very strange fact of what is called original sin? Have you asked yourself what it means, that you are suffering for something done thousands of years before your birth? All the questions raised by this enquiry we need not try to settle, but we may say that it means at least this, that in the divine plan the race falls and rises together; that mankind is not a collection of separate units, but an organised whole. Each individual is not, so to speak, complete in himself, but is a living stone in the great building—is so truly a member of one great body that, if withdrawn, there would ensue no less than a mutilation of the body. And so Adam's sin sent a shock through the whole race, exactly as when a hurt to any part sends a shock through our present body. This is the painful side, but it is only one side; and unfortunately the popular creed, as so often, persists in looking at one side only, and that the dark side, and in looking away from the bright side; or at least in so looking at it, as to miss its real aspect. But here the New Testament comes to our rescue and assures us that "as in Adam all die, so in the new and better Adam all shall be made alive." The race is fallen; true, but the race is risen; quite as true. Both facts strictly correspond; but, if so,

> "Of two such lessons why forget
> The nobler and the Christlier one?"

A partial salvation is thus in absolute conflict with this fundamental principle which the Fall affirms, and to which the Incarnation testifies; the organic indivisible unity of mankind. A partial salvation is no less in direct opposition to the great truth put by S. Paul so clearly: "If through the offence of one (the) many be dead, much more the grace of God, and the gift of grace, which is by one man, Jesus Christ, hath abounded unto (the) many * * * as by the offence of one, judgment came upon all men to condemnation, even so by the righteousness of one, the free gift came upon all men unto justification of life."—*Rom.* v. 15-8.

Observe, the offence is a thing actually imparted to, actually staining, ruining all men. And Jesus Christ came to bring to every man, to humanity, a salvation which shall be to mankind MUCH MORE than the Fall. But the popular view reads MUCH LESS; and in millions of cases, as much less as hell is less than heaven. I may in passing point out the tendency of modern scientific thought towards the conception of an unity underlying all the various forms of life. The facts of evolution and the facts of heredity confirm this. Individual responsibility is not the less true, because it requires to be supplemented by another fact, that of organic unity. Individuality does not contradict, but is complementary to solidarity. The individual is a whole; but the race is a whole as truly. The individual is truly free and responsible, and yet truly bound by those myriad ties of inherited capacity and character that link each inseparably to the whole. We are "members one of another" in the fullest sense, *i.e.*, parts of a whole from which no act of will can sever us. This far reaching conception of an unity of the race is S. Paul's too. See a striking passage, 1 *Tim.* ii. 4, 5, where he bases universal salvation not on God's love, but on God's *unity*. The connection is worth tracing : "God wills *all* to be saved. For He is ONE;" such is the Apostle's assertion. The meaning is—As an ultimate fact we have unity. It is the law of creation. The "All" run up into and are bound together into unity by His will, Who is "ONE."

I may here briefly note how scientific researches illustrate human solidarity. "The definite result of these researches —and the point is so important, that it must be again and again repeated,—is that heredity is *identity* as far as is possible : *it is one being in many.*"—RIBOT, *Heredity*, p. 280. This law may be traced everywhere. Not a sentiment or a desire exists : not an excellence or defect, bodily or mental, which is not capable of transmission, and actually transmitted. Why is this? "The cause of this heredity," says HECKEL, "is the partial *identity* of the materials which constitute the organism of the parent and child." This shews how vast a part heredity plays, and how close its relation to morality. We assert freely the facts of individuality; we forget the less obvious, but no less true, facts of heredity; we fail to see all that is involved in the Apostle's words, "we are members one of another."

But again, the traditional view conflicts with another great principle, viz., the unchangeableness of God. "If God be unchangeable, then what we see of Him at any moment, must be true of Him at every moment of time; true of Him also both before and after all the moments of time; always and for ever true of Him. If His purpose be to save mankind, that purpose stands firm for ever, unaffected by man's sin, unshaken by the fact of death, unaltered and unalterable by men, by angels, by aught conceivable."—*Salv. Mundi.* Redemption is no after-thought, it was planned in the full knowledge of all the extent of man's sin: knowing all, God declared His purpose to be to save the race. Redemption, then, is something indefeasible, except indeed God can change, or the will of the created be stronger than the will of the Creator. "The gifts and calling of God are without repentance."—*Rom.* xi. 29. That is, what God wills *must* be done; those whom God calls must obey finally. And this unchangeable purpose of God is stated afresh in the words that describe Jesus Christ as "*the same* yesterday, to-day, and for ever"—words deeply significant, and yet, whose true teaching so very often escapes attention.

And here let me illustrate this part of my argument by introducing a story, for whose truth I vouch, to shew how practical these considerations really are. In a certain quarter of London, one of the many evangelists employed for that purpose, had gone forth to preach to the people. When he had concluded an eloquent address, he was thus accosted by one of his hearers: "Sir," said the man, "may I ask you one or two questions?" "Surely," said the preacher. "You have told us that God's love for us is very great and very strong." "Yes," "That He sent His Son on purpose to save us, and that I may be saved this moment, if I will." "Yes," "But, that if I go away without an immediate acceptance of this offer, and if, a few minutes after I were to be by any accident killed on my way home, I should find myself in hell for ever and ever." "Yes." "Then," said the man, "if so, I don't want to have anything to do with a Being *Whose love for me can change so completely in five minutes.*"

"God so loved the world,"—dwell on these words. The world, then, must have been in some real sense worthy of love. He cannot *love*—He may pity—the unlovely. Has He ceased to love it? *If so, when?* I challenge a reply. "Love is not love that alters, where it alteration finds;" even human love, if true, never changes. Yet this love is but a faint, far-off, reflection of our Father's love. God is not love and justice, or love and anger. He is Love, *i.e.*, love essential. Therefore His wrath and vengeance, while very real, are the ministers of His love. To say that God cannot change, is to say that His love cannot change. Hence His love being changeless, pursues the sinner to the outer darkness, and, being Almighty, draws him thence. An earthly parent, who, being able to help, should sit unmoved, month after month, year after year, watching, but never helping, the agonies of his own offspring, is a picture more hideous than any the records of crime can furnish. What shall we say to those who heighten enormously, infinitely, all that is shocking in such a picture, until its blackest details become light itself; and then tell us that the parent in this ghastly scene is one who is Love, love infinite, almighty, and our Father?

And this brings us face to face with a blunder of our traditional creed, which is radical. It talks of God's love as though that stood merely on a par with His justice though it were something belonging to Him which He puts on or off. It is hardly possible to open a religious book in which this fatal error is not found; fatal, because it virtually strikes out of the Gospel its fundamental truth, *e.g.*, GOD IS LOVE. The terms are equivalent. They can be interchanged. God is not anger though He can be angry, God is not vengeance though He does avenge. These are attributes, love is essence. Therefore, God is unchangeably love. Therefore, in judgment He is love, in wrath He is love, in vengeance He is love—"love first, and last, and midst, and without end." But in fact the traditional creed knows nothing of what love really is. For love is simply the strongest thing in the universe, the most awful, the most inexorable, while the most tender. Further, when love is thus seen in its true colours, there is less than ever an excuse for the mistake still so common, which virtually places at the centre of our moral system sin and not grace. This it is which the traditional dualism has for centuries been doing, and is still doing. Doubtless retribution is a most vital truth. Universalists rejoice to admit it; nay, largely to *base* on it their system; but there is a greater truth—which controls, and dominates the whole, the truth of Love. We must not, in common phrase, put the theological cart before the horse. Retribution must not come first, while love brings up the rear; nor must we put the idea of probation, before that of God's education of His human family. In a word, to arrive at truth is hopeless, so long as men virtually believe in a quasi-trinity—God and the Devil, and the Will of Man.

I desire in closing these chapters to point out that, in

proportion to the excellence of christianity, are its corruptions especially vile—*corruptio optimi pessima*. These flow mainly from the characteristic unwillingness of theologians to accept as *fundamental*, the dictates of the moral sense; a reluctance which is the opprobrium of the noble science of theology. Those versed in the great controversy (so imperfectly discussed in these pages) must have noticed how constantly the advocates of endless evil *evade the great moral issues*. They will not face the question of the utter injustice of visiting finite guilt with an infinite penalty. They prefer to observe a discreet silence. They practically ignore the clear evidence of experts, which shews that moderate penalties are far more effective in repressing crime, and reforming the sinner, than are excessive punishments. They will not meet the arguments, which prove that the true conception of penalty is one, which, recognizing the need of retribution, yet lays the chief stress on its reformatory character. They, in fact, substitute the "Great Taskmaster" for "Our Father," thereby obscuring, nay, almost denying, the fundamental fact of christianity. They are strangely blind to the VITAL question of the dualism virtually involved in teaching eternal evil. They do not seem aware that so to teach is to proclaim the defeat of Jesus Christ. They forget how indefensible is a dogma which, in fact, divides God into two Beings, which represents the unchanging One as changing from love here, to wrath hereafter. They have never explained *when* God Who "so loved the world" has ceased to love it, or how such a change is possible to Him, Who never can change. They attempt no answer when the moral degradation is pointed out, which a heaven involves, where we are to rejoice while our dear ones, or our fellow-men, for ever agonize. They are dumb, when asked to explain how sympathy can expire at the very gate of heaven ; or how, if sympathy with the lost survive, the Blessed can know a moment's true joy. They do not explain how a process of degradation in hell can be endless : how moral rottenness can share the dignity of immortality : or how God can go on punishing His own children for ever, when all hope of amendment is past. They will not face the awful difficulty involved in God's free creation, in His own image, of myriads whom such a doom as hell to His certain knowledge awaits. They evade the difficulty, no less great, of conceiving a God, Who is Love, as watching to all eternity, unmoved and unloving, the agonies of His own children. They will not tell us why the savage is wrong, who mutilates his body to please his God ; and the christian is right, who mutilates his moral sense, his noblest part, by calling those acts good in God which he loathes in his fellow-man. This list, incomplete as it is, is sufficient to explain why those who would gladly, yet dare not, remain silent. God's honor is at stake : God's truth is at stake, when, in place of the Gospel, horrors are taught that especially wound that which is best within us, horrors that contradict alike man's conscience, primitive christianity, and the express teaching of Holy Scripture.

## CHAPTER IV.

## "*WHAT THE CHURCH TEACHES.*"

"Just as any teacher in christianity towered aloft, so in proportion did he the more hold and defend the termination of penalties at some time in the future."—DŒDERLIN, *Inst. Theol.*

"Indeed, beside ORIGEN, GREGORY of Nyssa also, GREGORY of Nazianzus, BASIL, AMBROSE himself, and JEROME, taught everywhere the universal restitution of things, asserting simultaneously with it, an end of eternal punishment."—C. B. SCHLEUTER, *pref. in Erig,* (*Migne.*)

PFAFF says "The ultimate restoration of the lost was an opinion held by very many Jewish teachers, and some of the Fathers."—*Frag. anec.*

REUSS says, "The doctrine of a general restoration of all rational creatures has been recommended by very many of the greatest thinkers of the antient church, and of modern times."—*Hist. de la theol. Apost.*

"From two theological schools there went forth an opposition to the doctrine of everlasting punishment."—NEANDER, *Church Hist.* iv. p. 444., Lond., 1853.

"The dogma of ORIGEN had many, and these the most celebrated defenders."—PAGE, *In. Bar. ann. A.D.* 410, p. 103.

"The school of Antioch had no hesitation in hoping for an end of the pains of the other world."—MUNTER.

"Universalism in the fourth century drove its roots down deeply, alike in the East and West, and had very many defenders."—DIETELMAIER.—*Comm. fanat.*

The learned and candid HUET names several Fathers as in sympathy with the larger hope.—*Origen.* ii, pp. 159, 205 : *Cologne,* 1685.

GIESELER says, "The belief in the inalienable power of amendment in all rational creatures, and the limited duration of future punishment was general even in the West."—*Text Book* i. p. 212. *Phil.* 1836.

I TRUST the candid reader will weigh the above testimonies with all care, coming as they do, so far as I know, in almost every case from those who are not friendly to universalism. We shall see how they are supported by a vast body of evidence, from all quarters, in the earliest centuries; and confirmed by the express testimony (which I shall quote) of co-temporary witnesses so famous as AUGUSTINE, JEROME,

BASIL, (and DOMITIAN of Ancyra,) who attest the very wide diffusion of the larger hope in their age. The following pages will, I hope, shew clearly how groundless is the widespread opinion which represents universalism as the outcome of modern sentimentality, and will establish clearly (1) That it prevailed very widely in the primitive Church, especially in the earliest centuries, often in a form embracing all fallen spirits. (2.) That those who believed and taught it, more or less openly, or held kindred views, were among the most eminent and the most holy of the christian Fathers. (3.) That it not only has never been condemned by the Church, but is, far more than any other view, in harmony with the antient catholic Creeds. (4.) That in our Prayer Book are some passages, which shew a leaning towards universalism. Such an enquiry seems indispensable, not alone because this branch of the question has been usually neglected, and the argument for universalism thereby weakened; nor because to many minds the Fathers speak with special weight, as a link connecting us with the Apostolic age, and preserving Apostolic tradition; but on grounds common to every serious student. For all such will surely admit that in dealing with a historic faith like christianity, its doctrines cannot be adequately treated, their growth and development rightly comprehended, or studied with intelligence, except when viewed from the standpoint of history, as well as of the moral sense, and of Holy Scripture. Further, if this historical enquiry were not entered on, we should have no sufficient answer to a very possible, and very fair objection, viz.: why, if the larger hope be in the Bible, did not those great minds of old find it there? And our faith in the larger hope will gain fresh vigour, as we see it very widely taught by many of the wisest and best men in primitive times, and taught (*a*) not alone on the direct authority of the Bible, but (*b*) by those especially to whom Greek was a living tongue, was indeed their native tongue. It is a striking fact that the weight of opposition to universalism in primitive times is found in the Latin Church, is found most vigorous where, as in AUGUSTINE'S case, the Greek language was never really mastered.

The period into which I propose to enquire will fall naturally into three divisions—(1.) Down to the opening years of the 4th century. (2.) Thence during the Church's "Augustan era," to the year 430 or 440 A.D. (3.) From that period to the 11th or 12th century. The two earlier divisions may be said to include all that is of most value and originality in patristic literature. These centuries are especially characterised by the preponderance of the Eastern theologians, and their broad and hopeful teaching. All the early influences that moulded christian thought are of the East, and not of the West. The language hallowed by the New Testament, carried to the East by the tide of conquest and colonisation, and there naturalised, continued for several centuries the language of theology. The earliest christian writings, even in the Church of Rome, are in Greek. The great councils that fixed the Creed of the Church were all held in the East, and there, too, were the early schools of theology—centres of christian light and learning. At first the East was active, while the West slumbered: Italy, Spain, and Greece were sunk in theological torpor, while Alexandria and Cæsarea were vigorous and active. Not only what is Roman, but in a wider sense what is Latin, counted at first as almost nothing in the theological scale, till the fatal genius of an African turned the balance, and the dark shadow of S. AUGUSTINE'S cruel and novel theology fell as a blight on the whole Western Church.

Before we can hope to understand the Fathers, or rightly to estimate the force of the testimony they bear to universalism, we must try to place ourselves mentally where they stood. The Church was born into a world of whose moral rottenness few have, or can have, any idea. Even the sober historians of the later Roman empire have their pages tainted with scenes impossible to translate. Lusts the foulest, debauchery to us happily inconceivable, raged on every side. To assert even faintly the final redemption of all this rottenness, whose depths we dare not try to sound, required the firmest faith in the larger hope, as an *essential* part of the Gospel. But this is not all: in a peculiar sense the Church was militant in the early centuries. It was engaged in, at times, and always liable to, a struggle, for life or death, with a relentless persecution. Thus it must have seemed in that age almost an act of treason to the Cross to teach that, though dying unrepentant, the bitter persecutor, or the votary of abominable lusts, should yet in the ages to come find salvation. Such considerations help us to see *the extreme weight attaching even to the very least expression in the Fathers, which involves sympathy with the larger hope,*—a fact to be kept in mind in reading these pages. Especially so when we consider that the idea of mercy was then but little known; (and that truth, as we conceive it, was not then esteemed a duty.) As the vices of the early centuries were great, so were their punishments cruel. The early Fathers wrote when the wild beasts of the arena tore alike the innocent and the guilty, limb from limb, amid the applause even of gently nurtured women; they wrote when the cross, with its living burden of agony, was a common sight, and evoked no protest. They wrote when every minister of justice was a torturer, and almost every criminal court a petty Inquisition: when every household of the better class, even among christians, swarmed with slaves, liable to torture, to scourging, to mutilation, at the caprice of a master or the frown of a mistress. Let *all* these facts be fully weighed, and a conviction arises irresistibly that, in such an age, no idea of universalism could have originated, unless inspired from above. If, now, when criminals are shielded from suffering with an almost morbid care, men, the best men, think with very little concern of the unutterable woe of the lost, *how*, I ask, *could universalism have arisen of itself in an age like that of the Fathers?*

Consider further. The larger hope is not—we are informed—in the Bible; it is not we know in the heart of man naturally: still less was it there in days such as those we have described, when mercy was unknown, when the dearest interest of the Church forbad its avowal. But it is found in many, in very many, antient Fathers, and often in the very broadest form, *embracing every fallen spirit. Where, then, did they find it? Whence did they import this idea*, not taught in the Old Testament and forbidden by the New Testament, as we are assured: totally out of harmony with every prevailing belief: totally at variance with the obvious interests of the Gospel in such days? *Whence*, I repeat the question, *Whence did this idea come?* Can we doubt that the Fathers could only have drawn it, as their writings testify, from the Bible itself?

I am aware that it will be said that patristic teaching is often not consistent on the question of the larger hope. This inconsistency, so far as it exists, it may be confidently said in reply, (*a*) is *precisely what we might expect under the circumstances;* (*b*) is very largely apparent only, and due to the use of ambiguous phrases which are misunderstood; (*c*) and where it is real, it is amply accounted for by the remarkable doctrine of Reserve. These propositions I hope now to establish clearly, taking the last first. It is the fashion to confine the doctrine of Reserve to the duty of suppressing a truth deemed inexpedient to disclose. I am prepared to shew by the Fathers' own words that it went very much farther, *e.g.*, to the advocacy of falsehood as a distinct duty, *when the supposed interests of piety were at stake*, a limitation to be carefully noted.

In considering this doctrine, we must remember that the principle of a so-called *fraus pia* pervaded the whole legislation of antiquity. So great a teacher as PLATO regarded falsehood as a kind of moral medicine. Thence this teaching passed to Philo; thence in turn to Alexandria, the birthplace of theology. The fruits of such teaching are only too apparent in the early centuries. A swarm of apocryphal Gospels and forged writings appear; fraudulent Oracles, Acts and Canons of Councils, Gospels, Legends abound. Writings were interpolated, glossed, mutilated, even wholly forged. "For a good end," says an eminent scholar (speaking of the *innocent* primitive times), "they made no great scruple *to forge whole books*."—DALLÆUS, *De usu Pat.* The illustrious scholar CASAUBON speaks very strongly. "This vehemently moves me, that I see in the first times of the Church how many there were, who thought it a palmary deed, that heavenly truth should be aided by their own figments. These *falsehoods* they call *dutiful*, excogitated with a good end; from which fountain, without doubt, sprang *600 books*, which that and the next age saw published, under the name even of the Lord Jesus, and other saints."— *Exerc.* i. N. x, *Baroni App. in Ann.* Of the 4th century MOSHEIM says, an error, almost publicly adopted, was "that to *deceive and lie is a virtue*, when religion can be promoted by it."—*Eccles. Hist.* i. p. 357, words that not unfairly describe the teaching prevalent in the early centuries. Thus EPIPHANIUS tells us that Catholics blotted out from S. LUKE's Gospel a statement "that Jesus wept."—*Ancor.* xxxi. I cite this story (which may not be true), as clear proof that Catholics were thought capable of most fraudulent usage of Holy Scripture itself. At Carthage, 419 A.D., FAUSTINUS tendered the canons of Sardica as though genuine canons of the Council of Nice. Only thirty years later LEO attempted the same fraud. CASSIAN, a friend of CHRYSOSTOM, is author of a collection of spiritual precepts; one of his chapters bears this striking heading: "Even the Apostles teach us that *falsehood is very often permissible, and the truth hurtful!*"— *Coll.* xvii. 20. S. CHRYSOSTOM openly advocates deceit (*apate*) as a spiritual medicine,—*De sacer. lib.* i. and ii., and having planned and carried out a fraud, and thus entrapped his friend BASIL into ordination, he exults in his success, and defends by Scripture his deceit. He also maintains that S. PETER and S. PAUL were merely dissembling in the scene recorded in Galatians (ch. ii.) And this was the common opinion since ORIGEN's time, and is asserted by S. JEROME very earnestly. He even says, writing to AUGUSTINE, "Tu veritatis tuæ saltem *unum adstipulatorem* proferre debebis," —*Ep.* lxxxix., words which any comment would weaken. What is this but to attribute a lie to the Apostle, and, in some sense, a partnership in lying to the Spirit of inspiration? Nor is this strange, for several Fathers do not hesitate to attribute dissimulation to our Lord Himself; *e.g.*, the author of ninety-two sermons found in some editions of S. AMBROSE (possibly MAXIMUS of Turin, 422, A.D.), says of Christ, "sitire se *simulat*,"—*Ser.* xxx.: this he repeats, adding that Christ circumvented the devil by *fraud.—ib.*

xxxv. Compare a striking passage in an old writer—*De sanc. Trin.* (in S. CHRYSOSTOM's works). S. GREGORY, of Nyssa, remarks that our Lord used *deceit* for purposes of salvation. —*Cat. or.* xxvi. S. HILARY asserts that Christ in saying He was ignorant of that day, was not in fact ignorant of it, *De Trin. lib.* ix., and that Christ's fear, and sadness, and suffering in His Passion were not real.—*ib. lib.* x. p. 235. S. AMBROSE says, "Neque fallitur Pater neque fallit Filius, verum ea est in Scripturis consuetudo * * ut Deus dissimulet se scire quod novit. Et in hoc ergo unitas divinitatis in Patre * * probatur et Filio, si quemadmodum Deus Pater cognita dissimulat, ita Filius, etiam in hoc imago Dei, que sibi sunt nota dissimulet."—*De fide lib.* v. 8. The Son of God *se fingit infantem.*—S. ZENO. *lib* ii. *tract* viii. S. BASIL teaches that Christ pretends ignorance.—*Ep.* cxli. *ad Cesar.: Adv. Eun. hom.* iv. and he expressly commends fraud employed for a good end.—*Hom. in prin. prov.*

From this evidence (which might be easily increased) it plainly follows, that such writers would have had no scruple whatever in employing threats, which were not true, to terrify obstinate sinners.

<small>Those desiring further information may consult FABRICIUS.—*Bibl. grec.*—" Tot fraudes a preposterá pietate profectæ ;" MILMAN—*Hist. of Christ*, iii. p. 358; S. GREGORY, of Nazianzus—*Orat.* xxxvi. ; TERTULLIAN—*De pud.* xix. ; RUFINUS—*In sym. Apos.*; DIONYSIUS of Alexandria—*On S. Luke* xxii. ; VICTORINUS—*De Phys. lib.* xxiii. vi. ; PROCLUS—*Or.* xiii. *In san. Pasch.*; S. LEO—*In Nat. Dom. Ser.* ii., *De Pass. Dom. Ser.* xvii. ; MAXIMUS—*Quest. et dub.* lxvi.; CLEMENT of Alexandria—*Strom.* vi. ; HUET—*Orig.* ii. *prop. fin.* and lib. iii. 2, 3 ; DODWELL—*De pauc. mart.* xiii. and viii. ; NEANDER—*Eccl. Hist.* vi. 325 ; CAVE—*Hist. liter., On S. John Damascene* ; GIESELER—*Eccles. Hist.* i. 298 ; *ed. Philad.* 1836 ; GROTIUS—*De jur. bell.* iii. 1. In fact the evidence seems clearly to shew that dissimulation was regarded as perfectly legitimate, and even as a duty, when (as in the case of the larger hope), the good of others seemed to require it. I am not for a moment charging the Fathers with a general advocacy of lying. I am but stating, in their own words, the limits they set to the duty of truth in one particular direction, and *in that only.*</small>

Finally, let me place side by side the two following views of this doctrine:—

S. HILARY.

Commenting on *Ps.* xv. 2, "And speaketh the truth in his heart," this Father, after enforcing the duty of truth, proceeds thus: "But this is difficult by reason of the sins and vices of the age. For *a lie is very often necessary.* (*Est enim necessarium plerumque mendacium*), and *sometimes falsehood is useful:* as when we tell a lie to an assassin lying in wait, or upset evidence on behalf of one who is in danger, or deceive a sick man as to the difficulty of cure."

Dr. PUSEY.

"The principle of accommodation was that of our Lord. 'I have many things to say unto you, but ye cannot bear them now' * * its limit was in not declaring as yet all the truth on a given subject, *never in saying what was untrue.*"—"*What is of faith as to everlasting punishment.*"—p. 250.

[*The italics are mine.*]

Dr. PUSEY's book is so often quoted by those who do not read the Fathers, that a striking instance of the way he has done his work will be useful. I might add *much more*, but forbear, desiring no controversy with an honoured name, and letting facts speak for themselves.

I turn next to shew the wholly inconclusive nature of the arguments drawn from the patristic use of such epithets as *aionios*, &c., when applied to future punishment. The least reflection will suffice to shew that everything depends upon *the sense* in which these terms are used. No early universalist hesitates to use *aionios*, which the Bible admittedly uses of future punishment. So far is this from proving the traditional creed, that it is even asserted, by both CÆSARIUS (?) —*Dial* iii., and by LEONTIUS, that ORIGEN and his adherents argued *from the very term aionios, as being finite, that future punishments were temporary*.—HUET, *Orig.* ii. p. 161. In fact we should remember what our own experience amply teaches. Almost every conversation we take part in, every book we read, offers ample proof that such terms as "for ever," "eternal," "ceaseless," &c., are habitually used in a purely conventional sense, without *so much as a thought of absolute endlessness*. And this is even more true of the Fathers, whose training was largely rhetorical; whose whole habit of mind was totally unscientific.

To come to definite proofs: just as the prophet calls that incurable, of which in a moment after he asserts the cure—*Jer*. xxx., 12, 17, just so do the Fathers often employ, in a limited sense, words that seem to assert the opposite. Thus S. JEROME, commenting on *Zephan*. ii. 9, explains the *eternal* desolation of Amon as ending in their conversion. See, too, his comment to the same effect on *Ezek*. xxv. 4. Of Jerusalem, he says on *Ez*. xxiv., that the city was burnt with *eternal* fire by Hadrian. He says Israel is delivered over to *eternal* woe.—*In Amos* viii.: a flame is kindled against them which shall not be quenched (*in Jer*. vii. 20); yet he asserts repeatedly the final salvation of Israel—*In Hos*. xiii., *in Zeph*. iii., *in Ezek*. xxxix., xxi., xxxv., &c. Again, he says that Edom is to be banished to *eternal* desolation.—*In Ezek*. xxxv., that Edom and the host of Egypt are to lie (slain) in a *perpetual* sleep.—*In Ezek*. xxxii.: And God is wroth with Esau (Edom) *for ever*, a fact S. JEROME repeats three times over; yet Edom is to be finally converted.—*In Obad*. i.: And Egypt is represented as restored and converted.—*In Ezek*. xxix. To S. JEROME the "outer darkness" permits an escape; and after "the uttermost farthing" is paid, salvation comes.—*In Micah* viii. Nay, JONAH's three days' imprisonment in the whale is "*eternal*" night!—*In Jon*. ii. And the very fire of "hell" (Gehenna) cleanses (and is, therefore, temporary).—*In Nahum* iii. In S. JEROME's works I have noted many cases in which *eternus* (&c.) means in fact temporary. Nay, so wholly ambiguous and inconclusive are such terms that we shall see ORIGEN asserting that obstinate sins are to be *extinguished* by the "*eternal fire.*" So, the antient author of the second Sybilline book tells us (in words that recall the statement in *Rev.* xx. 14, about the second death), that "hell" (Hades) and all things and persons are cast into "*unquenchable fire*" for CLEANSING. The author of the sermons printed in S. AMBROSE's works, *ed. Par.* 1569, who bids his hearers consider "the day of judgment" and the "*unquenchable*" flames of hell, yet says that baptism extinguishes the flame of hell, and opens Tartarus.—*Ser.* xxxi. So DOMITIANUS says those assigned to *eternal* punishment are saved.—FAC, *Pro def. tr. cap.* iv. 4. Another old writer, as we shall see, tells us that the worm "that dieth not" dies.

LEO (Augustus) says *eternal* prisoners were released from hades by Christ.—*Or.* vii. EUSEBIUS twice calls *unquenchable* the brief fire which consumes a martyr.—*Church Hist.* vi. 41. ORIGEN calls, without hesitation, that fire *eternal* which he believed to be finite. He even says that obstinate sins are to be *extinguished* by the *eternal* fires.—*Hom.* xiv. *in Lev*: (So DE LA RUE, his best editor, reads) a sentiment he repeats in *Hom.* viii. *in Josh.* Again, in the rival school of Antioch, THEODORE of Mopsuestia (a strong opponent of ORIGEN) agreed with him in calling "eternal" that future penalty which he taught would be in all cases TEMPORARY. Or if we take other words we may find a similar usage: thus to PAMPHILUS, "*limitless*" ages, and to RUFINUS, "*infinite*" ages have an end.—*Apol. pro. Orig.*: as also to S. JEROME —*In Jon.* iii. S. GREGORY of Nazianzus, calls ceaseless (*apaustos*) that which is terminable.—*Adv. Jul. Or.* ix. Next, let us take S. AMBROSE: He says—Christ freed the dead from *perpetual* chains.—*In Ps.* xliv. *ad fin.*, and says the rejection of the Jews is their *perpetual* death.—*In Ps.* cxix. 9, 10. And he very strikingly teaches deliverance from *the eternal fire prepared for the devil and his angels*, for he says that DIVES is to be set free.—*In Ps.* cxix : and teaches distinctly that DIVES was *in this very fire.*—*ib.* v. 17. An old author in EPIPHANIUS' *Works, Paris*, 1622, says that *eternal* bars, and *eternal* gates are shattered.—*In. sep. Christi.* Patristic usage, again, is well illustrated by no less an authority than S. ATHANASIUS, who calls the sin against the Holy Ghost "*unpardonable*," and its punishment "*eternal ;*" and yet asserts that this "*unpardonable*" and "*eternal*" sin might, on repentance, be pardoned.—*See Bingh* ii. p. 970. And let us carefully note that this eminent writer states, that this was the *general opinion* of the Antients—a very suggestive fact. The author of *Christus Patiens* begs to be loosed from bonds which "*cannot be loosed.*"—v. 2540. A similar instance may be found in ATHANASIUS.—*Rescrip. ad. Lib.* So CLEMENT of Alexandria calls that *incurable* which he goes on to shew may be cured.—*Strom.* i. THEODORET intimates that "*eternal*" death admits an escape.—*In Zach.* ix., and that "*eternal*" disgrace may be only temporary.—*In Jer.* xxiii. S. HILARY, like S. JEROME, says JONAH escaped from "*eternal*" bars.—*In Ps.* lxix. And such teaching is common as to the meaning of "*eternal*" S. GREGORY of Nyssa calls an *interval limitless*, and says it can be crossed over.—*In Ps. ch.* xiv. ; and he calls an interval which has an end, and a beginning *eternal.*—*ib.* ch. vii. He describes even the "second death" as cleansing.—*De an. et. Res.*, and in two passages, in the same work, plainly treats "the eternal fire" as purifying—*ib.* pp. 658, 691, *ed. Par.* 1615. S. BASIL teaches that "sins unto *death*" admit a cure.—*In Is.* iv. 4, and that God's wroth, that "will *not* cease," ceases on repentance.—*In Is.* i. 24. He teaches also that where it is said, Moab shall be shut out "*eternally*" (from God), this "*eternal*" is not really more than temporal.—*In Ps.* lx. 8.

We have seen S. JEROME calling the flame of *Gehenna*, purifying, and S. GREGORY of Nyssa teaching the same of "eternal" fire: and ORIGEN asserting that these fires extinguished sin. So does S. CHRYSOSTOM term *incurable* what may be cured in many passages, *e.g.*, —*In Ps.* cxl. v. and cx.; *In Gen.* vi. *Hom.* xxii. He calls perpetual (*dienekes*) what is temporary.—*In Heb.* ii. *Hom.* iv., and *in Eph.* iv. *Hom.* xiii. He also calls the fire which destroyed Sodom (the *eternal* fire of S. JUDE) beneficial.—In *Ps.* cxi. Similar phrases occur in the antient homilies printed in most editions of this Father, *e.g.*, the sleepless, *i.e.*, undying worm is said to die.—*In trid. Res.* An old commentator on the Psalter (in S. JEROME's works) calls the *eternal* blotting out of the wicked their conversion. PRUDENTIUS calls the brief darkness at the Crucifixion *eternal.*—*Hymn.* ix.: and the gloom of a martyr's prison *eternal.*—*Hymn. ad Vincen.* I have not exhausted the instances I might adduce: but I have brought very ample evidence to shew, how *absolutely groundless* is the argument still commonly urged in favour of endless penalty, from the mere use of terms like *aionios*, &c., &c. If the "eternal" can be finite, if the "incurable" can be cured, if the "undying" worm does in fact die, if hell (Gehenna) cleanses, *how vain* to build on the mere use of such terms a proof in favor of a penalty literally endless.

Canon FARRAR gives good reasons for thinking that even the terrible threats of such writers as Dr. WATTS, the poet YOUNG and JEREMY TAYLOR cannot be literally pressed. *Mercy and Judg.*, pp. 275-6, 401. I will give a stronger instance, viz.: Dr. BURNET in his *De statû mort*, p. 366, after teaching the larger hope, uses these significant words: "*Whatever your opinion is within yourself, and in your own breast, concerning these punishments, whether they are eternal or not, yet always with the people, and when you preach to the people, use the received doctrine, and the received words in the sense in which the people receive them.*"

These considerations fully dispose of very many passages quoted as proof that the Fathers teach endless penalty.

They no less apply to any similar expressions, that may be brought forward from those Fathers I am about to claim as universalists. And if any passages remain, that seem too positive to admit of this explanation, I point at once to the doctrine of Reserve, which quite distinctly authorised dissimulation, and specially applied to such questions as the larger hope. And this is to state the case moderately and to refrain from pressing this doctrine, to its legitimate bounds. For plainly, any one holding it may *continuously deny universalism, and yet secretly believe it.* But I merely apply it to cases of so-called inconsistency, *i e.*, where the larger hope is apparently at once held, and yet contradicted by the same Fathers. Such I claim as universalists, because no other view can possibly explain all the facts. Therefore I feel obliged to lay down this simple rule as the fair test of the Father's real meaning, viz., that *no hypothesis other than strong conviction of its truth can account for universalistic teaching ;* while the desire to terrify sinners, added to the ambiguous character of most or all of the terms they employ ; and lastly the doctrine of Reserve, easily account for apparent, or even real, inconsistency which we find in certain of the Fathers.

I may sum up by saying that the method usually employed in case of these writers, seems to *violate every rule of fair criticism.* Practically it takes account of but a single factor in their writings, and misunderstands that ; *e.g.,* if *aionios,* or kindred terms, are applied to future punishment, such a writer is at once labelled as teaching endless sin and pain. But (i.) this is (very often) to neglect that most important indication, viz., a writer's tone and general drift. Next (ii.) this is to assume that such terms are used in a strict and extreme sense, which, as we have seen, is certainly not (necessarily) the case, or even usually so. Professed universalists have no hesitation in using such terms. (iii.) It is to ignore the highly significant doctrine of Reserve; (iv.) and it is no less to ignore the great mass of evidence, direct and indirect, in so many Fathers, which *admits of no explanation other than sympathy with, or belief in the larger hope.* This I shall now adduce; premising that evidence abundant enough to fill a volume must, I fear, suffer in cogency when compressed into a few pages. The quotations I shall make will fall under these heads—(*a*), shewing a drift and tone of thought totally out of harmony with the perpetuity of evil; (*b*), involving the larger hope by fair inference; (*c*), or by direct statement; (*d*), at times teaching the restoration of every fallen spirit.

But first, it is well to note a fact, which it seems to me vain to deny, viz., that some very early writers appear to have held the final annihilation of the wicked. Thus CLEMENS (Romanus) seems to confine the Resurrection to the righteous. "Can we think it strange," he asks, "if the Maker of *all* shall cause a Resurrection of those *who serve Him holily.*" —*ch.* xxvi. Compare a passage in *ch.* l. The epistle of the Pseudo-Barnabas, 120 A.D., seems to teach annihilation. Perhaps the most decisive passage is that in which he says, (ch. xxi.), that "the wicked shall perish with the wicked one," meaning apparently the cessation of existence. There are also passages in the Ignatian epistles—*Ad Smyr.* ch. vii. : *Ad Trall.* ch. ix.—and in S. POLYCARP—*Ad Phil.* ch. ii. and v.—that seem to indicate that they expected a resurrection of the just only. The *Didache ton Apostolon,* while devoting a considerable space to eschatology seems to speak of the resurrection of the righteous only. This is perhaps the teaching of HERMAS—*Lib.* iii. *simil.* vi. v. 11—3 : *simil.* viii.

vv. 54, 59, 63, 68, 69, &c.—*ed. Glasg.*, 1884. JUSTIN MARTYR also almost certainly takes this view; for though his language is hardly consistent, yet the terms applied by him to the lot of the wicked, seem to imply their final extinction. God delays the destruction of the world, he says, "by which wicked angels, and demons, and men shall cease to exist."—*Second Apol.* ch. vii. "Some which have appeared worthy of God never die, others are punished so long as God wills them to exist."—*Dial.* ch. v. "Souls both die, and are punished."—*ib.* "The soul partakes of life since God wills it to live. Thus, then, it will not even partake of life, when God does not will it to live."—*ib.* ch. vi. A fragment (*Ex Leont. Adv. Eut.* ii.) seems to take the same view. IRENÆUS also, I believe, teaches annihilation: it is true that he ascribes a natural immortality to the human soul and spirit.—*Adv. her. lib.* v. ch. 4, 7, 13,—perhaps as surviving the body. For elsewhere he argues in a way that involves the final annihilation of the evil: *e.g.*, souls and spirits endure "as long as God wills," he who rejects life "deprives himself of continuance for ever."—*ib. lib.* ii. ch. 34. See also the argument—*lib.* iii. ch. 19, *ad fin.*: *lib.* v. ch. 2 *ad fin.*: and *ib.* ch. 27.

Further proof of the existence in very early times of a belief in conditional immortality is afforded by ORIGEN's words, which are given by EPIPHANIUS—*Hær.* lxiv. 10. To the early writers who teach the final extinction of the wicked should be added HERMOGENES.—Neander, *Eccles. Hist.* ii. p. 350. I may point out that THEODORET (referred to by NEANDER) adds that HERMOGENES taught the final extinction of all evil spirits.—*Hær. fab. com.* i. 19. And I believe THEOPHILUS of Antioch, 168 A.D., to have maintained the final extinction of the wicked.—*Ad. Autol.* ii. ch. 26-7. The

CLEMENTINE homilies, though inconsistent, teach in one or two passages the annihilation of the wicked, *e.g.*,—*Hom.* iii. 6. ARNOBIUS, 303 A.D., is the latest writer whom I can name as holding similar opinions. He speaks at length on this subject.—*Adv. gent. lib.* ii. 14, 19, 31—6, &c. The soul is, according to him, of intermediate quality, *i.e.*, not naturally immortal, yet capable of immortality by God's grace, cut off from which it perishes absolutely. This phase of opinion, though short-lived, and confined to but few writers, is of interest, because appearing at such an early date : and because it affords fresh and distinct evidence of the very slender claims, which the dogma of endless evil has to being the genuine representative of primitive teaching. The annihilation of the wicked was, it may be noted, the teaching of certain Jewish Rabbis, in our Lord's day and later. If dogmatic considerations were not so certain to warp the judgment, I believe no doubt would be thrown on the existence of *this remarkable phase of early teaching.*

I now turn to the task of adducing a portion, and it can only be a portion (on account of my limited space), of the mass of evidence which exists, both direct and indirect, in favour of primitive universalism. Our first class of proofs shall be drawn from the very remarkable doctrine of Christ's descent into hades. The number of texts formerly alleged in proof of this was very large, *e.g.*, from the Old Testament were quoted *Is.* ix. 2 ; xlv. 2, 3 ; xlix. 9, 25, *Zech.* ix. 11— 2 ; *Ps.* lxviii. 18 ; lxix. 33 ; cvii. 16. From the New Testament, not only S. Peter's famous statement, 1 *Pet.* iii. 21, but *S. Matt.* xii. 29 ; *Phil.* ii. 9, 10 ; *Col.* ii. 15 ; *Eph.* iv. 8, 9, were alleged. Very striking is the contrast between the universal acceptance of this doctrine in primitive days, and its universal disregard\* in our days. Very instructive, too, is this contrast; for, doubtless, the explanation is, that the Gospel preached to the dead, and still more to those who were in life *disobedient* to direct preaching (and who died so) was felt instinctively to strike a blow fatal to the traditional creed. To us this doctrine is thus of the highest interest; the more so when we regard the widespread belief of antiquity in the liberation from hades† of ALL SOULS by Christ. It is surely impossible to deny that this involves universalism as a necessary conclusion. For if all the dead, without any exception, were delivered by the preaching of Jesus Christ; then, as an eminent writer has tersely put the case, " it argues absolute *fatuity* to suppose that those who lived after the Incarnation can be worse off than if they had lived before it." I do not mean that this view was everywhere held, nor do I mean that all the writers holding it were themselves universalists. It is enough for our argument to shew that the doctrine so held does logically involve universalism.

A very early statement of this doctrine is that of the Gospel of NICODEMUS (perhaps of the second century). "Of course, to us, this fiction speaks with an authority no greater than that of the Pilgrim's Progress. But just as from BUNYAN's great allegory we might very safely infer what the puritan conception of the christian life was in the seventeenth century, so from this Gospel of NICODEMUS, we may very safely infer what conception the christians of the second century formed of Christ's descent into hades."—*Salv. Mundi.* The

---

\* For although adopted by nearly all commentators, it has never passed into the current theology of the day.

† Both Jews and early christians seem to have taught that the spirits of the departed were in one common abode (*Sheol—hades—apud inferos*), though with separate regions for the just and unjust. TERT., *De animâ* lv.; ORIGEN. *Hom.* ii. *in lib. reg.; &c.*

story is told dramatically. A great voice echoes through hades, crying, "Lift up your heads, ye gates, and the King of glory shall come in." Immediately the brazen gates are shattered, and *all* those bound come out; and hades (personified) exclaims, "*Not one* of the dead has been left in me." Jesus then turns to ADAM, extending His right hand and raising him. Then to the rest He says, "Come *all* with me, as many as have died through the tree which he (ADAM) touched, for behold I raise you *all* up through the tree of the Cross."* We may note also that the antient (so-called) *Acts of the Apostle* THOMAS addressed Christ as the "Saviour of *every creature* * * Thou Who wentest down even to hades. * * And didst bring out thence those shut in for many ages." A statement, perhaps even earlier, of the same fact is given by EUSEBIUS, as found by him at Edessa, in the archives, to the effect that Christ had descended into hades * * and brought up the dead. ORIGEN, on *Ps.* lxviii. 18, says, that Christ drew up and set free from the recesses of hades, the souls that were held in captivity. I quote next from an interesting homily, probably by EUSEBIUS of Alexandria, 289 A.D. He supposes that JOHN the Baptist† announced in hades the descent of Christ.—*Hom.* xiii. Another homily says "Christ will descend that in order that *all*, both on earth and in heaven and in hades, may obtain

---

* See also ch. vi. vii., *Latin* version (and a contradictory passage ch. ix. 2nd *Latin vers*). *ed. Edin.*, 1870.

† This opinion is almost peculiar to Greek Fathers. Some writers teach that the Apostles also preached in hades, *e.g.*, CLEMENT—*Strom.* ii. p. 379; and vi. p. 637. *Col.* 1688 : HERMAS, iii. ix. 156. Some say that the BLESSED VIRGIN did the same. Some even say that SYMEON went before Christ to hades.—PHOTIUS—*fide* LEO. ALL. An old writer in EPIPHANIUS' works asserts the same of the archangels GABRIEL and MICHAEL.—*In sep. Christi.*—this curious homily is worth perusal.

salvation from Him."—*Hom.* xii. EUSEBIUS of Cæsarea, 315 A.D., writes as follows : " Christ, caring for the salvation of *all* \* \* and bursting the eternal gates, opened a way of return to life for the dead bound in chains of death."—*Dem. evan.* iv. 12. To S. ATHANASIUS is ascribed a treatise (certainly very antient)—*De pass. et cruce Dom.* It says, " While the devil thought to kill one he is deprived of *all* \* \* cast out of hades, and sitting by the gates, sees *all* the fettered beings led forth by the courage of the SAVIOUR." In a treatise, certainly genuine, this Father tells how Christ broke the bonds of the souls detained in hades.—*De Inc. Christi.*

I quote next an antient homily—perhaps by BASIL of Seleucia. "That which happened to the visible tomb (of Christ—*i.e.*, its being *emptied* on His rising), the same happened to hades the invisible."—*In sanc. Pascha.* (*apud* ATHANAS. *ed. Col.* 1686) I take next S. HILARY, 354 A.D., who says, " Christ ascending on high \* \* took (captured) those who had been captured by the devil."—*In Ps.* lxviii. 18. M. F. VICTORINUS, 360 A.D., says, "The Saviour descends into hades by that Passion of the Cross in order that He may set free *every soul*."—*In Eph.* ch. iv. In a translation, or paraphrase, of DIDYMUS, 370 A.D.—*De Spir. Sanc.*, by S. AMBROSE, are these words : " In the liberation of *all* no one remains a captive ; at the time of the Lord's Passion he alone (the devil) was injured, who lost *all* the captives he was keeping." S. BASIL, 370 A.D., seems to teach this universal liberation, for he says the true Shepherd brought out of the prison of hades, and handed over to the holy angels, the sheep for whom He died.—*In Ps.* xlix. 14. But Christ died for all. S. EPHREM (Syrus), as will be seen in the note on him in this chapter, teaches the liberation of *all* from hades. From S. GREGORY of Nazianzus, 385 A.D., I take the following: "Until Christ loosed by His blood *all* who groan under Tartarean chains."—*Carm.* xxxv, v. 9, *ed. Lyons*, 1840. In this Father's works a remarkable poem is usually printed, entitled CHRISTUS PATIENS; it is of antient, but uncertain, authorship. Speaking of Christ's descent, it says: *All* of whom (*i.e.*, the dead) Thou shalt bring forth as Thy spoils from hades."—v. 1391-2. So again: "I believe Thou wilt bring forth from hades as many mortals as it has imprisoned."—*ib.* v. 1934-5 From S. AMBROSE 375 A.D., I take the following: "The Lord descends to the infernal world, in order that even those, who were in the infernal abodes, should be set free from their *perpetual* bonds."—*Enar. in Ps.* xliv. Here note that perpetual bonds are really temporary. Elsewhere S. AMBROSE says, Christ, when amongst the dead, "gave pardon to those in the infernal abodes, destroying the law of death."—*De Incarn.* ch. v.

Quite as emphatic is the AMBROSIASTER in his teaching. "Christ descending to the infernal abodes condemned death, taking from him those whom he was keeping."—*In* 1 *Tim.* ii. 6, 7. "Christ snatched from hades *all* * * the devil, lost, together with Christ, *all* whom he was keeping."—*In Rom.* iii. 22-4. My next witness shall be an early treatise (wrongly ascribed to S. AMBROSE), which says: "Christ went down to the *depths* of *hell* (*Tartarus*) and recalled (the) souls, bound by sin, to life, out of the devil's jaws." The context seems to imply the rescue of all sinners.—*De myst. Pasch.* Next I take the words of an old writer (MAXIMUS of Turin?) whose sermons are bound in S. AMBROSE's works.—*Ed. Paris*, 1569. He says: "hell (*Tartarus*) yields up those it contains to the upper world: the earth sends to heaven those whom it buries."—*Serm.* lii. S. JEROME, 378 A.D., bears clear testimony to the same effect: "Our Lord descends * * and was shut up in (the) eternal bars, in order that He might set free *all* who had been shut up."—*In Jon.* ii. 6. "In the blood of Thy Passion Thou didst set free those who were being kept bound in the prison of hell (*inferni*)."—*In Zech.* ix. 11. We may note that, in the context, S. JEROME asserts that DIVES was kept in this prison; the inference being, that in his opinion, the "great gulf" may be crossed by Christ. Indeed, the words that I next give, seem to say so quite plainly. "The Lord descended to the place of punishment and torment, *in which was the rich man*, in order to liberate the prisoners."—*In Is.* xiv. 7. This liberation of all (as it seems) is taught in an old document, perhaps by CÆSARIUS of Arles, printed in S. JEROME'S works.—*Ed. Paris*, 1623. "The *eternal* night of hell (*infernorum*) is illuminated as Christ descends * * the bonds of the damned, torn asunder, fell away * * every cry of the groaning is still * * The captive souls loosed from bonds go forth from hell (Tartarus), and the Apostle's words come true, *i.e.*, in Jesus' name *every* knee bends of things in heaven, and earth, and under the earth."—*De Res. Dom.* Here note that the *eternal* night is only temporary,—the whole is worth reading as a specimen of early teaching. An old homily in EPIPHANIUS' works (*Paris*, 1622,) says, "Christ, like a swift-winged hawk, snatched away *all* that He had from the beginning, from the devil and left him deserted." —*In Assump. Christi.* Another homily affirms that "Christ arose, and the prison of hades was emptied."—*In Res. Christi.* I take next the testimony of S. CHRYSOSTOM, 398 A.D. (from whom further evidence will be quoted in the next chapter). He writes: "While the devil imagined that he had got hold of Christ (in hades), he lost *all* in fact whom he was keeping." —*In Col.* ii. In this Father's works are usually included some homilies of antient, but uncertain, authorship. Anonymous writings of this sort, of which I have already quoted a few, afford excellent proof of the beliefs then current among christians. "The wood of the Cross recalls from hades those who went down thither."—*In sacr. Pascha.* "I see the earth trembling * * (the) dead preparing their escape * * Jesus Christ receives all."—*In sanc. et magn. Par.* Another homily teaches that Christ puts forward (pretends) fear to draw on the devil, so that, attacking Him as man, he should be routed, and *all* be set free who were held captive by him.—*De sanc. Trin.* This whole description is highly characteristic and suggestive. A passage perhaps even more striking is the following: "The fire of *hell* (Gehenna) *is extinguished*, the sleepless worm (evidently the '*worm that dieth not*') dies * * those who were in hades are set free from the bonds of the devil."—*In trid. Res.* Another witness is S. Asterius, Bishop of Amasea, 401 A.D., who writes: "Death swallowed up life, and becoming sick, vomited forth even those it had previously swallowed."—*Hom.* xix. Few Fathers have taught the deliverance of all from hades more clearly, (see especially his Paschal homilies,) than Cyril of Alexandria, 412 A.D. He describes Christ as having spoiled hades, and "left the devil there *solitary* and *deserted.*"—*Hom. Pasch.* vii. And again, "Christ, wandering down even to hades, has *emptied* the dark, hidden, unseen treasuries."—*Glaphy in Gen. lib.* ii. I understand Maximus of Turin, 422 A.D., to teach the same. "Christ," he says, "carried off to heaven man (mankind) whose cause He undertook, snatched from the jaws of hades."—*In Pent. Hom.* ii. From Theodoret, 430 A.D., I take the following: Christ says to the devil, "I mean to open the prison of death for the rest, but will shut up thee *only* * * Thou wast justly despoiled of *all* thy subjects."—*De prov. Or.* x. My next quotations are from S. PETER CHRYSOLOGUS, 433 A.D.: "The rule of hell perishes * * and *all* obtain pardon(?)" (*constat de venia jam totum*).—*Ser.* lxxiv. PROCLUS, 434, A.D., Bishop of Constantinople, says: "To-day Christ emptied the entire treasury of death."—*In Dom. Pass. Or.* xi. "*All* the dead, wondering at His Passion, cry for joy, 'we are healed by His stripes.'"—*In Dom. Res. Or.* xii.

My readers can now judge of the significance rightly attaching to such a catena of authorities, (which I might increase,) comprising as it does almost all the greatest names in the first four or five centuries. Fresh evidence might very easily be given down to the tenth or eleventh century, did space permit. I am wholly unable to perceive any reasonable grounds on which the argument can be met, which regards universalism as the logical outcome of such teaching. If Christ delivered from hades EVERY SOUL OF ADAM'S RACE up to the time of His Incarnation; if, *e.g.*, every murderer, if every blasphemer and adulterer, though dying unrepentant, were at last evangelised and saved by Christ, then on what grounds can it be fairly or reasonably asserted that less mercy will be extended to that half of our race, who differ in this, that by no fault of their own they were born after the Incarnation? Is salvation—the final salvation or damnation of millions of immortal spirits—a question of chronology?

Those who are students of this subject may be asked to draw their own inference from the significant silence in which writers, on the traditional side, *e.g.*, Dr. PUSEY, have left this branch of the question. I have already noticed the very striking fact of the disappearance, practically, in modern days, of this truly primitive and scriptural doctrine; and will now sum up, in the following beautiful lines of WHITTIER:—

> "Still Thy Love, O Christ arisen,
> Yearns to reach those souls in prison:
> Through all depths of sin and loss,
> Drops the plummet of Thy Cross;
> Never yet abyss was found
> Deeper than that Cross could sound."

Before dealing with the more direct evidence for early universalism, I may as well here notice a significant element in many Father's writings, *i.e.*, their attitude towards the question of evil. Pressed by the Manichean controversy, the Fathers were forced to consider this question. Their answers to the difficulty are often very significant; they frequently prove their point, either by asserting that *all evil shall one day cease*, or else that evil is nothing. Even AUGUSTINE is forced to make admissions, which seem to involve the final disappearance of evil. It is a strange sight to see the great dialectician caught in the toils he has himself set. Any struggle seems to me vain against the inevitable conclusion from his own premises, *i.e.*, the final extinction of evil. Evil, he maintains, tends to what is less, and what is less tends to *absolute non-existence*. His arguments may be seen,—*Cont. Sec.* ii. xv., and in the context; and *In De Mor. Manich.* ii. 2, &c. AUGUSTINE no doubt denies the extinction of evil. My point is that his denial seems vain on his own theory. So in the dispute between ARCHELAUS and MANES, 275 A.D., which, if not genuine, is antient, it is said on the catholic side, "that death, *has an end*, as it had a beginning."—Ch. xxix. So an old commentator (in. S. JEROME's works), on *Rom.* viii. 20, says: "Vanity is that which at some time *comes to an end.*" And so S. AMBROSE says: "For whatever is of the devil is nothing, which cannot have any perpetuity nor substance."—*De Jacob.* ii. 5. S. GREGORY of Nyssa, also often asserts the non-perpetuity of evil. From SERAPION, the friend of ATHANASIUS, I shall quote a passage to the same effect a few pages further on. TITUS of Bostra, quoted in this chapter, teaches the same. The passages just given seem conclusive against any creed which teaches the permanence of evil. I have ventured to call the traditional creed a dualism thinly disguised. Thoughtful readers will note its marked affinity with the Manichean heresy, in so far as both agree in the *essential fact of teaching the perpetuity of evil.*

To the arguments just stated, which are indirect, but, as it seems to me, significant, may be added, as an indication of primitive teaching, the undoubted fact—that in the very earliest representations of christian thought, in the Catacombs, everything is bright and joyous. Terrorism is conspicuously absent. No figures appear indicating pain, or anxiety; not even the Cross. Flowers, winged genii, and the play of children; such are the prevailing ornaments.

I will now take the more direct testimony in favour of universalism, which abounds in the writings of the Fathers. The earliest of all christian authors, CLEMENS (Romanus) has left us an Epistle about as long as S. MARK's Gospel. It is significant that though he devotes three chapters to the Resurrection, not a line can be quoted from him in favour of the traditional creed. This, though important, is negative evidence only, but there is a passage in RUFINUS—*Inv. in Hier., lib.* i., *prop. fin.*—from which we may, I think, infer, that CLEMENT, with other Fathers, was a believer in the larger hope. We have already noted that the antient *Didache ton Apostolon* is silent as to any endless punishment. Again, if we turn to the striking epistle to DIOGNETUS, which probably dates from about the middle of the second century, we shall find the author describing God as One Who always was, is, and will be, "*wrathless*,"—ch. viii.; he describes the "eternal" (æonian) fire as chastising not "without an end," but "*up to an end.*" (*Mechri telous*)—ch. x.

For many years after the apostolic days we possess but scanty records of christian thought, yet we are able to supply the blank indirectly. PAMPHILUS, the martyr, 294 A.D., wrote, in conjunction with EUSEBIUS, an Apology for ORIGEN, which has almost wholly perished; but we possess very valuable information as to its contents. Two early writers, anonymous, it is true, but whose testimony there seems no reason to doubt, agree in stating that this Apology contained VERY MANY TESTIMONIES of Fathers earlier than ORIGEN, in favour of restitution (and pre-existence).—ROUTH, *Rel. sac.* iii. p. 498. Now, as ORIGEN was born about ninety years after S. JOHN's death, these very numerous testimonies would carry back these doctrines very close, or altogether up to, the apostolic age. Nor is this all: DOMITIANUS, Bishop of Ancyra, whose words are quoted farther on, writing in the sixth century, is very positive indeed. He seems to assert the *universality* of such teaching *before* and after ORIGEN's days: a very significant statement. To this evidence must be added that of the passage respecting CLEMENT just referred to. Indeed, when the great scantiness of early records, during the three first quarters of the second century, is considered, it is cause for deep thankfulness that we possess such strong evidence, as that just quoted, of the extreme antiquity of the doctrine of universalism.

We may be said to emerge into the full daylight of christian history, with the famous CLEMENT of Alexandria, 190 A.D., head of the catechetical school there, and who perhaps may be called the founder of a christian philosophy. Of the great school of Alexandria I shall not attempt to speak at length, but we should note (*a*) how early it was founded, (*b*) how widespread was its influence in leavening christian thought; existing as it did without a rival practically for 150 years; and (*c*) how that influence was exercised in favour of the doctrine of restoration. As to CLEMENT, I may say that his nearness to the apostolic age (he speaks of having learned from a disciple of the Apostles—*Strom. lib.* ii.) his wide and various learning, and his sympathetic spirit combine to give special weight to his teaching. Few, if any, of the Fathers, appeal so little to terrorism, or so uniformly dwell on God's mercy, even in His punishments, as does CLEMENT. "It is manifest," says the learned DALLÆUS, "that CLEMENT thought all the punishments God inflicts upon men are salutary, and executed only for reformation."—*De usu Pat.* So CLEMENT's best editor, POTTER; so GUERICKE—*De schol. Alex.* I proceed to quote:

"All men are Christ's, some by knowing Him, the rest not yet." "He is the Saviour, not of some (only) and of the rest not" (*i.e.*, He is actually Saviour of all) * * "for how is He Lord and Saviour if He is not Lord and Saviour of all?" But He is indeed Saviour of those who believe * * * while of those who do not believe He is Lord, until having become able to confess Him, they obtain through Him the benefit appropriate and suitable (to their case) * * He by the Father's will directs the salvation of all * * For all things have been ordered, both universally and in part, by the Lord of the universe; with a view to the salvation of the universe. * * * But needful correction, by the goodness of the great overseeing Judge, through (by means of) the attendant angels, through various prior judgments, through the final (*pantelous*) judgment, compels even those who have become still more callous to repent.—*Strom. lib.* vii. pp. 702-6, Cologne, 1688. These words seem to teach that all (even those who are callous) are finally restored (*a*) by correction, (*b*) or by angelic ministries, (*c*) by previous judgments, (*d*) by the final judgment. Thus he says that the evil, by chastisements far harder, shall be moved, though unwilling, to repentance.—*Strom.* vi. "The universe has become ceaseless light * * The Sun of righteousness who traverses the universe, pervades all humanity alike. * * Giving us the inalienable inheritance of the Father * * Writing His laws on our hearts. What laws are those He thus writes? That *all* shall know God from small to great. * * It is always the purpose of God to save the human flock (humanity)."—*Adm. ad gent.* p. 71. CLEMENT's teaching as to the design of penalty, is conceived in the spirit of the larger hope. God's "blame is censure concealed in an artful mode of help, ministering salvation under a veil."—*Pæd. lib.* 1. ch. ix. p. 123. And again: "David very plainly states the motives of God's threats (by saying). 'when He slew them they sought Him and turned to Him.'"—*ib.* p. 126. Commenting on Deut. xxxii. 23-5, where God uses very bitter threats of destruction, CLEMENT says: "The divine nature is not angry, but is at the very farthest from being so, for it is an excellent artifice to affright, in order that we may not sin."—*ib.* ch. viii. p. 116. The drift of CLEMENT's teaching may be thus stated. God is training the universe with a resolve to save all. If men are disobedient to the message of salvation, then by discipline and by punishments, He sooner or later brings all to repentance. He says, "So Christ saves *all* men. Some He converts by penalties, others who follow Him of their own will * * that *every knee* may be bent to Him, of those in heaven, on earth, and under the earth, *i.e.*, angels, men, and souls, who, before His coming. passed away from this mortal life."—*In* 1 *S. John*. Before passing on I may point out that CLEMENT, like many of the Fathers, seems to regard death (not of the righteous merely), but death in itself, as a provision designed in mercy for healing sin. He asserts that "when any one falls into *incurable* evil * * it will be for his good if he is put to death." —*Strom.* i. p. 353. Of Sodom, CLEMENT writes: "The just vengeance on the Sodomites became to men an image of the *salvation* which is well calculated for men."—*Pæd.* iii. ch. viii.

There is much that is interesting in a writer earlier than CLEMENT, ATHENAGORAS, 177 A.D.

He nowhere alludes to endless penalty, though he speaks of future judgment His conception of the Resurrection seems to be that it is the crown and completion of man's rational nature. "If this takes place (the Resurrection) an end befitting the nature of man follows also."—ch. xxv. He speaks of the future body as not liable to suffering,—ch. x., and of the Resurrection as a change for the better (apparently in every case) ch. xii. ATHENAGORAS, though little known, writes with a grace and vigor too often wanting in more famous names.

Further evidence of early teaching is afforded by a fragment—assigned to IRENÆUS by PFAFF, its discoverer, but certainly very antient. "Christ will come at the end of the times in order to annul everything evil, and to reconcile again all things, that there may be an end of all impurities." *Frag.* iv. These words fairly express the larger hope.

Further proof of the prevalence of universalist views at a very early date in the Church may be drawn from the so-called SIBYLLINE books, which were composed (except a certain portion, which is pre-christian), at various dates, and by various authors, in the second and following centuries. These books furnish us with most valuable evidence as to the beliefs current in those days. It will be seen how sharp is the contrast between them and our modern notions. In one of them a very striking picture is drawn of the end of the world. All things, *even hades*, are to be melted down in the divine fire in order *to be purified*. All, just and unjust, pass through *unquenchable* fire. The unjust are further committed to *hell* (Gehenna); they are bound in fetters not to be broken; they pray vainly to God; yet these men—apparently all the lost—are finally to *be saved* at the request of the righteous. They are to be "removed elsewhere to a life eternal for immortals."—*Lib.* ii., vv. 195-340. Another passage—*Lib.* viii. 412, seems to teach an universal purification. These verses belong perhaps to the second century; so far from exhibiting any sentimentality, the picture drawn of the end of the world is awful:—even infants at the breast wail in the unquenchable fire; how significant then is it to find mercy finally triumphing. "The Sibyl asserts that the pains even of the damned * * are to be terminated."—FABRIC., *Bibl. grec.* i. p. 203. (So, too, say OPSOPOPŒUS, MUSARDUS, GALLÆUS, &c.) In passing, too, we may at any rate note that the APOCALYPSE OF MOSES (in part, probably very antient,) represents God as saying to satan: "There shall not be granted to thee ear, or wing, or one limb of all which those have whom thou hast enticed by thy wickedness." Even if the primary reference be to Adam and Eve, still the drift and spirit of these words is quite in harmony with the larger hope.

I give next a few quotations from the famous ORIGEN,

234 A.D., born at Alexandria, and when only eighteen called to preside over its school of theology.

Writing on 1 *Cor.* xv. 28, he says: "When the Son is said to be subject to the Father, the perfect restoration of the whole creation is signified."—*De prin.* iii. ch. v. 7. And again, speaking of the end, "God will be all * * seeing evil nowhere exists, for God is all things." "When death shall no longer exist, or the sting of death, nor any evil at all, then, verily, God will be All in All.—*Ib.* iii. ch. vi. 3.

"All things shall be re-established in a state of unity * * all rational souls restored."—*ib.* vi. 6. "We assert that the Word will subdue to Himself all rational* natures, and will change them into His own perfection."—*Cont. Cels.* viii. 72. Such was the teaching that at first leavened all christendom: the fearless assertion of a restoration embracing not all men merely, but all fallen spirits. Such was the teaching of one who stands perhaps foremost, since the Apostle's day, in the union in one person, of genius, learning, industry, holiness, "whose life was one continuous prayer." "Everyone with hardly an exception adhered to ORIGEN."—HUET, *Orig.* p. 197. "Provided one had ORIGEN on his side, he believed himself certain to have the truth."—DOUCIN, *Hist. de l'Origenisme.* Three points may be briefly noted, (*a*) the wide diffusion at this early date of the larger hope; (*b*) the stress ORIGEN frequently lays on the guilt of sin, and the need of retribution; (*c*) his use of *aionios* to express a limited punishment.

Another antient universalist, as I think we may conclude, is S. GREGORY (Thaumaturgus), 254 A.D. Born of heathen parents, he was converted by ORIGEN, whose friend and pupil he became.

As Bishop of Cæsarea, he was distinguished for orthodoxy and numerous (alleged) miracles. He there converted nearly the whole

---

* Some critics think ORIGEN to have taught a possibility of falling away after restoration. This is not certain, but he certainly taught an *universal* restoration.

population to christianity. Bound as he was to ORIGEN by the closest possible ties, he would naturally, in turn, teach the larger hope; and thus, from so important a centre as Cæsarea, a vast district would in turn be leavened. That S. GREGORY did, in fact, so teach, we can infer from a passage in RUFINUS, *Invec. in Hier. Lib.* i. *prope fin.* Of his writings hardly anything has survived.

I have next to cite some extracts from METHODIUS, A.D. 293, Bishop of Tyre, and a martyr (probably). Extracts of his work on the Resurrection have been preserved in EPIPHANIUS, and PHOTIUS.

His teachings seem logically to involve universalism. Thus he asserts that death was given for the destruction of sin in man: "God for this cause pronounced him mortal and clothed him with mortality, that man might not be an undying evil (*i.e.*, that evil in man might not be endless) * * in order that, by the dissolution of the body, *sin might be destroyed root and branch from beneath*, that there might not be left even the smallest particle of root, from which new shoots of sins might break forth." He goes on to employ the illustration of a fig tree growing in the walls of a splendid temple, to preserve which the fig tree is torn away by the root and dies. "In the same way also, God, the Builder, dissolved, slaying by the seasonable application of death, man His own temple, when (man) had fostered sin like a wild fig tree * * * in order that the flesh, after sin is withered and dead, may, like a restored temple, be raised up immortal, while sin is *utterly* destroyed from its foundations."—*Apud.* EPIPH., *Hær.* lxiv. 24-5. He adds that if the Artist wishes that, that on which he has bestowed so much pains, shall be quite free from injury, it must be broken up and recast, in order that all disfigurements * * * may disappear while the image is restored again. "*For it is impossible for an image under the hands of (Kata) the original artist to be lost*, even if it be melted down again."— —*ib.* 27. He says that, what the melting down is to a statue, that is death to man, and the recasting in full beauty is man's resurrection. It is possible no doubt to minimise and explain away all this, but such teaching as that quoted seems clearly to imply in its natural meaning, that God's image cannot be lost, and that death and resurrection (the common lot) involve the cure of sin. To the African school death is simply a penalty. To the great Eastern theologians death is in fact a *mode of cure*—a striking difference. I may add that METHODIUS says in one passage, "Death is good, if it be found like stripes to children for correction;" not the death of sin (sinners?) —*ib.* 22. He adds that God sent death in order that all sin in man might perish.—*ib.* PHOTIUS asserts, that METHODIUS maintains, that even the power of thinking evil thoughts is eradicated by the presence of natural death.—*Cod.* ccxxiv. "Man, after having been formed for God's worship * * *cannot* return to discord and corruption."—*Frag.* i. *from a Hom. on the Cross.* "It is incredible that we, who are the images of God, should be altogether destroyed as being without honour."—*Frag. on Jonah.* Christ was sacrificed and rose again, in order that He might "be by *all created things* equally adored, for to Him 'every knee shall bow, of things,'" &c.—*Or. on the Palms.*—This treatise is in one manuscript assigned to S. CHRYSOSTOM.

We may now be said to have entered on the second of those periods into which our enquiry is divided. The years stretching away from the present date to 430 or 440 A.D., are crowded more than any other with names illustrious in the annals of the Church. And it is noteworthy that precisely in this period universalism finds some of its ablest, and most outspoken advocates, as we shall see in the course of these pages.

EUSEBIUS of Cæsarea, 312 A.D., was a notorious Origenist. "He in the most evident manner acquiesced in ORIGEN's tenets," (except on the Trinity) says S. JEROME.—*Adv. Ruf. lib.* ii.

Commenting on *Ps.* ii., he says: "The Son's 'breaking in pieces' His enemies is for the sake of remoulding them, as a potter his own work; as *Jer.* xviii. 6, says: *i.e., to restore* them once more to their former state." "Even the impious, when the day of the Lord arrives * * shall cast forth and fling away every false opinion of their mind with regard to idols."—*In Is.* ii. 22.—words that are certainly suggestive when speaking of the universal judgment, as here. "Christ will therefore subject to Himself *everything* (the universe), and this *saving* subjection it is right to regard as similar to that, according to which the Son Himself shall be subjected unto Him, Who subjected to Himself all things * * But after the close of everything, He will not dwell in a few, but in all those who are then worthy of the kingdom of heaven. So then shall come to pass (God's being) all in all, when He inhabits as His people all (absolutely, *tous pantas*). —*De eccles. theol.* iii. 16.

EUSEBIUS has preserved some fragments of the writings of MARCELLUS of Ancyra, 315 A.D. I may quote one :—

"For what else do the words mean, 'Until the times of restitution' (Acts iii. 21) but that the Apostle designed to point out that time, in which all things partake of that perfect restoration."—*Cont. Mar.* ii. 4.

I take next a brief passage from SERAPION (ATHANASIUS' friend), 346 A.D.. His words seems certainly to involve the final extinction of evil. In his view, evil, as consisting in choice merely, has no real existence, and easily passes away, leaving no trace behind. "It is of itself nothing, nor can it of itself exist or exist always; but is in process of vanishing, and by vanishing proved to be unable to exist."—*Adv. Man.* ch. iv.

I do not design to discuss S. ATHANASIUS' teaching at any length. It has never been my intention to deny the existence of a school of thought adverse to universalism, in early times. But I do not feel certain, by any means, that ATHANASIUS belonged to this school.

(*a*) There is undoubted evidence seeming to point the other way, *e.g.*, the learned and candid BINGHAM shews that he teaches the possibility of repentance, and pardon, for even the sin against the Holy Ghost. (*b*) Of ORIGEN he speaks, more than once, with respect and even admiration. (*c*) In his treatises, *De Incarn. V. D.*, and *In illud, Om. mihi trad.*, there is much teaching as to Christ's work, &c., which seems in perfect harmony with the larger hope. (*d*) His teaching as to the Descent into hades is significant. He says, that the whole population of the world, which existed in the first ages, and was detained by death, bend the knee as being freed from it. "For He spake to those in bonds, 'Come forth' * * But that they who were formerly disobedient and resisted God were set free, that PETER shewed."—(1 *Peter* iii. 18.)—*Fragm. in verb. Laud. Dom. dracones.* "Christ captured over again the souls captured by the devil, for that He promised in saying, 'I, if I be lifted up, will draw all men unto Me.'"—*In Ps.* lxviii. 18. (*e*) Let us note the following: "'But when all things have been subjected unto Him, then shall the Son also Himself be subject, that God may be All in All:' now this is so, when, as he (PAUL) says, we all are made subject to the Son, and *are found members of Him*." This seems to teach an universal subjection to Christ—a subjection of obedience.—*De hum. nat. suscepta.* Again, elsewhere, after remarking that all things are not yet subject to Christ, for that He is to the Jews a scandal, and to the Gentiles folly, He proceeds, "when, then, the *whole creation* shall meet the Son in the clouds, and shall be subject to Him, then, too, shall the Son Himself be subject to the Father, as being a faithful Apostle, and High Priest of all creation, that God may be All in All."—*Serm. maj. de fide.* (*f*) Lastly, I may notice a remarkable comment on *Ps.* ix. 5. 'Thou hast rebuked the nations, Thou hast destroyed the wicked, &c.'—the devil is meant since *rebuke* (*Epitimesis*) *signifies emendation* * * these words may also be understood of the Last Judgment, for then sinners (*ton hamartolon*—all sinners) being rebuked, the devil who is rightly the wicked one is destroyed."—*Frag. in Ps.* ix.

We now turn to S. HILARY, 354 A.D., Bishop of Poictiers,

one of the most distinguished champions of orthodoxy. His leaning to ORIGEN is evident, of whom he translated, says JEROME, nearly 40,000 lines.—*Adv. Ruf.* i.

Of *S. Luc.* xv. 4, he says, "This one sheep is man, and by one man the *entire race is to be understood* \* \* the ninety and nine are the heavenly angels \* \* and by us (mankind) who *are all one*, the number of the heavenly church is to be filled up. And therefore it is that every creature awaits the revelation of the sons of God."— *In S. Matt.* xviii. This extract, in its obvious sense, teaches universalism. The whole human race, *who are one*, are the one lost sheep, which is destined to be found by the Good Shepherd. Again, S. HILARY has a long and interesting comment on *Ps.* ii. 8-9, pervaded by the spirit of the larger hope. In giving to Christ the ends of the earth as His possession is meant, he says, a dominion, absolutely universal, one to be summed up in S. PAUL's words, which teach: "That every knee of things in heaven, and earth, and under the earth, are to bend in Jesus' name." And as to the nature of this supremacy over all, S. HILARY proceeds to say that by Christ's "ruling the nations with a rod of iron" is indeed meant the care of the Good Shepherd; and by "breaking them in pieces like a potter's vessel" is really signified the vessel's *restoration.* "In this way God will bruise and break the nations of His inheritance, so as to reform them." And the breaking of the vessel, he says, takes place "when the body, being dissolved by death, and thus broken up, the *restoration* shall be effected by the artificer's will." This surely is the same process as that in *Rev.* xix. 15, where Christ smites the nations and rules them with His rod of iron, "treading the winepress of the fierceness of the wrath of Almighty God." But if all this means *salvation*, do we not arrive at the larger hope? By God's slaying sinners, he says that their *conversion* is meant. "'Wilt Thou not slay the sinner,' can He Who came to save that which was lost, and to redeem the sinner, (really) pray that the sinner may be slain? Far be it from Him to desire that he should be slain. But the sinner is slain *when he dies to the world* \* \* In this way is the sinner slain, when the birth of spiritual life is renewed, by the death of all vices and sins."—*In Ps.* cxxxix. 19. This Father is not easy of quotation, being often diffuse, involved, and at times inconsistent; (this latter a fact in perfect harmony with his explicit advocacy of dissimulation), yet his writings convey to me a distinct impression of an inner belief in the larger hope; as, *e.g.*, when writing on *Ps.* cxix. 39, he says that the Psalmist knows a life of immortal glory to have been promised to him by the fact of his being formed in Gods image—"an arrangment of *unalterable* truth," he adds, (and true of every man.) Or again, take the following comment on Christ's words: "'As Thou hast given Him power over all flesh in order that He should give eternal life to all that Thou hast given Him,' \* \* so the Father gave all things and the Son accepted all things \* \* and honoured by the Father, was (in turn) to honour the Father, and to employ the power received in *giving eternity of life to all flesh* \* \* \* now this is life eternal that they may know

Thee," &c.—*De Trin.* lib. ix., p. 206-7, *Paris*, 1652. "When the poor in spirit shall have been set in the heavenly kingdom, then *every creature*, together groaning and mourning, is to be set free from the bondage of corruption."—*In Ps.* lxix. 32-3 " Even the abode of hell "—*inferni*—is to praise God, he says.—*ib.* v. 34.

Our next witness shall be F. M. VICTORINUS, 360 A.D., a distinguished rhetorician at Rome (where he was converted to christianity). Though of African birth, this writer's sympathies are wholly with the Neo-Platonic school and its liberal theology. Such a system whose essence is the outflow of all rational beings from God, and their return to God through Christ, Who is the Universal Word and Saviour, (and Who is also the final centre of unity to all creation,) leads without doubt to the larger hope. VICTORINUS' rugged Latinity has prevented due recognition of his merits as a thinker and theologian.

"And because Christ is the life, He is that by Whom all things have been made, and for Whom (in quem *into Whom*) all things have been made, for *all things cleansed by Him return into eternal life*."—*Adv. Ar.* lib. iii. 3. "In assuming our flesh Christ assumed (the position of) universal word (*logos*) of flesh * * and therefore succoured all flesh ; as is said in Isaiah, 'All flesh shall see Thee the salvation of God ;' and in the Psalms, ' To Thee shall all flesh come ' * * for in Him were all things universally—the universal soul and the universal flesh—and these were lifted up on the Cross and cleansed by the life-giving God the Word, by (Him Who is) universally (the Word) of the entire universe. For by Him all things were made."—*ib.* VICTORINUS' periods are harsh and involved, but his meaning seems clear. Christ is, he says, *universally, i.e.*, to the entire universe at once, and *actually* Creator, Word (*logos*), and Saviour—actually the Saviour ; for the whole train of thought, excludes any such idea as that of a merely potential salvation. And so, he adds, "He is Jesus Christ, because He will save all things unto life."—*ib.* iii. 8. "Christ fulfilled the mystery in order that *all* life with the flesh (*i.e.*, after the resurrection,) filled with eternal light, should return free from all corruption into the heavens."—*ib.* i. 57. "*All things* shall be rendered *spiritual* at the consummation of the world." (1 *Cor.* xv. 28)—*ib.* i. 36. "At the consummation *all things* shall be *one*."—*ib.* "Therefore *all things* converted to Him, *shall become one, i.e.,* spiritual * * through the Son all things shall be made one, for all things are by Him * * for *all* things that exist are ONE, though they be different. For the body of the entire universe is not like a mere heap, which becomes a body only by the contact of its particles ; but it is a body chiefly in that—its several parts being closely and mutually bound together—it forms a *continuous chain*. For the chain is this—God : Jesus Christ : the Spirit : the Intellect (*nous*) : the Soul : the Angelic host : and lastly, *all* subordinate bodily existences."—*ib.* i. 25. To VICTORINUS the universe is one organic whole : a living chain clasped and bound together to the very throne of God. "The *logos* was made 'all in all,' He begot *all things* and saved them."—*ib.* i. 26. Again, commenting on *Eph.* i. iv., he says : "Thus the mystery was completed by the Saviour in order that, perfection having been completed throughout *all things* and *in all things* by Christ, *all universally should be made one through Christ and in Christ.*

VICTORINUS' system shews clearly, what I have elsewhere maintained (p. 54), the natural connection between the dogma of Christ's Deity, and the larger hope.

The next witness I shall call is TITUS, Bishop of Bostra, 364 A.D., in whose writings we see the larger hope taught in Arabia by one whom his editor, CAILLOU, describes as "the most learned among the learned bishops of his age, and a most famous champion of the truth." S. JEROME reckons him as one of those, in whom you are at a loss whether to admire most, their learning or their knowledge of Holy Scripture. On TITUS' Origenism see HUET—*Origen.* ii. p. 199. From EUSEBIUS we learn that ORIGEN thrice visited Arabia, and taught there, once certainly at Bostra.—*Eccles. Hist. lib.* vi. 19, 33, 37.

I transcribe a striking passage, in which TITUS is speaking of evil spirits. "The very pit itself is a place of torments and of chastisement, but is *not eternal* * * It was made that it might be *a medicine and help to those who sin.* Sacred are the stripes *which are medicine* to those who have sinned * * 'Therefore we do not complain of the pits (of hell)—*abyssis*—but rather know that they are places of torment, and chastisement, being for the correction (amendment) of those who have sinned.'"—*Adv. Man. lib.* i. 32. Such words are very significant, as seeming to teach the salvation of all evil spirits. Again, his view of death is significant, and quite inconsistent with the doctrine of never-ending punishment, or of annihilation. He teaches that death is universally, and from its very nature a blessing. Indeed, TITUS maintains significantly that, "if death were an evil, *blame would rightly fall on Him Who appointed it,*" (God)—*ib.* ii. 27. He goes on to say that it comes "not as an injury to the just, nor as a vengeance to the unjust, for that which *is natural cannot be a vengeance*, but as an example, or for the chastisement of evils (*otherwise*) incurable."—*ib.* This, I believe, from the context, and his whole tone, to be TITUS' meaning. Thus he teaches that "Death, which is assigned by law to nature, is not evil in what way soever it come." * * to those who are killed (in war) it brings *an end of* sin * * for as to the unrighteous death is *an end of unrighteousness,* so also to the righteous * * it is a beginning of their crown."—*ib* ii. 12. "Death is not appointed by God to cause men hurt, but is appointed for the greatest benefit both to the *righteous and the unrighteous.*"—*ib.* ii. 16. He goes on to say that death if inflicted on a great number is just the same natural event as in the case of individuals, and even indicates more clearly the divine care: for it "*by the show of indignation,*"—*te kata to phainomenon aganaktesei*—(which the death of many causes) "*benefits,* as explained, those who die, and converts the living."—*ib.* Thus, as he remarks elsewhere, war is permitted by God to raise a surmise, that it is for the punishment of sin, "while in fact it is to put an end to sin."—*ib.* 12. And thus he teaches that evil has a beginning *and an end.*"—*ib. lib.* i. 35. I need hardly pause to point out the significance of all this.

I give next a few sentences of a little known author, MACARIUS MAGNES, who flourished about this time.

> Death was sent to our first parents "in order that, by the dissolution of the body, even all the sin arising from the bond (of body and spirit) should be totally destroyed."—*Not. et. frag.* xix.

Of S. EPHREM (Syrus), 370 A.D., it is enough to say that however strong his language may be as to future penalty, yet he teaches very clearly the liberation of all souls from hades. "Christ burst open the most voracious belly of hades * * seeing this Death trembled * * and sent forth *all* whom from the first man up to that time he had kept in bonds."—*Serm.* xviii. *De sanc. Cruce.*—*Ed. Caillou.*

Another very great name there is whose testimony must be given here, S. GREGORY of Nazianzus, 370 A.D., president of the second great Ecumenical Council, "the most learned bishop in one of the most learned ages of the Church." With S. GREGORY we come to the first of the very celebrated group of teachers, who, in the fourth century, throw lustre on the Cappadocian school.

(a) Let us take a few examples of the way in which S. GREGORY hints, to say the least, his belief in the final salvation of all men

Speaking of the dead, he tells us that God brings them to life as partakers either of fire, or of illuminating light. "But whether *even all* shall hereafter partake of God, let it be elsewhere discussed." —*Carm.* i. v. 548. This striking statement is *concealed* in the Latin version. —*ed. Col.* 1690. S. GREGORY says elsewhere—"I know also a fire not cleansing but penal * * which, more to be dreaded than all, is conjoined with the undying worm, which is not quenched * * unless anyone pleases, even in this instance, to understand this more humanely and worthily of Him Who punishes."—*Orat.* xl. "*It is manifest,*" says PETAVIUS, "that in this place, GREGORY doubted about the pains of the damned, whether they would be endless, or whether they are to be estimated rather in accordance with the mercy of God, so as at some time to be brought to an end." It is no less manifest that he, GREGORY, who was perhaps the foremost man in all christendom, evidently knew of no ecclesiastical objection to teaching the widest hope: nay, there is strong reason to think that he himself believed it. (*b*) He teaches that when Christ descended into hades, He liberated not some, but *all* the souls there in prison. This view, as already shewn, logically implies universalism. "Until He loosed by His blood *all* who groan under Tartarean chains."—*Carm.* xxxv. (*ed. Lyons,* 1840.) "To-day salvation has been brought to the universe to *whatsoever* is visible and *whatsoever* is invisible * * (to-day) the gates of hades are thrown open."—*Or.* xlii. (*c*) Again, it is significant that S. GREGORY speaks of death as a gain to man, because it puts an end to sin, and of penalty as a mercy. "ADAM receives death as a gain, and (thereby) the cutting off of sin ; that evil should not be immortal : and so the vengeance turns out a kindness, for thus I am of opinion it is that God punishes."—*Orat.* xlii. "When you read in Scripture of God's being angry or threatening a sword against the wicked * * understand this rightly and not wrongly. * * How, then, are these metaphors used? Figuratively. In what way? With a view to terrifying the minds of *the simpler sort.*"—*Carm. iamb.* xxi. vv. 370-85. These words recall at once a striking passage of S. GREGORY (of Nyssa), elsewhere quoted : God's judgment uses threats to the lazy and vain, "but by those who are more intelligent, it (the judgment) is believed to be a *medicine*, a *cure* from God."—*Cat. orat.* viii. I believe such teaching to be most highly significant S. BASIL, too, uses very similar words : "Fear edifies the *simpler* ones," speaking of God's slaying sinners.—*Quod Deus non est auct. mal.* (*d*) Again, S. GREGORY seems to treat the human race as made one organic whole by Christ's death, "A few drops of blood renew the whole world, and become for *all* men that, which rennet is for milk, uniting and drawing us into one."—*Or.* xlii. Again : "Christ, stretching His sacred body to the ends (of the earth), brought thence that which is mortal, and bound it into one man."—*Carm.* ii. v. 167. Christ is man that He may be "like leaven for the entire mass (of mankind), and having made that which was condemned (or 'damned'), one with Himself, frees the whole from condemnation (damnation)."— *Or.* xxxvi. (*e*) In a brief iambic poem, he uses language recalling the Neo-Platonic view, saying among other things that God is "end of all things."—*Ad Deum.* (*f*) Again, having used language that seems to favour the ordinary view, S. GREGORY goes on to say "that everything (*ta panta*) shall be subdued to Christ, and they shall be subdued by a full knowledge (*epignosis*) of Him, and by a remodelling * * Now God will be All in All at the time of restitution."—*Or*. xxxvi. (*g*) It is certainly noteworthy again, that this Father speaks of the Novatians (who die in *heresy*, and in a way not that of Christ), as follows: "Perhaps there (in the other world), they shall be baptized with the fire, the last and more laborious, and more protracted baptism, which devours the substance like hay, and *consumes the lightness of all evil.*"—*Or*. xxxix. These words are abundantly suggestive. On this "It is clear," says PETAVIUS, "that pains *by no means endless*, though very long, are appointed for the lost * * and, those dying in heresy."—*De Ang*. iii. 7, § 13. The passages just quoted, if read together, can leave little doubt indeed as to S. GREGORY's views, but there remain two pieces of evidence to complete our proof: (i) Is is certain that S. GREGORY's authority as teaching "restoration" was appealed to by the monks of the New Laura early in the sixth century.—*Vit. S. Cyril, c*. 10. (ii) We have, finally, a passage of RUFINUS, a contemporary, from which the same may be inferred.—*Invec. i, prop. fin*.

Next in the list of Cappadocian teachers are two illustrious names—(brothers) BASIL and GREGORY, Bishops of Cæsarea and Nyssa respectively, to whom should be added a sister, S. MACRINA the younger. BASIL's teacher in childhood had been another S. MACRINA, his grandmother, herself a disciple of that GREGORY who was ORIGEN's bosom friend and pupil, and almost without a doubt an universalist. —p. 110. In such a family the larger hope might be expected to find a congenial home. Certain it is that S. MACRINA (the younger), to whose holy counsels BASIL largely owed his choice of a religious life, was an ardent, nay, an extreme universalist. And no less certain is it that GREGORY of Nyssa taught openly and strongly the same creed. I know what may be alleged from BASIL'S works to prove that he did not share these views; but I also know that one who scruples not expressly to approve pious frauds, and to attribute dissimulation, for a good end, even to our Blessed Lord, may be supposed very likely in his own person to copy such a pattern. And I feel also quite unable to reconcile with the doctrine of endless evil such passages as I shall here quote from S. BASIL.

Take, *e.g.*, these words: "The peace (coming) from the Lord is co-extensive with all time (eternity). For *all* things shall be subject to Him, and *all* things shall acknowledge His empire; and when God shall be All in All, those who now excite discords by revolts, having been quite pacified, (all things) shall praise God in peaceful concord."—*In Is.* ix. 6. Such a prospect is in absolute harmony with the larger hope, and with it only. "Therefore, since *all* are to be made subject to Christ's rule according to the saying, 'He must reign till He put His enemies under His feet,' (the prophet) said His throne shall be restored, (for) the things made subject to His rule are to *obtain restoration*."—*In Is.* xvi. 4-5. That is, Christ's rule is to be one day universal, and this rule involves the restoration of those who come under it (including His enemies). Again, on *Is.* ii. 17 (reading thus): "Every man shall be brought low," BASIL says it means that "every kind of wickedness in man shall cease"—a very remarkable description of the result of the Judgment Day, to which the passage refers: he adds on v. 18 the significant words that "*every rational nature* shall bear witness that true loftiness and greatness belongs to God alone." In another passage this Father teaches that "sins * * *unto death* * * require the fire of judgment" (for their cure).—*In Is.* iv. 4,—a noteworthy statement. In the same spirit he explains the words: "My fury shall not cease on My enemies," (reading *ou pausetai mou ho thumos*) "consider the good issue of righteous judgment * * *My anger will not cease*, I will burn them. And why is this? In order that *I may purify. Thus it is that God is angry in order to bestow benefits on sinners.*"—*In Is.* i. 24. Here note that *ceaseless anger* on God's part is said to mean *mercy*. On *Is.* ii. 9, he says, reading, "'I will *not* forgive,' *even this* the Good (Lord) works for beneficence * * the not being forgiven is not a hurtful threat, but a saving discipline." This passage refers to the final consummation, it must be remembered, (see BASIL's comment on v. 2). On *Is.* i. 28, he says, "'Therefore the sinners and transgressors shall be destroyed (crushed) together,' in order that they may *cease to be disobedient and unruly;* and 'they that forsake the Lord shall be consumed,' *i.e.*, the sin whereby they have offended against God shall no more be committed." S. BASIL goes on to imply that the destruction of the Man of sin, by Christ at His coming, is the removal of his sin, as JEROME teaches.—(*In Mic.* v. 8) "For we have often observed that it is the *sins* which are consumed, not the very persons to whom (the sins) have happened."—*ib.* S. BASIL says on v. 31, that we have once more their case referred to here: first they are to be consumed, and here it is added they are to be burned. This burning he refers to Gehenna (hell), and the whole context seems to render it clear that he regards this as a healing and purifying fire. Again, commenting on *Ps.* xlix. i., this Father says that Zephaniah's words (ch. i. 8-18) about God's wrath devouring the earth, at the Last Day, is in order that all men "may call upon the name of the Lord, and serve Him under one yoke." With this, he says, such Psalms as the present agree, pointing to a time when all things are subdued by Christ, and every knee bends to Him (evidently in harmony). So on *Is.* ix. 19, God's burning up the whole earth is, he declares, for the soul's benefit, for its cleansing. Again, on *Is.* xiii. 19, Babylon's destruction, like that of Gomorrha, is, he says, for its healing. To see the significance of this we must remember (*a*) that the context threatens Babylon with a final and hopeless ruin, v. 20, and (*b*) that Sodom and Gomorrha suffer the vengeance of eternal fire (*S. Jude*).

Before passing on we may relieve the tedium of quotations by noticing a touching family picture, not unworthy to take its place side by side with the famous scene of AUGUSTINE and his mother.—*Confess. lib.* ix. S. MACRINA (the younger), of whom I have just spoken, is lying on her death bed, to which S. GREGORY (of Nyssa) has come, that they may together mourn for S. BASIL, their brother, just taken to his rest. The dying MACRINA, strong in faith and in hope, cheers her surviving brother, by noble thoughts and assurances of the true extent of Christ's Redemption—as destined to embrace savingly all humanity, destined to blot from the universe every stain of sin. This most remarkable conversation of two famous saints, in which "THE PURIFICATORY NATURE OF THE FIRE OF HELL IS UNMISTAKABLY SET FORTH" —(*Dict. of Christ. Biog.* iii. p. 780) has been recorded by S. GREGORY in a well-known book.—*De an. et Res.* The list of early female saints contains, I think, no name illustrious in so many ways, as that of S. MACRINA; illustrious at once for wisdom and energy in practical life; for the deepest devoutness; and for intellectual vigour.

Our next witness deserves special attention—the famous GREGORY of Nyssa, 380 A.D., at once the very flower of orthodoxy, and, like his sister, the most unflinching advocate of extreme universalism, which he teaches in almost countless passages.

I proceed to quote in proof of this. S. GREGORY, in a remarkable passage, speaks of Christ as "both *freeing mankind* from their

wickedness, and healing the *very inventor of wickedness* (the devil)."
—*Cat. orat.* ch. 26. In another treatise the same great Father writes, "for it is needful that at some time, *evil shall be removed utterly and entirely* from existence * * For since by its very nature evil cannot exist apart from free choice, when free choice becomes in the power of God, shall not evil advance to *utter abolition, so that no receptacle for it shall be left?*"—*De an. et. Res.*, vol. ii. p. 659, Paris, 1615. Here it is quite clear that the saint anticipates the utter extinction of evil at some future day, and bases its extinction largely on man's free will. Again, writing on *Phil.* ii. 10, S. GREGORY says that " in this passage is signified, that when *evil has been obliterated* in the long circuits of the ages, nothing shall be left outside the limits of good ; but even from them (the demons) shall be unanimously uttered the confession of the Lordship of Christ."—*ib.* p.644.
"The word seems to lay down the doctrine of the *perfect obliteration of wickedness*, for if God shall be in all things that exist, obviously wickedness shall not be in existence."—*ib.* 661. In another treatise, the *Orat. in* 1 *Cor.* xv. 28, vol. i. p. 844, there is the widest possible assertion of universalism, viz., "At some time the nature of evil shall pass *to extinction, being fully and completely removed from existence ;* and divine unmixed goodness shall embrace in itself *every rational nature :* nothing that has been made by God falling away from the Kingdom of God : when, all the evil that is blended with existence * * being consumed by the melting action of the cleansing fire, everything that has had its being from God, shall become such as it was at first, when as yet untainted by evil." In this strain S. GREGORY continues all through this treatise. Every form of evil is to be swept away ; every rational creature, *without exception*, shall bow the knee in love and peace to Jesus Christ. " For it is evident that God will, in truth, be 'in all' then when there shall be *no evil seen* in existence." And again, "when *every created being* is at harmony with itself * * and every tongue shall confess that Jesus Christ is Lord ; when *every creature* shall have been made one body (then shall the body of Christ be subject to the Father) * * Now the body of Christ, as I have often said, is *the whole of humanity*." (*pasa he anthropine phusis*)—*ib.* p. 849. Again, in the clearest manner S. GREGORY maintains that subjection to God is reconciliation to God. Where it is said that God's enemies shall be subjected to God, " this is meant that the power of evil shall be taken away, and they who, on account of their disobedience, were called God's enemies, shall *by subjection* be made *God's friends.* * * When, then, *all* who once were God's enemies, shall have been made His footstool, because they *shall receive in themselves the divine imprint*, when death shall have been destroyed * * in the subjection of all, which is not servile humility, but immortality and blessedness, Christ is said, by S. PAUL, to be made subject to God." A favourite doctrine of this Father's is that the Resurrection involves restoration—as undoing of all the work of the Fall. It brings immortality and incorruption—things, says S. GREGORY, peculiar to the divine nature, and in themselves a blessing. There is a long and striking passage to this effect in the *De an. et Res.* p. 689. The apostle's words seem to me to imply " what our definition contains,

*i.e.*, that (the) Resurrection *is nothing else than the restoration of our nature to its antient state* (of blessedness) \* \* This corruptible must put on incorruption. But incorruption and honour and glory are confessed to be peculiar to the divine nature. \* \* So we, too, severally divested of mortality and blended with the earth, are born again in the Resurrection after the fashion of our pristine beauty." Doubtless, he adds, the evil are to look for great severity from the Judge; but after due curative treatment, and when the fire shall have destroyed all foreign matter, then the nature, even of these, shall improve by the copious nurture they receive, and at length they too shall regain the divine impress. In this and in a former passage (vol. ii. p. 650), this Father expressly attributes cleansing properties to the "*eternal*" fire,—a fact concealed in the Latin version.

Let us here note the length to which S. GREGORY goes. Universalism, not in isolated sentences, but as the centre of his teaching, and in a form embracing all fallen spirits, characterizes this great Father. And this universalism is as fearless as it is clear. With the Dean of Wells, I say, "That S. GREGORY claims to be taking his stand on the doctrines of the Church in this teaching, with as much confidence as when he is expounding the mysteries of the divine nature, as set forth in the Creed of Nicæa." Let me proceed to quote:—

"By which God shews that neither is sin from eternity, *nor will it last to eternity.* For that which did not always exist shall *not* last for ever \* \* (The Lord) will \* \* in His just judgment, destroy the wickedness of sinners, *not the nature* \* \* *wickedness being thus destroyed* and its imprint being *left in none* all shall be fashioned after Christ, and in *all* that one character shall shine, which originally was imprinted on our nature."—*In Ps. Tract* ii., ch. viii. On the words, "Arise, O Lord, in Thy wrath, and be exalted over the end of Thine enemies" (so the words run in S. GREGORY'S text). "The term 'wrath,'" he says, "shews the retributive power of the just judge, and that which follows (shews) the *extinction of sin:* for that alone is contrary to nature which is seen to be opposed to good, which is sin, whose end is *extinction* and *a change to nothingness.*" He then goes on to explain that to put an end to the enemies of God, means not to allow to human life any power of turning to evil; for as the end of disease is health "so here the Psalmist calls the change of the nature of *mankind, from evil to a state of blessedness. the end of* (God's) *enemies.*"—*ib.* ch. x. Here let us notice the stress laid on *wrath, justice,* and *retribution* and the conclusion so strictly drawn, that these involve the termination of sin. Again, S. GREGORY writes on *Ps.* lvii. 1: "For the nature of sin is unstable and *transitory* * * nor lasting for ever in the universe * * It is like a plant on a house top, not *rooted*, not sown, not ploughed in, and though for the present it may cause trouble with its unsubstantial shoot, yet in the time to come, in the restoration to goodness of all things, it passes away and vanishes. So not *even a trace of the evil, which now* abounds in us, shall remain in the life that is promised as an object of our hope.—*ib.* ch. xiv. So, too, writing on *Ps.* cvii. 42: "And all iniquity shall stop her mouth," this Father says: "How blessed is that life in which the mouth of iniquity shall be for ever stopped * * This is the crown of all blessings, the head of all hope * * that nature shall no longer be troubled by wickedness, but that He shall put a stop to all iniquity, that is to say (to) the very inventor of iniquity" (the Devil). —*In Ps. Tract* i. ch. viii. Again, on *Ps.* cl. 5: "Praise Him upon the high-sounding cymbals," there is a very striking comment. "These cymbals," he says, "joined with cymbals, shew the (future) harmony between the human and the angelic natures, when human nature shall have attained its end. One cymbal is the heavenly nature of the angels. The other is the rational creation of mankind; but sin separated the one from the other; when, then, the goodness of God shall have united once more one with the other, then shall both, brought together, chant forth that hymn, as the great Apostle says, 'Every tongue, of things in heaven, and on earth, and under the earth, shall confess that Christ is Lord, to the glory of God the Father.' Which done, the voice of these cymbals shall chant their song of victory, which arises * * for the extinction of war: which being *wholly extinguished* and *reduced* to *nothingness*, ceaselessly shall there be, with like honour, fully rendered by *every spirit alike* praise to God *for ever:* for since praise is not comely in the mouth of a sinner, but then there shall be no sinner, (sin no more existing,) *every spirit* shall by all means praise God for ever. S. GREGORY sums up: Such is the meaning of this final *Psalm* "in which after the complete abolition of sin, praise shall be sung to God; which praise contain (implies) our being *incapable* of turning to sin * * *when every created being shall be harmonised into one choir* * * and when, like a cymbal, the reasonable creation, and that which is now severed by sin * * shall pour forth a pleasing strain, due to mutual harmony * * Then comes the praise of every spirit for ever * * abounding with increase unto eternity."—*ib.* chap. ix. It may be questioned* whether a nobler exposition of the true spirit of the Psalter, and the true hope of the Gospel, can be anywhere found than the above.

As some readers may not grasp the full significance of this evidence, let me point out that, even if it stood alone, it should dispose of the pleasing fiction, for such it is, that the Church of the fourth or fifth centuries, was unfriendly

---

* Dr. PUSEY thinks it *fair* to describe this Father's teaching as '*mists*' (of Origenism): such are the ways of theological controversy.

to universalism. What are the facts? Very few of his day were so prominent, or so famous, as S. GREGORY: none more thoroughly orthodox; a Confessor and most able champion of the Nicene faith; next to GREGORY of Nazianzus, the most famous member of the General Council of Constantinople; chosen to draw up that Creed, which we to this day recite; appealed to by subsequent Councils as *a very bulwark of the catholic Church*. Such was GREGORY, this fearless advocate of universalism; nay, of an universalism *wide enough to embrace every rational being*.

With the celebrated DIDYMUS, 380 A.D., we return to the school of Alexandria, of which he was the last distinguished head. "DIDYMUS," says S. JEROME, a scholar of his, "surpassed all of his day in knowledge of the Scriptures." The same Father styles him "a most avowed advocate of ORIGEN." But a small portion has survived of his numerous writings, and little, if any, in a perfect condition, mostly in translations, or as fragments in *Catenæ*.

He argues "that as by the Son all things endowed with reason received their being, so by Him the salvation of all of them has been wrought out. * * For Christ brought peace to all things through the blood of His Cross, whether in heaven or on earth * * For as men, by giving up their sins, are made subject to Him, so, too, *the higher intelligences*, freed by correction from their wilful sins (*correcta spontaneis culpis*) are made subject to Him, on the completion of the dispensation ordered for the salvation of all."—*In* 1 *S. Pet.* iii. 22. These words seem to involve the salvation of the fallen angels. DIDYMUS, elsewhere, speaks of a time when *all* are to come to the knowledge of the fulness of Christ, *i.e.*, of God made All in All.— *In* 1 *S. John* iii. 2. Another passage (the text is unfortunately corrupt) on 1 *Pet.* i. 12, evidently contains a hint as to the salvability of evil spirits. With many Fathers, DIDYMUS, from the fact that sin resides in the will, argues its final abolition; and holds that beings who sin voluntarily, are from that very fact not essentially evil. Therefore, even the devils themselves are not *radically* evil; their will has been deflected, but not their substance, not their essential being. Hence all evil spirits are capable of salvation. On *Ps.* x. 15, we have a striking comment—"Break Thou the arm of the wicked," &c. This wicked one, DIDYMUS says, is satan, whose arm is broken, and his sin is not found, "receiving its end in its very completion, for evil is no substance, but a quality. And so shall come that end for all things, for the sake of which all things came into being;" evidently these words intimate the final extinction of evil. And so he says, "God desires to destroy evil, therefore evil is (one) of those things liable to destruction. Now that which is of those things liable to destruction will be destroyed."—*Cont. Man.* ii. So we find DIDYMUS earnest in teaching that the destruction of God's enemies is practically their conversion. Thus, when it is said that God burns up His enemies (*Ps.* xcvii. 3), DIDYMUS explains this of the removal of their sins. And so again in *Ps.* lviii. 8, the melting away of God's enemies is explained by him of life absorbing death. On *Ps.* xviii. 43, where God is said to beat His enemies "small as the dust before the wind," DIDYMUS explains this of their *conversion*. And, he says, God "destroys liars, *so far as they are liars*."—*In Ps.* v. 6. On *Ps.* ix. 5, a comment to the same effect will be found, and other passages might readily be quoted from this Father to the same effect. I may next point to DIDYMUS' teaching on penalty; he argues that divine correction (even vengeance), and promise, have the same object in view.—*Adv. Man.* ch. xviii. I should like to add that he teaches the liberation from hades of every soul by Christ, for he says that Christ "descends to hades and brings back the souls, there detained *on account of their sins.*"—*In Ps.* lxxi. 20. See, too, *De Trin. lib.* iii. 21, &c.

I can hardly feel any doubt that DIDYMUS held the final conversion of all evil beings. So, too, think BASNAGE (*Migne Tom.* 39, p. 176): LUCKE, *ib.* p. 1740: GUERICKE, *De schol. Alex.* pp. 359, 368, 390: *cfr.* HUET—*Orig.* p. 199.

## CHAPTER V.

## "WHAT THE CHURCH TEACHES."

"The Eastern Church of that time (fourth and fifth centuries) was permeated, from GREGORY of Nyssa downwards, with the wider Hope. (See *Spirits in Prison*, ch. iv., *The Eschatology of the Early Church*; and GIESELER, *Church Hist.* Per. ii. ch. ii. 85)."—*The Dean of Wells.*

"Of course I was aware that several of the Fathers are in favour of a restoration of all things."—Cardinal NEWMAN. (*Spirits in Prison.* p. 351.)

WE have already noticed (p. 82) the dominant influence exercised over early christian thought, not by Greeks (for Greece itself was singularly barren theologically), but by Eastern theology, couched in the language of the New Testament. Even at Rome the Church continued, down to the end of the second century, or later, a Greek speaking body — reared under Oriental influences — and whose earliest teachers, like CLEMENT and HERMAS, wrote in Greek, as S. PAUL had written to them, and not in Latin: indeed the very name Pope is Greek. This influence is very marked in the writings of the Latin Fathers, excluding North Africa, of the first four centuries. AMBROSE and the AMBROSIASTER, HILARY, VICTORINUS, JEROME, alike bear evident traces of the more liberal theology of the East. Doubtless to Alexandria, with its cosmopolitan culture, its varied learning, and its school of theology, at once the most antient and most famous in the world, is due the largest share in thus moulding christian thought to a broader and truer catholicity. Its influence may be traced far and near. Thus when

Pamphilus, the martyr, founded towards the end of the third century a library and school at Cæsarea, (or, perhaps, restored the school founded there by Origen in his exile from Alexandria,) we find him giving the place of honour to the works of Origen, transcribing the greater part of them with his own hand—inspired by the influence of Alexandria, where he had studied. When, again, about the same epoch, the presbyters, Dorotheus and Lucian, laid the foundation of the celebrated school of Antioch, it is very significant that, though representing a healthy reaction against the allegorizing interpretations of Origen, the new school retained the dogma of restoration. The same advocacy of the larger hope may be found in the famous teachers of Cappadocia, whose spiritual ancestry is to be traced to the first Gregory, Origen's bosom friend and pupil, and so to Alexandria finally.—(p. 110.)

But there is this to be noted and frankly admitted, that if Africa gave birth to a theology broad and truly catholic in its sympathies, so it furnished what to some may seem the antidote. North Africa was in a special sense the home of a theology cruel and remorseless in its eschatology. Let us hear Tertullian gloating and revelling over the future torments of the heathen. He is to "laugh," "rejoice," "exult." He tells us why "when I behold so many kings * * groaning in the lowest darkness; so many magistrates liquefying in fiercer flames than they ever kindled against christians * * sapient philosophers blushing as they burn with their disciples: then shall we see the tragedians more tuneful under the fire * * the charioteer all red in his burning car."—*De Spectac.* xxx.—Tertullian rejoices *because* the condemned are for ever burning; we are to rejoice *while* they are burning, even though our nearest and dearest are in those flames! Is the moral difference very great?) And when, exhausted by faction and strife, this Church fell hopelessly before the advance of ISLAM, the teachings of its greatest bishop not only survived, but gained a wider sphere. Extinct in their birthplace, the cruel doctrines of AUGUSTINE flourished as a graft on the Roman stock, thence leavening by slow degrees the whole of Latin christendom, with an element novel and uncatholic. The moment was auspicious for their success, for now the churches of Italy were fast rising to power. The great Greek Fathers had spoken and passed away: their very language rapidly becoming unknown in the West. Thus no obstacle was left to stem the fast rising tide of Augustinianism, naturally triumphant in an age cruel, corrupt, and superstitious. And so by degrees no less than a doctrinal revolution was accomplished, and the whole framework of Western theology, to its infinite loss, bears to this day the imprint of Africa, and its pitiless creed, which slanders at once God and Man, true sign of an ignoble and false theology. The mediæval schoolman and the modern puritan, alike wear with complacency the spiritual fetters forged at Hippo, by one who, despite his genius, never so much as fully mastered the language of the New Testament,—a fact I commend to those who claim the authority of Scripture for the traditional creed.

Let us now turn to some Latin Fathers, whose works attest plainly this widespread influence of Greek theology. I take first a very distinguished name, S. AMBROSE of Milan, 390 A.D. We shall see what his teaching is on the question of the divine punishment of the wicked. Their very destruction is, in his view, a mode of cure.

"Many ask an important question here, whether Holy Scripture asserts the perishing of our nature, especially because it elsewhere says: 'I will beat them small as the dust before the wind. I will *destroy* them as the mire of the streets.'—*Ps.* xviii. 42. * * What, then, hinders our believing that he who is beaten small as the dust is not annihilated, but is *changed for the better ;* so that, instead of an earthly man, he is made a spiritual man, and our believing that he who *is destroyed, is so destroyed that all taint is removed*, and there remains but what is pure and clean. And in God's saying to the adversaries of Jerusalem, 'they shall be as though they were not,' * * you are to understand they shall exist substantially and as *converted* (to God), but shall not exist as (God's) enemies."—*In Ps.* i. On the words : " I have set Thee over nations and kingdoms to root up, to destroy, to ruin, to build, and to plant." S. AMBROSE says this means Christ's "destroying *every vestige of sin* * * this it is to destroy and to plant, viz., that what is sinful should be rooted out, and what is better planted in."—*In Ps.* xliv. p. 1370. *ed. Par.* 1569. In harmony with this, but in hopeless contradiction to the traditional creed, stands S. AMBROSE'S teaching as to death, which to him is not a penalty but *a mode of cure.* "Why, then, do we blame death," asks S. AMBROSE, " * * if life is a burden, death is freedom ; if life is a punishment, death is a *remedy.* * * In every way, then, death is good * * because it does not change one's state for the worse. We shall find death to be the end of sin. The Lord suffered death to enter in order that guilt might cease."—*De bon. mort.* ch. iv. "Death is a passage to better things, for if the guilty, who will not recall their steps from sin, die even against their will, yet they receive not an end of nature, but of their guilt." —*De Cain et Ab.* ii. 10. "God gave death, *not as a penalty*, but as a *remedy ;* * * death was given for a remedy as the *end* of *evils* * * God did not appoint death from the beginning, but gave it as a *remedy*."—*De fide Res.* p. 471.

In the next chapter we shall discuss the true meaning of the Resurrection, and shall quote S. AMBROSE (and many other Fathers) as teaching that it involves restoration, as being a gift of life in Christ to all. (See *e.g.*, *De fide Res.*) Next we see S. AMBROSE asserting that from its very nature sin cannot last for ever.

"That which is of the devil is nothing, and can have no perpetuity and substance."—*De Jacob* ii. 5. "How shall the sinner exist in the future, seeing the place of sin cannot be of long continuance?" —*In Ps.* xxxvii. p. 1302. Again (writing of the wickedness of evil spirits) : "They will not always remain, nor can their wickedness be perpetual."—*In S. Luc.* viii.

The next class of quotations consists of those, in which S. AMBROSE argues from the divine image in man.

" That image may indeed be obscured, but *cannot be destroyed*, by reason of its nature" (per naturam).—*De fide Res.* (*frag.*) p. 487. For as S. AMBROSE asks ; " Shall He Who has not permitted those things to perish, which belong to man's needs, permit man to perish, whom He made after His own image?"—*De fide Res.* p. 473. "Because God's image is that of the one God, it like Him starts from one, and is diffused to infinity. And, once again, from an infinite number *all things return into one* as into their end, because God is both beginning and end of all things."—*Epis. lib.* i. 1.

The closing words of the last passage recall that Neo-Platonism, which we have noticed in VICTORINUS, and shall see fully elaborated by the so-called DIONYSIUS (the Areopagite), and his imitators. We shall next quote S. AMBROSE's teaching as to the subjection of all things to Christ, which breathes the very spirit of universalism.

"How, then, shall (all things) be subject to Christ? In this very way in which the Lord Himself said: 'Take my yoke upon you.' For it is not the untamed who bear the yoke, but the humble and gentle * * so that in Jesus' name every knee shall bend." * * S. AMBROSE asserts that subjection to Christ is loving submission, and that in this sense *all* must become Christ's subjects. He proceeds to discuss Christ's subjection to the Father. "Is this subjection of Christ now completed? Not at all. Because the subjection of Christ consists not in few, *but in all* (becoming obedient). * * Christ will be subject to God in us by means of the obedience of *all* * * (then) when vices having been cast away, and sin reduced to submission, one spirit of *all* people, in one sentiment, shall with one accord begin to cleave to God, then God will be All in All; * * when *all*, then, shall have believed and done the will of God, Christ will be All and in All; and when Christ shall be All in All, (then) God will be All in All."—*De fid. lib.* v. 7. Again, on *Ps.* cxix. 91: "For all things serve Thee;" he says, "At present we do not all serve God. But, when Christ shall have delivered His kingdom over to God, then shall *all* things be subject to Him, Who has subjected the universe to Himself; acquiring *the faith of all*, through the Passion of His only begotten Son; * * when, therefore, *all* shall have believed in the Lord, then shall *the universe* serve God, so that He may be *All and in All*." "By a profound design the Apostle declares that Christ shall be subject to the Father in us, when there shall exist in *all* the fullness of faith. * * At present He is over *all* by His power, but it is necessary that He be in *all* by their free will."—*In Ps.* lxii. 1.

S. AMBROSE, I may add, teaches that the sin against the Holy Ghost may be forgiven.—*De pænit.* ii. 4—a chapter worth reading. Lastly, the following passages shew clearly the tone of his theology.

"The mystery of the Incarnation is the salvation of the *entire creation* * * as it is elsewhere said, 'the *whole creation* shall be set free from the bondage of corruption.'"—*De fide lib.* v. 7. "The Father has committed all judgment to Christ; shall then He be able to condemn thee for whom He gave Himself? * * Will not He say, what use is there in My blood if I condemn him whom I have saved?"—*De Jacob* i. 6. "*All* nations shall come and worship before Thee * * for *all* flesh shall come to Thee, no longer subject to the world, but united to the spirit."—*De fide Res.* p. 486. "The mercy of the Lord is to all flesh, in order that *all flesh* * * may ascend to the Lord."—*In Ps.* cxix. 156. "So the Son of Man came to save that which was lost, *i.e.*, *all*, for as in Adam *all* die, so, too, in Christ shall all be made alive."—*In S. Luc.* xv. 3.

In S. AMBROSE's teaching "death is altogether to be desired, * * the terrors of the future state almost entirely disappear * * he affirms that, even to the wicked, death is a gain."—*Dict. of Chris. Biog.* (*Smith and Wace*). Thus, while S. JEROME with perfect truth asserts that, nearly all of S. AMBROSE's books are full of Origenism,—*Adv. Ruf.* i., and the learned HUET confirms this.—*Orig.* ii. pp. 159, 199. we must note that even ORIGEN lays more stress on sin and future penalty than does S. AMBROSE.

I next proceed to quote an early and able writer (not certainly identified), whose works are usually bound with those of S. AMBROSE, and who wrote during the Popedom of DAMASUS, 366-384 A.D. (see his words on 1 *Tim.* iii. 14-5.) He teaches clearly the liberation of all souls by Christ from hades (p. 100). I quote some further specimens of his teaching.

"This seemed good to God * * to manifest in Christ the mystery of His will * * namely, that He should be merciful to all who had strayed, whether in heaven or in earth * * *Every being, then, in* the heavens and on earth, while it learns the knowledge of Christ, *is being restored to that which it was created.*"—*In Eph.* i. 9-10. On the two last verses of the same chapter may be found a striking comment—tracing the salvation of all through Christ to His creation of all. Since *all* were made by Christ He is to be Head and Lord of of all. "In speaking of the whole Church (reading *omnem ecclesiam*), the Apostle summarily comprehends the *totality of that which exists in heaven and on earth* * * for when they shall have returned to the confession of one God, bending the knee to Christ, He is fulfilled in all, so as to be all, for all comes from Him." Again, we find the same argument for universal salvation. "Christ rose that He might create anew once more those things which He had first made ; * * that He should restore all those things which He (God) made through Him \* \* and *all things* that have been made by Him should live in Him as in their Author"—(compare VICTORINUS' teaching already quoted).—*In Col.* i. 20. A striking passage is the following, recalling VICTORINUS, and the Neo-Platonic school : "The creation was formed by God through Christ, so that \* \* it should be as it were a chain linked together (*concatenatio*), descending in ordered arrangement to the firmament, so as to form an *united whole* \* \* This, then, is the point aimed at, that the creation (*creatura*) may be brought back to one mind \* \* so that it may be harmonious in love of the Creator \* \* For it is rebuilding itself into a temple of the Lord."—*In Eph.* iv. On 1 *Cor.* xv. 27, this writer says : "When every creature learns that Christ is its head, and that Christ's head is God the Father, then God is All in All ; that is to say, that *every creature* should believe alike, that with one voice *every* tongue of things in heaven and earth and under the earth, should confess that there is one God from Whom are all things." The following is interesting on Christ's enemies being made His footstool : "They are made to bow under His feet who \* \* return to the Lord, and as a footstool to the feet so are bent to His preaching. Without doubt this is said of those enemies who, having been corrected, are set on His right hand."—*In Heb.* i. 13. "The Father has granted to the Son that, after the Crucifixion, all things should be saved in the name of the Son."—*In Phil.* ii. 10.

In S. AMBROSE'S works is generally printed a treatise—*De Sacramentis*, assigned by most critics to a contemporary, or it may be, a later author. It is of interest as further tending to shew the tone of the current beliefs of christian antiquity.

"God," it teaches, " desiring to undo everything hurtful \* \* sentenced man to death \* \* It was assigned as a *remedy* that man should die and rise again : \* \* death interposing puts a stop to sin. \* \* Christ brought in the Resurrection : \* \* We have on our side both (*i.e.*, death and resurrection), because death *ends sin*, and resurrection is a remoulding of our nature."—*lib.* ii. ch. 6. "What, then, is the Resurrection except our rising from death to life."—*ib.* iii. 1. These words are in harmony with a very large body of primitive teaching (as my readers can see), and are in hopeless antagonism to the views now general, which regard death as essentially penal.

Our next witness shall be one who is, with the exception of AUGUSTINE, the most striking figure among the Latin Fathers ; one to whom in learning and in critical acumen even AUGUSTINE cannot be compared—I mean S. JEROME. It is impossible not to pause as we survey these two great contemporaries, who corresponded, indeed, but never met

In Jerome are represented the tendencies, broad and sympathetic, of Eastern theology (already beginning to wane.) In AUGUSTINE are summed up the cruel and uncatholic dogmas of the rising school of North Africa. In a true sense S. JEROME is the last of a long line of Latin Fathers, drawing their inspiration from Eastern sources.—AUGUSTINE is the founder of a new theological dynasty. The lengths to which S. JEROME went in teaching universalism may be seen from what follows.

"Christ will, in the ages to come, shew, not to one, but to the *whole number of rational creatures*, His glory, and the riches (of His grace)." He adds that the saints are to reign over the *fallen angels, and the prince of this world, Lucifer, even to them bringing blessing.* \* \*—*In Eph.* ii. 7. This remarkable passage is followed by one even more explicit and outspoken. Both should be read in the original rather than in my brief summary, especially that which follows.—"In the end of (all) things \* \* the whole body which had been dissipated and torn into divers parts shall be restored. \* \* Let us understand the *whole number of rational creatures* under the figure of a single rational animal \* \* let us imagine this animal to be torn \* \* so that no bone adheres to bone, nor nerve to nerve." S. JEROME proceeds, And then suppose some wonderful physician to come and restore to its place every part. \* \* "So in the restitution of all things, when the true physician, Jesus Christ, shall have come to heal the body of the whole Church, *every one* \* \* shall receive his proper place \* \* What I mean is, the *fallen angel will begin to be that which he was created,* and *man*, who has been expelled from Paradise, *will be once more restored to the tilling of Paradise.* These things, then, will take place *universally.*"—*In Eph.* iv. 16. What an idea may not unprejudiced readers gain of the breadth of early teaching from these words. If, he says, we see one falling into sin we indeed are sorry, and hasten to rescue him, but we cannot be saddened, knowing that "with God *no rational creature perishes eternally.*"—*In Gal.* v. 22. "Death shall come *as a visitor to the impious;* it will *not be perpetual;* it will not annihilate them; but will prolong its visit, *till the impiety which is in them shall be consumed.*"—*In Mic.* v. 8. Again, speaking of the consummation of all things, S. JEROME says, on *Zeph.* iii. 10: The prophet, here aware of the extent of God's mercy, is like the Psalmist communing with his heart and asking, "'will the Lord cast off for ever?' \* \* of which the meaning is—I did think God would abandon sinners for ever \* \* but now I perceive that it was done for this end \* \* to *change everything*, and that He might *shew mercy* on those whom *He had before* cast away." "In the Cross and Passion of the Lord, all things have been summed up." He goes on to shew what this means. It is, he says, as though one were to lend 100 pence in various sums and get all back in one sum. In other words. Christ is to get back all things.—*In Eph.* i. 10. To this idea he returns: "The Cross of Christ has benefited not earth only but heaven * * and *every creature* has been cleansed by the blood of its Lord."— *ib.* ii. 16. And on ch. iii. 14, he teaches clearly that "by every knee bending in Jesus' name is meant 'the obedience of the heart.'" "Christ is subject to the Father in those who are faithful, for all who believe, nay, *all the race of man is counted as His members.* But in those who are unbelievers, Jews, heathen, and heretics, Christ is said not to be subject, because a part of His members is not subject to the faith. But in the end of the world, when all His members shall have seen Christ, *i.e.*, their own body, reigning, they, too, shall be subject to Christ, *i.e.*, to their own body, so that the *whole body of Christ* may be subject to God and the Father, that God may be All in All."—*Ep. ad Aman.* This involves the final obedience of all, and teaches that Jews, heathen, and heretics are Christ's members.

Nor are these isolated instances: I have found *nearly 100 passages* in his works (and there are doubtless others) indicating S. JEROME's sympathy with universalism. Further, we should note that when towards the year 400 A.D., S. JEROME took part with EPIPHANIUS and the disreputable THEOPHILUS, against ORIGEN (whom he had hitherto extravagantly praised), he, as HUET points out—*Orig.* ii. p. 159 —kept a significant silence on the question of human restoration. "Though you adduce," says HUET, "six hundred testimonies, you thereby only prove that he changed his opinion." But did he ever change his opinion? and if so, how far? Thus, in his *Epis. ad Avit.*, where he goes at length into ORIGEN's errors, he says *nothing of the larger hope; and when charged with Origenism, he refers, twice over, to his commentaries on Ephesians, which teach the most outspoken universalism.*—*Epis.* lxv. *ad Pam.*: lxxv. *adv. Vigil.* As a specimen of his praise of ORIGEN, he says, in a letter to PAULA, that ORIGEN was blamed, "not on account of *the novelty of his doctrines, not on account of heresy, as now* MAD DOGS *pretend*," *but from jealousy.* So that to call ORIGEN a heretic is the part of a MAD DOG! Note this, from the most orthodox JEROME.

Certain it is, that his works abound in universalistic teaching: I proceed to quote.

On *Amos* ix. 2, we have this vivid (and *significant*) description of the fate of the sinful soul *after death:* "If despairing of safety, it shall try to avoid the eye of the Lord, and to fly to the utmost limits, * * even there shall the Lord command the old and crooked serpent, the enemy and avenger, and he shall bite it; * * it shall also be smitten by the sword of the Lord, * * in order that, by means of tortures and punishment, it may *return to the Lord.*" On *Nahum* ii. 2, this striking comment occurs: At the end of the world satan and his hosts shall fly in terror. * * "Now while they (the devil and his hosts) are thinking over this, *every thing that they have captured shall be brought forward* (*i.e.*, rescued). * * Further, *all the substance of the world*, and *all its servants* after they have submitted themselves to Christ, * * shall be led along in joy and gladness * * And then shall be fulfilled that which is spoken (*Ps.* lxviii. 18) of the Saviour's victory, when ascending on high, 'He led captivity captive.'" Here there seems to be taught the final liberation from satan of all his captives. In this spirit this Father says that Christ's final coming is "to destroy *sins*" (not sinners) and so, "at the consummation of the world, every creature shall have been set free."—*In Hab.* iii. 2, 11.

S. JEROME'S teaching as to God's vengeance and destruction of His enemies is very significant.

What shall I do to thee, Ephraim? * * I will destroy thee unto dust and ashes. And when the harsh, nay, cruel sentence has been passed * * he appeases the austerity of the Judge by the love of the Father * * for I do *not strike in order to destroy for ever*, but in order to *amend.*"—*In Hos.* xi. 8. "The Jews think the original word may be translated, not only 'judgment' but 'gold,' meaning that in the valley of judgment, which they believe to be Gehenna, the taint of sins being purged away, thou (the sinner) mayest remain pure gold.—*In Joel* iii. 14—suggestive words. Again he says, commenting on *Zech.* xii. 9: "He will destroy, not for their ruin, but for *their amendment*; * * for if He created all things out of nothing, He did not do so in order to destroy that which He had created, but in order that by His mercy the things created should be saved;"—words that recall VICTORINUS' teaching as to creation.

From an early writer (not certainly identified), whose commentary on the *Psalms* is bound with S. JEROME'S works, *ed. Paris* 1624, I quote some passages, wholly breathing the larger hope.

Thus, on the destruction of God's enemies, he writes: "When the Psalmist says, 'Thine enemies, O God, shall perish,' * * *every one* who has been Thine enemy shall *hereafter be made Thy friend*: the man shall not perish, the enemy shall perish."—*In Ps.* xcii. 9.

No less striking is the comment on *Ps.* ix. 5: "Thou hast blotted out their name *for ever and ever.*" This Father says, in effect, that it means blotting out their sins and *their turning to God. Here an eternal blotting out is amending.* So again: "The devil is, as it were, God's executioner. They who walk not rightly are handed over to the devil. Wherefore? That they may perish eternally? And where then is the mercy of God? Where is the tender Father? * * What the Apostle says is this, 'I have handed over sinners to the devil, that, tormented by him, they may be converted to Me.'"—*In Ps.* cviii. 9. On the words, "His wrath will soon be kindled" —*Ps.* ii. 12—this Father (reading *in brevi*), says: "This means at the death of every one, or, with a *brief wrath* at the Day of Judgment, as that (verse means) 'sudden destruction shall come on them.'" This involves the opinion that the sudden destruction of the wicked, to which S. PAUL refers, would be satisfied by a *brief wrath* at the Day of Judgment. A significant passage holds out hope of pardon even to satan. "Thou who wast first a dragon * * Look ye what the Psalmist says * * Do thou *not* then despair, *repent* and *straightway thou art converted.*"—*In Ps.* cxlviii. 12.

Nor should the name of DIODORUS, 378 A.D., Bishop of Tarsus, be absent from the roll of early universalists. He was one of the greatest ornaments of the famous school of Antioch, with whose teaching we are now to make acquaintance. In his lifetime he was noted for untiring zeal in defence of the Nicene Faith, and was praised by men like BASIL, THEODORET, CHRYSOSTOM, and CYRIL, and died in universal honour; having, says THEODORET, saved the bark of the Church from being submerged under the waves of unbelief. Of his numerous writings but mere fragments have survived. The following is from his book *De Œcon.*— ASSEM. *Bibl. Or.* iii. p. 324.

"For the wicked there are punishments not perpetual.* * but they are to be tormented for a certain brief period, * * according to the amount of malice in their works. They shall therefore suffer punishment for a short space, but *immortal blessedness,* having no end *awaits them;* * * the penalties to be inflicted for their many and grave crimes are very far surpassed by the magnitude of the mercy to be shewed them. The Resurrection, therefore, is regarded as a blessing not only to the good but also to the evil."

We may next note that RUFINUS, 390 A.D., certainly taught that the future punishment of the wicked would be *temporary,* in his exposition of the Creed. He plainly so teaches, says HUET, *Orig.* ii. p. 160. He contrasts the *perpetuity* of glory of the just, with a (merely) lengthy punishment of the wicked. There remain two other facts by which we may ascertain RUFINUS' views. In his preface to ORIGEN—*De prin.*, he states, in effect, that he had removed what was "discordant with our belief" from that book. But he certainly left there *very distinct* assertions of universalism. Again, it seems hardly possible to doubt that in his work on the Creed, he taught the liberation from hades of all souls by Christ.

I quote next from S. PAULINUS, Bishop of Nola, 393 A.D. (not attempting to decide what he at heart believed).

PAULINUS' brother DELPHINUS, seems to have died in sin: so far from abandoning his case as quite hopeless, PAULINUS begs S. AMANDUS to pray for him, because "*doubtless* the dew of God's indulgence will penetrate hell (*inferna*), so that those burning there * * may be refreshed."—*Epis. ed Aman.* He, too, teaches that the destruction of the heathen by Christ is really their *cure*. His iron rod "breaks their hearts as though vessels formed of clay, in order to remake them (for the) better." How far this principle logically goes—for Christ is to have possession of the whole earth—any one can judge —*Par. of Ps.* ii. A common disobedience shut up all, in order that faith might heal *the whole;* so that *all the world* may be made God's servant."—*Carm. Ad Cyth.* p. 494, ed. Antwerp, 1622.

I take next S. CHRYSOSTOM; trained in the school of Antioch, a pupil of DIODORUS of Tarsus, his education can hardly have been otherwise than decidedly universalistic in character. And when all the evidence is fairly weighed, I think that but little doubt can remain, as to his very strong sympathy with, or, indeed, adoption of the larger hope; notwithstanding his apparent teaching of the ordinary creed. For, on the theory of his really holding that creed, I can find no explanation of such passages as I shall quote; while his threats of future punishment, however terrible, may be easily explained (I.) as coming from a great preacher in cities stained with horrible vices, like Antioch or Constantinople—(*e.g.*, see *Hom.* ix. *on Rom.* v., where he speaks of lusts worse than those of Sodom: perhaps civilisation has nowhere assumed so base a form as in the Byzantine empire.) (II) By the rhetorical and ambiguous character of the terms used. (III) By the notorious advocacy of deceit—*apate*—as a spiritual medicine, which we find in his works. (*a*) We may note, too, the fact that he was charged with a leaning to Origenism in the controversy between JEROME (and EPIPHANIUS), and JOHN of Jerusalem. (*b*) Again, he sanctions prayers and almsgiving on behalf of those who have died in sin (*i.e.*, unrepentant).—*In S. Jno. Ser.* lxi. *In* 1 *Cor., Serm.* xli. (*c*) Nor should his enthusiastic praise of the universalists, DIODORUS, and THEODORUS of Mopsuestia, be forgotten.—FAC. *Pro def. tr. cap.* iv. 2; vii. 7. These facts raise a strong suspicion, at least, of his sympathy with the larger hope. Let us therefore try to gather his views from his own words. Writing on *Rom.* v. 16 (*Ser.* x.), he uses language inconsistent with the perpetuation of evil in hell. S. PAUL is speaking of the result of Christ's work; on this CHRYSOSTOM comments as follows:

"By this is inevitably shewn that death is plucked up root and branch; * * not only was the sin (of ADAM) *abolished*, but *also all other sins whatsoever.*" * * Of death "*not a trace remains*, nor can *its shadow* be discerned, as it is *utterly* destroyed." Again, on the words, God shall be "All in All" he says: "Some maintain that the Apostle asserts here the *abolition of evil*, so that *all* shall henceforth willingly yield (to God), and *not one resist or be under the power of* evil, for when sin shall no longer exist, it is evident that God will be All in All." He closes his comment with these words: "For when *evil has been taken away*, much more shall death cease." The abolition of sin is surely a synonym for the larger hope. And so, on *Col.* 1 (*Hom.* iii.), where the Apostle is speaking of Christ as first creating all things, and then reconciling *all things*, CHRYSOSTOM says that it was needful that He should reconcile them "*perfectly*, so that they should *never again* become His enemies:" and on v. 18 says that the Church stands for the whole race. I cannot see any escape from the conclusion that these words involve universalism, in their natural meaning. Again, on *Eph.* i, *Hom.* i., this Father says that all, angels and men are to be brought under one head.

"Thus, then, shall there be an unity * * when *all things* (the universe) shall have been brought under one head, having a necessary bond of connection from above." On *S. Jno.* xii. 32 : " ' I will draw all men unto me.' Had Christ said, 'I will rise,' it is not clear that (He would have implied that) they (all) would believe, but in saying that they shall believe, He combines both."

The following extracts again teach a view of "vengeance" and "penalty" and "death" which seems to point clearly in the direction of the larger hope.

"Tell me on what account do you mourn for him that is departed? Is it because he was wicked? But for that very reason you ought to give thanks, because his evil works are put a stop to."—*De dorm. Serm.* xxx. "Death has been ordered for our *benefit* by the Lord * * for such a Master is ours that in His vengeance (*timoria*) no less than in His benefits, He shews His care of us. Had He known that sinning without vengeance *i.e.* (with impunity) would make us no worse, He never would have inflicted vengeance on us. * * To extirpate our wickedness * * He kindly inflicts vengeance."—*In Gen.* iii. *Hom.* xviii. "If punishment were an evil to those who sin, God never would have added evils to evils. * * It is, then, no evil to the offender to be punished, but that one so acting should not be punished (is an evil), just as for a sick man not to be cured."—*In Rom.* ch. v. *Hom.* ix. "God is *equally* to be praised when He chastises, and when He frees from chastisement. For both spring from goodness. * * It is right, then, to praise Him *equally* both for placing ADAM in Paradise, and for expelling him, and to give thanks, not alone for the kingdom (of God), but for *hell as well* (Gehenna)."—*In Ps.* cxlviii. 10. Note, too, the following: "What great goodness did it not shew to restrain from sin those who, at the time of the Deluge, were *incurably* diseased * * and to employ, as a medicine, the common debt of nature, and to bring on them the easiest death by water."—*In Ps.* clxv. 8. "God does all things through love, as, *e.g.*, to benefit man He set him in Paradise, and to benefit him He turned him out of Paradise. * * To benefit him He sent that fire on Sodom,"—*In Ps.* cxl. 1,—the "eternal" fire of S. JUDE.

The drift of S. CHRYSOSTOM's teaching is further shewn by his attitude toward the so-called unpardonable sin, as quite capable of pardon. *Many*, though guilty of it, were, he tells us, pardoned subsequently on their repentance.—*In S. Matt.* xii. *hom.* xlii.. I commend to the thoughtful and unprejudiced to consider the light thrown by this teaching on the patristic use of such terms as "never," "for ever," "eternal" (see pp. 88-92).

Again, I may appeal to CHRYSOSTOM'S very clear assertion of the liberation of *every soul whatsoever* from hades by Christ, and of the subversion of hades itself in consequence. I give a summary of his striking words:

Christ, he asserts, not merely opened, but broke in pieces the gates of brass, in order to make the prison useless; where there is neither door, nor bar, *whosoever enters is not detained*. What God destroys, who can set up again? Earthly kings indeed set free prisoners, yet leave untouched the prison gates; but Christ broke in pieces the gates of brass. Christ went to the utterly black and joyless portion of hades, and turned it into heaven, transferring *all* its wealth, the *race of man*, into His royal treasury. In this, too, Christ surpasses kings, for they send messengers, but He went in person to set the captives free.—*De cam. et cruce. Ser.* xxxiv. So again, he says: "Our Lord, when He was in hades, set free *all* who were kept prisoners by death."—*In magn. heldom.*

We now come to the famous THEODORE of Mopsuestia, 407 A.D., who enjoyed during his lifetime an extraordinary renown as a teacher of the catholic faith. "He was," says DORNER, *Pers. of Christ*, i. 50, "the crown and climax of the school of Antioch, and was called the Master of the East from his theological eminence."

THEODORE and (perhaps) DIODORUS, after they had rested for a century and a quarter in their honoured graves, were condemned as *Nestorians* in the Fifth Council, an assembly unrecognised by the English Church. *No question of universalism was thereby raised*, for the very promoters of this Council *were Origenists*, and intrigued against THEODORE on the *very ground of his hostility to* ORIGEN. That DIODORUS was condemned is uncertain, for though PHOTIUS states that he was, his name does *not occur* in the Acts of the Council. Certain it is that (1) THEODORE towered above almost all his contemporaries, and lived and died in honour. See a striking letter full of praise from CHRYSOSTOM, addressed to THEODORE.—*Epist.* cxii. Certainly, too (2), such posthumous attacks by Councils of very doubtful authority are most often rooted in paltry jealousy and intrigue. (3) And it is a painful reflection to compare the impunity enjoyed by those who blacken the divine *character*(*e.g.*, S. AUGUSTINE) with the sharp measure meted, too often, to those great men, who, (as in THEODORE's case,) *before* the Church has defined the point at issue, write, perhaps, incautiously, (but moved with zeal for the truth,) about the divine *nature*. (4) HUET has the candour to confess that, if the mere teaching, or originating heresy, unconsciously, and with a readiness to abjure it, (as distinguished from persisting in it when the Church has once spoken,) make a heretic, then *very many orthodox Fathers, e.g.*, CYPRIAN, IRENÆUS, &c., *may be called heretics.*

—*Orig.* ii. ch. iii. p. 195. And it is (5) certain, too, that, as his best editor says, "Every accesion to our knowledge of THEODORE adds strength to the conviction, that he was *entirely unconscious of deviating from the catholic Church.*" (6) And to talk of *heretics* is ground most unsafe for the advocates of endless sin. That dogma bears a deeply tarnished escutcheon. Who was its first distinguished advocate?— the heretic TERTULLIAN. What were the authors of the Pseudo-Clementines?—heretics, and forgers, and teachers of unending pain? What was TATIAN, another very early champion of this doctrine?— a Gnostic heretic. What was LACTANTIUS?—an ill-taught layman, "hovering ever on the verge of heresy." And who is the true fountain and source of the cruel heresy of CALVIN?—no less a name than AUGUSTINE himself. And what was PELAGIUS?—at once a heretic, and a champion of misery without end. (7) But did THEODORE and DIODORUS really teach what is known as Nestorianism? "The Syrian teachers, and NESTORIUS himself, in the opinion of *every one who understands the case*, are guilty of no error; and the dogmas which are known as Nestorianism have been neither taught by NESTORIUS, nor approved by the Syrian church."— MUNTER.—*Stœud. u. Tzsch. Archiv.* i. "THEODORE," says NEANDER, "sincerely adopted the doctrine of the Church respecting the divine Incarnation."—*Church Hist.* iv. p. 110. "Of all that the Church declared to be of the faith, he was the staunch defender," says his editor SWETE. (8) Certain it is that, practically, the Anglican Church has abandoned the term (theotokos), so strenuously contended for. (9) And it is also certain that the condemnation of NESTORIUS brought its Nemesis, it helped to pave the way for the cult of the Blessed Virgin, and its terrible abuses, and for the heresy of EUTYCHES.

Certainly THEODORE's immense influence must have spread very widely the larger hope, which lay at the root of his doctrinal system. Nor did his enemies charge him with this as a fault, so far as I have read, a fact to be noted; as is also this, that he calls those penalties "*eternal*"—as being out of time, which he yet taught to be finite (so little does the use of such terms prove). He lays great stress—with the school of Antioch—on the Resurrection as in itself, and to all, a blessing.

"Who *is so great a fool* as to think, that so great a blessing can be to those that arise, the occasion of endless torment?"—*Frag. Ex. lib. cont. pecc. orig.* "All have the hope of rising with Christ, so that the body having obtained immortality, thenceforward the proclivity to evil should be removed."—*In Rom.* vi. 6. Speaking of the Resurrection he says, "then, too, shall we be freed from sin, for being rendered immutable by the grace of the Spirit, we shall be set free from sin."—*ib.* viii. 2. God "recapitulated all things in

Christ * * as though making a compendious renewal, and *restoration of the whole creation*, through Him. * * Now this will take place in a future age, when *all mankind and* ALL POWERS (*virtutes*) POSSESSED OF REASON, look up to Him, as is right, and obtain mutual concord and firm peace."—*In Eph.* i. 10.

CYRIL of Alexandria, 412 A.D., frequently teaches the liberation of *every soul* from hades by Christ.

"The devil was deprived of all power of being able to do anything for the future. * * The souls of men who had been caught in his toils to their ruin, came out of the underground gates, and, leaving the hiding-places of the pit, escaped."—*Hom. pasch.* vi. "Traversing the *lowest recesses* of the infernal regions, after that He had preached to the spirits there, He led forth the captives in His strength.—*ib.* xx. For when death devoured Him who was the Lamb on behalf of all, it vomited forth *all men* in Him and with Him. * * Now when *sin has been destroyed*, how should it be but that death, too, should wholly perish?"—*In S. Jno.* i. 29. Speaking of the cities of Refuge are these words: "It is, perhaps, not improbable to think, that those who have been entangled in sins, are, as it were, homicides of their own souls; * * So, then, the wretched soul of man is punished by exile from the world and the body, and *residing in the recesses of death, as in a city of Refuge*, was spending these long ages: but was with difficulty set free when Christ, the High Priest died, * * and went down to hades and loosed their bonds."—*De adorat. lib.* viii. *ad fin.* This picture is suggestive. (All) sinners who die before Christ's visit to hades go thither, AS TO A CITY OF REFUGE, and are by Him set free: because, though sinners, yet they have been as it were forced to sin by a nature prone to evil (so he says). But if so, how can you fairly suppose Christ's work less efficacious after His death? On the death of Christ, "all iniquity stopped its mouth, and the rule of death was destroyed, all sin (*tes hamartias*, sin generally) having been taken away, * * so, then, the sin of *all* having been taken away, we can justly say, 'O death where is thy sting?'"—*In Hos.* xiii. 14. "Through Christ has been saved the holy crowd of the Fathers, nay, the whole human race altogether which was earlier in time (than Christ's death) for He died for all, and the death of all was done away in Him."—*Glaph. in Ex.* ii. *ad fin.*

CYRIL'S teaching as to the final salvation of all men before Christ is fairly clear. I fail to see how this can be logically held apart from the larger hope. I close with the following quotation. "The force of sin has been dissolved * * the evil that has grown out of it, *i.e.*, death has been plucked up *from the very root.*"—*Hom. pasch.* xxiv.

In S. AMBROSE'S works (*Paris*, 1569), there are included

ninety-two sermons, which may be by MAXIMUS of Turin, 422 A.D. The author seems to teach (I.) the liberation of every soul from hades, and (II.) to take the significant view of God's inflicting death to amend the sinner.

"By the Resurrection of Christ, hell—*Tartarus*—is opened * * hell yields up those it contains; * * so DAVID invites everything created to the festivity of this day."—*Ser.* lii. It illuminates, he adds, heaven, earth and *hell*. Christ "destroyed the sins of all believers. He must of necessity have destroyed the sins of all, Who bore the sins of all, as says the Evangelist: 'The Lamb of God Who taketh away the sins of the world.'"—*ib.* xxi. "We read in the Scripture, that the salvation of the entire human race, was won by the Redemption of the Saviour * * the everlasting safety of the entire world."—*ib.* li.

I take next THEODORET, the Blessed, 423 A.D. This great Father was, I cannot doubt, an universalist. He became Bishop of Cyrus, or Cyrrhus, in Syria, and is the last representative, that we shall quote, of the school of Antioch. THEODORET was perhaps the most famous, and certainly the most learned teacher of his age; uniting to a noble intellect a character and accomplishments equally noble. We notice in his writings great prominence given to the view which regards the Resurrection as being of itself restoration; as essentially a spiritual force, bringing to man's whole nature immortality and glory, and, therefore, immunity from sufferings; a view supported by very many Fathers, but surely fatal to all forms of the traditional creed.

S. PAUL, asserting that "the last enemy to be destroyed is death," and that "He hath put all things under Christ's feet," adds finally, "*in order that God may be All in All.*" * * In the present life God is in all, for His nature is without limits, but is not All in All. * * But in the future, when (by the Resurrection) mortality is at an end and immortality granted, and (consequently) sin has no longer any place, God will be All in All."—*In Eph.* i. 23. "For Christ has *wholly destroyed* the power of sin by His promise of *immortality;* for it (sin) *cannot trouble immortal* bodies."—*In Heb.* ix. 26. "In the future life, the body, when it has been made incorruptible, cannot admit the filth of sin."—*In Col.* ii. 11. On 1 *Cor.* xv. 20, he writes: "Now the mass shall certainly follow the 'firstfruits.'" This refers to the entire mass of humanity. For, says THEODORET, as all men became mortal through Adam, "so shall the whole nature of mankind (all men) follow the Lord Christ, and be made partaker of the Resurrection." The meaning of this is stated in a lengthy comment, of which I can only give a brief summary. No doubt there shall be a difference between good and bad, and so the Apostle writes: " Every one in his own order " (meaning probably a delayed Resurrection till Judgment has done its cleansing work). Then comes the end, *i.e.*, *the General Resurrection*, when Christ delivers up His kingdom, causing all to know God, for He must altogether subdue all men. In what sense? in that indicated by the Apostle— *Phil.* iii. 21, "Who shall change our vile body after the fashion of His glorious body." But how is the Son to be Himself subjected to God? The apostle shews by adding, "that God may be ALL IN ALL." So the Son is subject in the subjection of mankind (when that is complete). At present God is indeed in All, for in Him we live, " But He is not by obedience in All : for He is by obedience in those fearing Him * * even in those He is not All ; for nobody is sinless : * * But in the future life when corruption is at an end, and immortality granted, there is no place for *suffering* (*pathe*) but it (suffering) being *totally removed, no form of sin remains at work*. So shall God be All in All, *all* being out of danger of falling, and *converted to Him*, and not admitting an inclination to what is worse." So on *Phil.* iii. 21 he says, Christ " puts an end to corruption and death * * causing all to look up to Himself." In the same spirit THEODORET writes: "Christ being taken as 'firstfruits,' the whole nature of man (all humanity) shall know the true God, and chant praises for His loving kindness."—*In Ps.* lxxx. 18. " Afterwards the Psalmist speaks more plainly: ' All the kings of the earth shall adore Him.' Some, indeed, in the present life willingly, but all the rest after the Resurrection ; for not yet do we see *all things* subject to Him, but then every knee shall bow to Him."—*In Ps.* lxxii. 11. Here the context shews "all kings" to be used for "all peoples," and the subjection of all to Christ, is in THEODORET'S view their submission and adoration.

Finally, on two other points, let us note his teaching. (I.) He explicitly asserts the liberation from hades of every soul. I shall shut up thee only * * "Thou," says Christ to satan, "art justly despoiled of *all* thy subjects * * Thou shalt vomit forth *all* that thou hast already swallowed. * * I shall free *all* from death * * for I paid the debt for the *race*. * * As the debt has been paid, it is right that those confined on account of it should be set free from their prison."—*De Prov. Or.* x. (II.) He teaches that *death is a medicine, not a penalty.*—*Ques. in Gen.* xl., and even goes a great deal farther, for he says, that to imagine that God, in anger at a little eating, inflicted death as a penalty, is to copy the abominable (heretic) MARCION. This statement I commend to my readers' attention. Those who fancy God to have acted from wrath, shew, says THEODORET, their ignorance of the mystery of the dispensation. Can this teaching be reconciled with any modification of the traditional creed? Take, finally, the following: "*After* His anger, God will bring to an end His judgment; for He will not be angry unto the end, nor keep His wrath to eternity." —*In Is.* xiii.

From S. PETER CHRYSOLOGUS, 433 A.D. (so called from his eloquence), Bishop of Ravenna, I take the following, which refers to the great gulf separating LAZARUS and DIVES.

"Those assigned to penal custody in hades cannot be transferred to the repose of the saints, *unless*, having been redeemed by the grace of Christ, they be freed from this hopelessness by the intercession of the holy Church: so that what the sentence denies them, the Church may gain for them and grace bestow."—*Ser.* cxxiii.—suggestive words, coming from one who uses elsewhere such strong language as to the fate of the lost. Again, explaining the words, "Thy kingdom come," he says: "We thus pray for the coming of that time when the author of so great evil (satan) perishing, the *whole world*, the *whole creation*, may reign and triumph for the whole glory of Christ only."—*Ser.* lxxi. "We pray that the devil may perish, that sin may cease, death may die. * * This is the kingdom of God, * * when in *all* men God lives, God acts, God reigns, God is everything."—*Ser.* lxvii. This seems to involve an anticipation that all evil shall in the future wholly cease. So he says on the parable of the leaven: "In order that, as a woman had corrupted the whole mass of the human race in Adam, by the leaven of death, so (a woman) should, by the leaven of the Resurrection, restore in Christ *the whole mass of our flesh*" (all humanity?—*Ser.* xcix. On the parable of the hundred sheep he says, that the one lost sheep represents "*the whole human race lost in Adam*," and so the Good Shepherd "follows the one, seeks the one, in order that in the one He may find *all*, in the one He may restore *all*."—*Ser.* clxviii. I may finally cite a striking passage on the raising of LAZARUS. Hades, personified, is represented as addressing God, to this effect: "If I permit LAZARUS to escape, You lose *all* whom I have been keeping." Christ answers: "I, O Father, will pay ADAM's debt, in order that those who, through ADAM, are perishing in hades, may, through Me, live to Thee." On this the whole Trinity consent. And LAZARUS is ordered to leave the tomb, and "hell (Tartarus) was ordered to obey, and give up to Christ *all the dead.*"—*Ser.* lxv. Surely these teachings involve universalism, if taken logically: at least they may be set over against any passages that seem to teach the ordinary view.

I will now ask my readers to consider another very important piece of evidence. Within the first five centuries, the two great Creeds—the Apostles' and the Niceno-Constantinopolitan, received their present form, and the first four General Councils were held at Nice, Constantinople, Ephesus, and Chalcedon. Now it is a highly significant fact, that though universalist views were then widely prevalent, no syllable of condemnation was breathed against them at any of these councils. Nobody ever thought of including amongst the articles of the faith a belief in endless punishment; and this, be it remembered, though *the very question of the life to come was distinctly raised* at Constantinople, in the clauses then added to the creed. I say, without fear of contradiction, that this silence would of itself be an argument of irresistible weight in proving that universalism was, as an opinion, perfectly tenable in those days.

But this is a very small part of the evidence. If the silence of these councils is significant, so are the following facts still more significant. We have the faith of the Church defined in two documents, of an authority in its kind quite unique and fundamental—the two Creeds\* the Apostles', and that we call the Nicene. Rightly to estimate the weight of the testimony they bear, let us remember that in the second Great Ecumenical Council, where the Nicene Creed received its present shape, S. GREGORY of Nazianzus, (whose opinions are discussed p. 117-9) presided: while the chief agent in the task of adding to the Nicene Creed the new clauses then adopted, and ending with the significant words, "I believe in the life of the world to come," (in the *life*, be it remembered, and *in nothing more*), was, probably, S. GREGORY of Nyssa; whose words

---

\*Whatever we may think of the Athanasian Creed—its want of conciliar authority—its comparatively late date—its uncertain origin —its doubtful acceptance in the East—when it speaks of "everlasting," that term can mean no more than the Scriptural *aionios*, which it represents: and as it is clear that everlasting is not the necessary or even the usual meaning of *aionios*, this Creed is really quite consistent with the larger hope.

—see pp. 121-5, shew him to have been an unhesitating advocate of universal salvation. What can be more significant of the belief of the Church in those primitive days? Look at the facts. To a known and outspoken believer in universal salvation is entrusted principally, by the Church in her Great Council, the duty of defining the faith; and that definition runs thus, "I believe in the life of the world to come." *What but the larger hope* could such words, under such circumstances, have conveyed to the Council? And mark the position these words occupy in the Creed (as does the corresponding clause in the *Apostles' Creed). They close, and as it were, sum up the whole. The Creed opens with a statement of belief in the Great Creator; it speaks of the Father, Son, and Holy Ghost: of the work of salvation: of the Incarnation, &c. But the great procession of the christian verities ends, in both Creeds, in the expressive assertion of faith in everlasting life. It is as though both Creeds proclaimed—that to this all christian truth led, in this all christian hope culminated; in life, and not in death everlasting.

We have now reached the close of the second, and most important of the three periods embraced in our enquiry (p. 82), a point from which it is well to look back over the ground we have traversed. We have seen the tide of universalism, (so far from being censured,) rising, swelling, and broadening; till in that famous age of the Church's story, the period embracing the fourth and the earlier years of the fifth century, universalism seems to have been the creed of the majority of christians in East and West alike; perhaps even of a large majority. It had gained a footing in the most famous schools of theology: it had leavened Alexandria and its school; had leavened Palestine; had leavened Cappadocia; had even leavened Antioch—where ORIGEN's teaching was directly opposed; it had leavened the early Latin Fathers—(p. 127)—and in the roll of its teachers (or those, at least, in sympathy with it), were, as we have seen, most of the greatest names of the greatest age of primitive christianity. A crowd of witnesses, from almost every quarter to which the Gospel had reached, assure us of their belief that Christ liberated from hades every soul, without exception. And we have heard teachings that openly assert, or, by fair inference, involve the larger hope, from both East and West, from Gaul as well as from Alexandria; from Rome; from Milan; from Arabia; from Palestine; from Antioch; from Cappadocia; from Cilicia; from Constantinople; from the distant Euphrates. And this teaching, be it noted, is strongest where the language of the New Testament was a living tongue, *i.e.*, in the great Greek Fathers: it is strongest in the Church's greatest era, and declines as knowledge and purity decline. On the other hand endless penalty is most strongly taught precisely in those quarters where the New Testament was less read in the original, and also in the most corrupt ages of the Church.

Note carefully—the point is significant—that this universalism was *essentially and first of all based on Scripture;* on

---

*On the great significance of the clause—the Descent into hell—in this Creed I have already spoken.

those promises of a "restitution of all things," taught "by all God's holy prophets," repeated so often by the Psalmists; and echoed clearly and distinctly in the New Testament. Another point there is, whose importance in view of some modern teaching, seems to me very great; it is the teaching of so many, and such illustrious Fathers, that death is no penalty, but is, indeed, A CURE, that it is, in fact, the great Potter remoulding His own handiwork to restore it to its pristine beauty, and that the sinner's destruction means but the destruction of the sin, (the *sinner* perishes, the man lives). Such teaching would be significant even in a solitary instance; but here we have witness upon witness, to whom Greek was a familiar and a living tongue, repeating the same striking idea; teaching death to be no penalty, but the remoulding of our nature by the heavenly artist, and designed to cure sin; teaching, too, that the sinner's destruction by God is not loss but gain, is not annihilation, but conversion and reformation. To this point I shall return, and adduce fresh evidence from early writers, in the next chapter.

I have said enough, amply to prove the wide diffusion of universalism in the early centuries, alike in East and West, taught as it was, as in perfect harmony with the catholic faith. But it may be well to call three witnesses (whose testimony it is quite hopeless to gainsay). From S. BASIL I quote "The MASS OF MEN (*i.e.*, of christians) say that there is TO BE AN END OF PUNISHMENT to those who are punished." (quoting *S. Luke* xii. 47-8)—*Conc.* xiv. *De fut. judic.* This opinion the writer disputes: but his words prove, that a terminable penalty was the ordinary view, and he *does not even hint that this view was opposed to the Faith.* The passage is from the *Ascetica*, a work interpolated, and I do not claim it as certainly BASIL'S: its value as antient *testimony* is, however, not altered.

Again, S. JEROME (and no more competent witness can exist), writing towards the end of the fourth century, says— I know that MOST PERSONS understand by the story of Nineveh and its king, THE ULTIMATE FORGIVENESS OF THE DEVIL AND ALL RATIONAL CREATURES.—*In Jon.* iii. Now, if *most* believed the ultimate salvation of *every evil spirit*, ought we not to say that *all*, or nearly all, believed in the more moderate dogma of universal human salvation in S. JEROME's day?

But there is another witness of slightly later date, and of equal weight. S. AUGUSTINE tells us that, in his days, there were not only some, but "VERY MANY" or "THE MAJORITY" —*quam plurimi*, "who compassionated the eternal punishment of the damned, and believed that it would not take place."—*Enchir.*, 112.

In addition we have the testimony of DOMITIAN to be presently quoted, which, if indirect, is perhaps even stronger.

The significance of such testimonies is very great indeed. They state precisely the all important fact that universalism was the belief of half, *or more than half*, christendom, even in the West, during the fourth and part of the fifth century. S. AUGUSTINE speaks for the West, S. BASIL for the East, and DOMITIAN for the same, while S. JEROME, from his peculiar position, may represent both. How, indeed, shall any fact be attested satisfactorily, if such testimony, backed by the very words of so many Fathers (as quoted) be not decisive? And how hopeless and inveterate must be the prejudice which rejects such testimony because unwelcome.

In the succeeding ages as ignorance spread, and superstitions of every kind multiplied, with a wholly corrupt and licentious people, and a clergy venal and grossly ignorant, there is no reason to wonder that, by slow degrees, the earlier and nobler faith decayed everywhere (declining in almost exact proportion as knowledge declined and corruptions flourished); a process aided largely in the West by the preponderance of the cruel and uncatholic Augustinian theology, and by the consequent development of the doctrine of Purgatory. It would be difficult, and want of space forbids the attempt, to convey to general readers, an adequate idea of the degraded state of learning and morals, when, in the tenth century, the climax of darkness was reached in the West. Yet the creed even then current *was mercy itself* compared with our modern traditions, leaving as it did a door of hope widely open, beyond the grave, to all but a few exceptionally great sinners.

I now resume my task of quoting; from what has been said all can understand why in the period, into which we now proceed to enquire, our quotations are neither so numerous nor so striking as before. This period (the third of the divisions already made, p. 82) extends from about the middle of the fifth century to the eleventh or twelfth. I may begin by an extract from FACUNDUS, who was a man of considerable eminence, Bishop of Hermiane. "To all this is to be added the confession of DOMITIAN of Galatia, formerly Bishop of Ancyra; for in the book which he wrote to VIGILIUS \* \* he says, 'they have hastily run out to anathematize most holy and glorious teachers, on account of those doctrines which have been advanced concerning pre-existence and restitution; and this, indeed, under pretext of ORIGEN, but thereby anathematizing *all those Saints, who were before and have been after him.*'"—*Pro. def. trium cap.* iv. 4. It is clear from the context, that DOMITIAN believed in the salvation of all evil spirits—a noteworthy fact —indeed, we shall see this belief existing at a still later period.

There are also three branches of evidence to which I desire here briefly to refer. (*a*) First, we know on excellent authority that many of the followers of NESTORIUS, who were very widely diffused over the East, taught universalism. —See ASSEMANNI, *Bibliotheque Orientale*. Nor has their Nestorianism *the very least connection* with this particular opinion, which they drew, *not from Nestorius*, but from the general current of Church teaching in that age, and to which they thus become witnesses. "It is obvious," says the Dean of Wells, "that the special point on which NESTORIUS was condemned had no connection with this or that form of eschatology; and that it was derived by them from those whose orthodoxy, like GREGORY of Nyssa, was unquestioned." —*Spirits in prison*. (*b*) But next, it is also certain that in the sixth century, in the monasteries, erected in the wilds lying between Jerusalem and the Dead Sea, there was a strong party, of which DOMITIAN (just quoted) was a leader, teaching (with other tenets of ORIGEN) the restitution of all souls. (*c*) Further, several testimonies might be quoted from writers of the period now under discussion, teaching the liberation from hades, by Christ, of every soul whatsoever.

I proceed to quote GENNADIUS, Patriarch of Constantinople, 458 A.D.

The firstfruits shall obtain the *totality* and the rest of the body shall follow the head. * * For, said He, when lifted up, I will draw all men unto Myself."—*Rom.* ch. viii. 34. GENNADIUS also seems to hold the opinion shared by many Fathers—see next chapter—which regards the Resurrection, as in itself involving immunity from sin and suffering. "Thank God who has given us immortality, incorruptibility, and impassibility."—*ib.* vii. 24. Finally, as I understand his comments on *Rom.* viii. 19, there will be one day an *universal* regeneration. Other passages might be given; but I pass on to quote from ANDREW, Bishop of Cæsarea (500 A.D.). He is describing the great (future) Apocalyptic song of praise, thus: "By *all things* intelligible or sensible (*i.e.*, visible or invisible), both living and simply existing, God is glorified as author of all, in the modes of speech natural (to them)."—*In Rev.* v. 13. Neither GENNADIUS nor

ANDREW are consistent writers; and they probably do not design to teach universalism, but such extracts seem noteworthy, and *very hard to reconcile* with the dogma of endless misery and sin.

We now approach a striking incident in the history of religious thought. In the sixth century were published the (so-called) works of DIONYSIUS, the Areopagite. The influence exerted by these writings, and their profoundly mystical tone, was extremely great, and has lasted, in a true sense, even to our day. As the worship of the Church became more and more material, so contemplative minds gladly turned for relief to a theology which spiritualised, without rejecting, the external symbols. The system these writings embrace recalls the earlier teaching of Alexandria, and its Platonism; and asserting, as they do, that all things come out of God, and return to, (or into) Him, cleansed from all stain, they form a storehouse of universalism. Although challenged when first produced in 533 A.D., at Constantinople, yet, in an uncritical age, a belief in their authenticity prevailed. Thus viewed as belonging to the Apostolic era, their influence was widely felt, especially in the case of two remarkable men. Of these, one was MAXIMUS, head of a monastery near Constantinople, 645 A.D., the ablest theologian of his day. The other was J. S. ERIGENA—perhaps the acutest of the Schoolmen—if he be not rather their forerunner—who, two centuries later, taught at the Court of CHARLES the Bald. We thus find the East once more communicating an impulse, vital and fertile, to the colder West, warming with a diviner hope her narrow creed, now touched with a stern Africanism.

I append the following brief extracts to shew the tone of the writings of the so-called DIONYSIUS.

"Out of Him and through Him is every being and life * * every power, every energy * * and (all) are being turned into the good and beautiful. All things—whatsoever exist and are formed—exist and are formed for the sake of beauty and goodness ; * * and He is beginning and end of all things * * for (out) 'of Him and through Him, and unto Him are all things.'"—(*Rom.* x. 36)—*De div. nom.* iv. 10. "He makes all things, makes perfect all things. He holds together and converts all things (to Himself)."—*ib.* "With God are the causes of evils, they are beneficent powers."—*ib.* 30. "Even of all evils, the beginning and END is the good, because for the sake of good exist all things, both those which are good, and those which are opposed to it."—*ib.* 31. "What is good is the beginning and end of all things."—*ib.* 35. "Even to the *demons* that they exist both comes of good and *is good.*"—*ib.* 34. God "converts and holds together all things, as being the all powerful abode of all, safe guarding all things, * * nor permitting them to fall away from Himself, and perish by departing from the all perfect home."—*ib.* x. 1. "The good (or beautiful) is the beginning and end of all things."—*ib.* iv. 7. All this leads logically and naturally to the larger hope.

At this point I must ask attention to two names, as teaching the larger hope, whose personality has almost faded away in the mists of time.

The first is HIEROTHEUS, who is known only by a few brief extracts, which DIONYSIUS quotes, as from the writings of his master. HIEROTHEUS belongs, probably, to the school of Edessa, sometime in the fifth century. I give two brief specimens. "Towards the supreme love tends the total love flowing from *all* existences"—quoted—*De div. nom.* iv. 16. "There is one simple force, self moved, towards a blending together in unity (flowing) from what is good unto the last of those things that exist."—*ib.* 17. Inadequate as are these brief extracts to represent the man, yet his teaching is evidently in harmony with the PSEUDO-DIONYSIUS.

The other name is that of an Abbot of Edessa, BARSUDAILI, who, towards the end of the fifth century, taught (under the name of HIEROTHEUS) the broadest universalism. He asserts the termination of all penalties of the future world, and their purifying character. Even the fallen spirits are to receive mercy, and all things are to be restored, so that God may be All in All.—ASSEM. *Bibl. Orient.* ii. p. 291.

I now quote briefly from MAXIMUS, Saint and Confessor, 645 A.D., to whom I have alluded, p. 153. Having spoken somewhat unfavourably of GREGORY of Nyssa's teaching, he proceeds:

"For it is necessary that as *all* nature is to receive at the Resurrection immortality of the flesh, * * so, too, the fallen powers of the soul must, in the process of the ages, *cast off the memories of sin* implanted in them, and having passed all the ages, * * *come to God;* and so by the knowledge, not the fruition of good, receive strength and *be restored to their original state.*"—*Quæst. et Dub.* xiii. Again, in his *Aphorisms, sec.* xx., 'the reunion *of all rational essences with* God is established as the final end.'"—NEANDER, *Eccles. Hist.* v. p. 242.

This writer adds that the fundamental ideas of MAXIMUS seem to lead to the doctrine of a final universal restoration —a proposition which is, in my judgment, beyond question true, not only of MAXIMUS, but of the PSEUDO-DIONYSIUS, and of ERIGENA: while we may admit that an absolutely consistent enunciation of this was rendered difficult by the theology current in their days, (the language of which MAXIMUS indeed sometimes uses.)

In his *Scholia* on DIONYSIUS, we find him teaching that "God is end and measure of all things."—*In De div. nom.* iv. 20. "God moves, for He transforms and changes for the better all things * * as says DIONYSIUS, "He is beginning and end of all things.'"—*ib.* v. *ad fin.* And again, "God is made All in All, embracing all things." —*Ambig.* ii. p. 1210 (*Migne*), (from ERIGENA'S version). "All things made by God are gathered into God perpetually and unchangeably."—*ib.* p. 1200. "The rest—the Sabbath—of God is the *full bringing* back into Himself of the things that are created."— *Capit. theol.* i. 47. Again, with so many Fathers, MAXIMUS teaches that the passing away of the wicked, is the passing away of their wickedness. Thus on *Ps.* xxxvii. 36, he says the meaning is that evil will pass away and leave no trace.—*Schol. De div. nom.* iv. 18. MAXIMUS, as noted above, connects with the Resurrection the idea of restoration. I take one more passage: "At the Resurrection, through the grace of the Incarnate Son, the flesh will be absorbed by the soul."—*Quoted by* ERIG.—*De div. nat. lib.* v. 8.

Our next witness shall be ERIGENA, of whom I have spoken, whose remarkable writings may be heartily commended to every student of theology. Profound thinking

—conveyed in clear and vivid style—lends to them an unusual charm.

"It belongs in common to all things that have been made to return—as though by a perishing—into those causes which subsist in God."—*De div. nat. lib.* v. 21. In another very characteristic passage (to which I have unfortunately mislaid the reference), he argues that as Christ is maker and cause of all things. so "the universal end of the whole\* creation is the Word of God. \* \* Last of all, the universal creation shall be united with the Creator, and shall be one in Him, and with Him. *And this is the end of all things visible and invisible.*" Again he says, there is to be a return and a gathering together "into that *unity of all things*† *which is in God and is God:* so *that both all things may be God,* and God be all things."—*Pref. in Max. Ambig., Migne,* p. 1195. This passage gives the substance of MAXIMUS' version of the teaching of the PSEUDO-DIONYSIUS, and involves ERIGENA's agreement with both. "The whole human race has been both redeemed in Christ, and will return into the heavenly Jerusalem."—*De div. nat.* v. 38. "Nothing contrary to the divine goodness, and life, and blessedness can be co-eternal with it. Because the divine goodness will destroy evil, eternal life will absorb death, blessedness absorb sin."—*ib.* 27. "Sins and iniquities \* \* shall be completely brought to nothingness, so that they shall have no existence."—*De div. nat.* iv. 4. "Further, if the entire world, and *the entire creation* UNIVERSALLY, which has been made by God, is not destined to return into the eternal causes in which it subsists, then the whole of our reasoning so far, will fall away, as vain, and completely gone to pieces."—*ib.* v. 28.

There are still writers who (even at dates later than the present) teach the liberation from hades of all souls, but any direct evidence for universalism is now very rare. The following from ŒCUMENIUS, 990 A.D., shews evident traces of primitive teaching. He writes on the famous words: "That God may be All in All," "The abolition *of evil* (all

---

\*ERIGENA guards against Pantheism, by repudiating any blending in the future life of the human and divine."—*De div. nat.* v. 8.

†Is is true that ERIGENA, writing in the Latin Church of the ninth century, naturally *professes* a belief in endless punishment. But this stands in hopeless contradiction to his entire theological system; and the extraordinary process of jugglery with words, by which he attempts to teach that a thing can exist, and not exist, at the same time, may be read in the fifth book.—*De div. nat.* A curious and striking passage intimates that perhaps the ETERNAL PUNISHMENT of the devils will be *the universal abolition of their wickedness and impiety.* —*ib.* v. 27.

evil *tes kakias*) is shewn by these words, for when sin (*he hamartia*—all sin) has been taken away, it is evident that God will be All in All, when we are no longer divided between God and passions. Others have so interpreted it, that *all things* will be brought back to the Father as source." —*In* 1 *Cor.* xv. 28.

THEOPHYLACT, Archbishop of Achrida, in Bulgaria, 1077 A.D., shall be our next witness. By the parable of the ninety-nine, and the one lost, sheep, he understands the just and sinners. But as the lost sheep of the parable is found, then, if this represent the sinners of mankind, the passage seems logically to involve universalism. But there is more than this:

Some, he goes on to say, understand by the 100 sheep all rational creatures, and by the one lost sheep man (*i.e.*, mankind), * * and by the lost coin, the lost image of God. "The whole world is cleansed over again from sin, and plainly the lost coin (the royal image) is found." Both interpretations seem to involve the larger hope. On 1 *Cor.* xv. 28, he says: "Some understand by this *the removal of wickedness, for when sin* is no more, plainly God will be All in All." This seems to shew that the larger hope survived up to nearly the end of the 11th century: it is also *noteworthy* that THEOPHYLACT says nothing against it here. On *Eph.* i. 10: "Things in heaven were cut off from things on earth, and had not one head. For though by creation all had one God, yet by friendship (*oikeiosis domesticity*) they had not yet (one God): and so it was that the Father planned to bring back to one head the things in heaven and on earth, *i.e.*, to set Christ as head over all." On *Col.* i. 18-20, he says: "PAUL by the *Church* intends the whole human race. * * Christ, as firstfruits, has even (all) the rest following him (*kai tous loipous*). * * One sheaf being offered, the whole harvest is sanctified * * and one body rising, the whole nature (mankind) is deemed worthy of the Resurrection * * Christ is first begotten (from the dead) as firstfruits of the Resurrection, because that is regeneration." The train of thought in these passages is hard to reconcile with the perpetuity of evil, whatever the writer's views may have been.

Nor are later instances wanting. "Both S. THOMAS AQUINAS, and DURANDUS shew us that, even in their day, absolute universalism was not unknown. It was the opinion of the school of GILBERT of Poictiers—S. THOMAS AQUINAS,

*Sent.* iv. 45—and 'aliquorum juristarum'—DURANDUS,"—(*Mercy and Judgment,*) and, probably, of some mystics. Again, a great name, S. ANSELM, in the twelfth century, writes thus: "It is quite foreign to God's nature to suffer any reasonable creature wholly to perish."—*Cur Deus Homo*, ii. 4 (a striking proof of the survival of the earlier hope) " nor," adds the saint, " is it *possible* for the reasonable mind to think otherwise." To these testimonies may be added a highly interesting prayer, quoted by the Dean of Wells from an old English manual, *The Fifteen O's*, published by CAXTON; and illustrating the dominant tone of religious feeling in England, in the age immediately preceding the Reformation :—" Be merciful to those souls for whom there is no hope \* \* in their torment, save that they were made in thine image \* \* Put forth thy right hand and *free them from the interminable pains and anguish of hell*, and lead them to the fellowship of the citizens on high."

The three periods of the Church's history, embraced in the enquiry we have just made, may be said to correspond to early Spring time; to Summer, brief and bright; to Autumn, followed by wintry gloom. After some centuries of conflict and growth, the freedom won for the Gospel by CONSTANTINE was followed by an outburst of activity, theological and intellectual (such were the Church's Spring and Summertide). But in the very success lay unperceived the seeds of disaster. Elements of evil, repressed in adversity, soon revived; and the crowds who now flocked to christian teaching brought with them, too often, the superstition, the ignorance, the vices of heathenism. Bitter intestine strife, scandalous intrigues, virulent controversies, began more than ever to exhaust the energies of the Church, or to direct them into barren channels. And so the Autumn and its decay followed. To the Fathers succeeded—after a period of barrenness—the Schoolmen in the West; while, in the East, no successor appeared to the great names of earlier days. Other features of this period I can barely notice, *e.g.*, the break up of the Roman empire; the growth of the Papacy; the successive inroads of barbarians into Italy; the spread of Monasticism; the steady advance of superstition; the decay of learning; the ever-widening divisions between the East and West. Who can pretend to wonder that amid all this "hurly burly," the larger hope,—taught so freely in the Church's Spring and Summer time,—gained ever fewer adherents in its Autumnal decay, and well nigh died out in its dark Winter?

But any sketch of universalism would be incomplete without a discussion of the assertion still repeated, though often refuted, that the dogma of the final salvation of all men was condemned, in the person of ORIGEN, at the Fifth Council. This assertion is, as will be distinctly shewn, untrue. An attempt was indeed made to procure a condemnation of this doctrine—an attempt which *wholly failed;* and which was made, not at the Fifth Council, but at the Home Synod of Constantinople (*i.e.*, a committee of Bishops from a small number of sees near Constantinople, who, with some officers of the Metropolitan Church, formed a standing Council for the Patriarch). For a clearer understanding of the facts, which are very generally misunderstood, it must be premised that the larger hope was but a very inconsiderable part of what was known as "Origenism," and quite independent of it, *e.g.*, so that it was strongly held by ORIGEN'S determined antagonists in the school of Antioch. Origenism meant a widely spreading system, embracing amongst many other points: (*a*) certain highly speculative tenets, *e.g.*, pre-existence, and also (*b*) certain views, *e.g.*, on the Trinity, capable at least of easy misrepresentation, (*c*) and a doctrine of the Resurrection, in which this great writer was too far in advance of his day. These it was, the two latter especially, that led ORIGEN into grave disrepute; and *not his belief in the final salvation of all men.* The proofs of this are abundant and decisive. (I.) Those who taught simple universalism perhaps more fully than ORIGEN, *e.g.*, CLEMENT, of Alexandria, and GREGORY, of Nyssa, and many others, were held in universal honour, or if some were condemned, like THEODORE of Mopsuestia, (see pp. 141-2) no condemnation, direct or indirect, was made of their universalism. (II.) The larger hope was, in fact, widely held by those who opposed ORIGEN in nearly everything else (*e.g.*, the school of Antioch). Indeed, the intrigue against THEODORE was promoted by Origenists. (III.) We have several lists, more or less complete, of the alleged errors of ORIGEN, from 300 down to 404 A.D., *in none of them is any mention of the larger hope.* I may instance the lists\* of METHODIUS, 300 A.D., that given by PAMPHILUS and EUSEBIUS, in their Apology, 310 A.D.; that of EUSTATHIUS, 380 A.D.; of EPIPHANIUS, 376 and 394 A.D.; of THEOPHILUS, in a circular letter, and in three Paschal letters of 400, 402, and 404 A.D.; and more than one of S. JEROME, 400 A.D. I beg that this most significant fact may be noted, JEROME, THEOPHILUS, and EPIPHANIUS literally scrape together every possible charge against ORIGEN, *but never allude to his teaching of the larger hope as heretical.* How can any fair

---

\* Some other early writers against ORIGEN are known, *e.g.*, EUSTATHIUS of Antioch, 330 A.D., MARCELLUS of Ancyra, 320 A.D. But none of these touch on the doctrine of restoration. LEO the Great, in a letter—*Ep.* xxxv.—alludes to ORIGEN as condemned for teaching pre-existence.

mind refuse the inevitable conclusion, that this was, at least, a perfectly open question? Again I ask how these facts can be reconciled with the common prejudice, which asserts that ORIGEN's teaching of all men's final salvation, was that which brought him into disrepute? Indeed, so far from the larger hope, as we understand it, being something peculiar to ORIGEN, there is reason to believe that—while he certainly taught restoration and the limited duration of all future punishment (and thus give a great impulse to these opinions) —he himself held them in a peculiar form. I do not mean so much that he taught the final salvation of all evil spirits —a view held by several Fathers, but that he seems to have taught (I.) that all human beings would return to exactly the *same level*, so that a prostitute, as S. JEROME says, would finally be the same as the Blessed Virgin ; (II.) that, thereafter, fresh cycles would ensue, in which even the good angels might fall away, and so on for long periods, or, possibly, even for ever. These views naturally invited opposition on all sides, from the friends of the larger hope, as well as from its enemies.

Thus, from what has been stated, it is absolutely certain that to condemn "ORIGEN" or "ORIGENISM" in general terms, does not involve disapproval of restoration, even as he taught it; still less of the restoration of all human beings; (a tenet quite compatible with very strong hostility to Origenism—as in the school of Antioch). I repeat that all the evidence goes to prove that it was speculative tenets— at least tenets wholly unconnected with the larger hope— that brought ORIGEN into disrepute, aided, doubtless, by the jealousies of rivals. Equally misunderstood are the facts connected with the alleged condemnation of ORIGEN at the Fifth Council, so that it is needful to state briefly the salient points, which are these:—In 541 A.D., (the exact year is not certain,) the Emperor JUSTINIAN caused the Patriarch MENNAS to convene at Constantinople the *Home Synod*, expressly to condemn the larger hope, and certain other opinions attributed to ORIGEN. This is noteworthy, as being the first attempt to procure a distinct condemnation of the larger hope. Mark the result. "This Synod passed fifteen Canons, in which various theories of ORIGEN were condemned, but *deliberately omitted*" that concerning the larger hope, *i.e., deliberately refused to condemn it.* Twelve years later was convened the Fifth Council (born in intrigue and unrecognised by the English Church). It is said, but the fact is disputed by able and impartial writers, to have condemned ORIGEN by name in the eleventh canon, but only in general terms, which, as I have shewn above, proves *nothing at all* as to the condemnation of the larger hope. Further, special reasons exist which render any intention to condemn universalism, on the part of the Fifth Council, in the highest degree unlikely. (I.) The promoters *were themselves Origenists.* (II.) The object of the Council was to condemn certain Nestorian tenets, quite *distinct from universalism.* (III.) The Council expressly referred to S. GREGORY of Nyssa, as a prop of the faith, who was the most outspoken universalist of all the Fathers! Such is the true story of the so-called condemnation of universalism. The Home Synod distinctly refused to condemn it, even at the Emperor's bidding; while if, as is doubtful, the Fifth Council did condemn ORIGEN, it did so in general terms only, and *it did not thereby condemn the larger hope;* nor am I aware that this special point was *ever so much as submitted to any antient general council for decision.* In short, " we have no evidence that the belief in 'restitution,' which prevailed in the fourth and fifth centuries, was EVER definitely condemned BY ANY COUNCIL OF THE CHURCH."—*Spirits in Prison*, p. 141. A fact which I must ask my readers to impress most clearly on their minds; a fact further attested by a witness of most strict orthodoxy, in these words: "Whatever the amount, and quality of authority arrayed against ORIGEN's view may be, *conciliar decisions make no part of it.*"—*Church Times, Feb. 1, 1884.* No doubt some will ask, Does not the very fact that this belief in an endless hell was permitted to spread so widely, as to have become practically universal, prove its truth?

If so, I reply, why not then carry out your theory? Infant Communion was *universal* for centuries; slavery was universally defended from the earliest age of the Church. Are we, therefore, to adopt them? The duty of persecution for errors of faith was universally held—shall we adopt it? Shall we invoke saints and angels because the practice was once universal, or burn witches for the same cogent reason? It has pleased God to permit in numberless cases error to prevail, and obscure in this present age His truth. This very fact is but a louder call to us to work against all that hides or distorts that truth. Nay, it points not uncertainly to a conclusion in perfect agreement with the larger hope, this namely, that the present is but an initial stage of being; one of many ages, during which God is slowly, very slowly, working out a vast plan, and permits for a moment, as it were, an apparent triumph to error and to evil.

Let us now pass on and see what our own Church teaches on this point. We shall, I think, find, if we examine it carefully, in our Book of Common Prayer—moulded as it is on primitive lines, and on Scripture—not a few testimonies in favour of the larger hope. Not that I mean to represent the compilers as themselves universalists, far from it. But it is interesting to note the indications of a wider hope that emerge, even where indirect and unintentional.

Take, for instance, the service of Holy Baptism—what is the profession of faith required? "Dost thou believe in everlasting life after death," and not a *word or hint further*. Again, in our Litany, do we not pray God to have mercy, not on some men, but on *all men*? If this were in fact impossible, would it not be very like a sham to address such a prayer to God—just as the Inquisition used to hand over prisoners to the secular courts with a request that they would be merciful? Do we not also address, in the same Litany, Jesus Christ as the "Lamb of God that taketh away the sins of the world," and that twice over? Do we not, in Holy Communion, repeat, *three* times in one prayer, this truly catholic address to Christ, as "taking away the sins of the world?" And here it is right to ask, are words a mere pretence, and that in our holiest moments? How does Christ *take away* the sins of the world, if to all eternity in hell the sins of any men remain not taken away? On this point our Book of Common Prayer is specially emphatic, for in the proper preface for Easter Day we are bidden to remember how Christ "*hath taken away* the sins of the world? and has by His death *destroyed* death." But to abolish death in its Scriptural meaning is surely to abolish all that the Fall brought on man. Take next one of the Ember Collects: "To those who shall be ordained. grant Thy grace, that they may set forward the salvation of all men." Does the salvation of *all* men mean the damnation of *most men*, of *any* man? And so, too, when the Church bids us render thanks for a world Redeemed, and for our Creation, no less than for our Redemption, how can this be if Creation be not a certain promise of good? If Creation does, as a matter of fact, imply an awful, unutterable risk of hell's torment, why bid a man give thanks for that, which may be to him an occasion of endless pains? I will next ask your attention to a fact perhaps not always remembered, that our Church deliberately expunged that article which (adopted in 1552) condemned the belief in the final salvation of all men. "The 42nd article was withdrawn" (says the Bishop of Manchester), "because the Church, knowing that men like ORIGEN, CLEMENT, and GREGORY of Nyssa, were universalists, refused to dogmatise on such questions." Nor are other indications wanting of the hopeful teaching of our Prayer Book. Let us not fail to note the hope expressed for *all* in the Burial Service; the stress laid on the wide extent of the Atonement in the Catechism, and in the General Confession; the true force of all this is best seen when our formularies are compared with those of other reformed communions (a comparison for which I have not space). In a word, the tone of the Book of Common Prayer is frequently that indicated in the Collect for the Sunday before Easter—where the object of Christ's death is described as this—"that *all mankind* should follow the example of His great humility," and in that other prayer, which addresses God as one, "whose property is *always* to have mercy;" words which, if taken in their full meaning, certainly seem to teach the larger hope.

But there is further important evidence of our Church's teaching. Of Christ's descent into hades I have already spoken, and pointed out that to teach the liberation of *all* souls thence, is logically at least to teach universalism.—p. 103.

And this liberation of *all*, it can, I think, be shewn that our Church teaches: For the Church has intimated her belief in the fact of Christ's descent into hades, and preaching there, by the selection of *S. Peter* iii. 19, as the Epistle for Easter Eve, and of Zech. ix., as the first lesson (see v. 11, and its striking allusion to the "prisoners of hope.") Further, in the Homily (*Of the Resurrection*) appointed for Easter Day, we have the result of Christ's preaching in hades stated in the following words :—" He destroyed the devil and *all* his tyranny, and took from him *all his captives*, and hath raised and set them *with Himself among the heavenly citizens* above. His death *destroyed hell and all the damnation thereof*." These words, as I think, teach the liberation of *all* souls, without exception, from hades.

Nor has the larger hope wanted able defenders in English theology since the days of the Prayer Book. It is interesting to note, that amid the tumults of the Rebellion and the gross profligacy of the Restoration, there rose and flourished a school of devout men (trained, most of them, at Cambridge); partly Anglican, partly Nonconformists, who held, or sympathised with, the larger hope.

One of the earliest was GERALD WINSTANLEY, who taught a complete restoration of the whole creation in the *Mystery of God*, &c., printed 1669. To nearly the same epoch belong two very remarkable names, RALPH CUDWORTH and HENRY MORE, of the school of Cambridge Platonists, whose sympathies were distinctly in favour of the larger hope. More out-spoken in his teaching was PETER STERRY, Fellow of Emmanuel College, Cambridge—one of CROMWELL's chaplains—whose works published (after his death) in 1683 and 1710, evidence a strong leaning to mysticism, often stated with much beauty of imagery. I may note next, as of the same school of thought, SADLER, author of *Olbia*, and WHICHCOTE, a friend of CUDWORTH, and MORE, a Fellow of Emmanuel College, a contemporary of MILTON and JEREMY TAYLOR; and two less known authors, R. COPPIN, 1649, and W. ERBURY. At this time there also appeared not a few anonymous books, advocating the wider hope, which deserve mention, as illustrating the course of theological enquiry in the seventeenth century, e.g., *Enochian Walks with God*, and *The Revelation of the Everlasting Gospel Message*, by the same author; and *God's Light*, 1653; also *Of the Torments of Hell, the Foundation and Pillars thereof Shaken*, 1658, by S. RICHARDSON. A more distinguished advocate of the larger hope was Bishop RUST, successor of JEREMY TAYLOR, author of *De Veritate*, and *A Letter concerning the Opinions of Origen*. Another name almost equally eminent is that of JEREMY WHITE, Fellow of Trinity, Cambridge, chaplain to CROMWELL, and author of *The Restoration of all Things*, published (after his death) in 1712; a book, I may add, eloquent, devout, and breathing the deepest reverence for Holy Scripture. Towards the close of the seventeenth century, came R. STAFFORD and JANE LEADE, the latter a mystic, whose works are rare and valuable.

To these I may add TILLOTSON, who seems to have held that God was not bound to execute his threatenings pronounced against sinners ; a view in which he was followed more decisively by Bishop STILLINGFLEET ; and by Dr. BURNET, Master of the Charter House, a pupil of his at Cambridge, who, in his *De Statu Mortuorum*, teaches universalism openly The movement in favour of the larger hope was continued during the eighteenth century by WILLIAM WHISTON, in his *Sermons and Essays*, London, 1707, and by many others. I may name Dr. CHEYNE, in his *Discourses*, published 1742, and (probably) Bishop WARBURTON.—(See ch. viii. note on *Rev.* xx. 14), Bishop NEWTON, 1750, in a sermon on the *Final state of man*; and WILLIAM LAW, 1766, in his *Letters* and *Way to Divine Knowledge*. To the latter may probably be due, ultimately, the whole revival movement in England. To this era belong also two books, little known, *De Vitâ Functorum Statu*, by J. WINDET, and *Glad Tidings to Jews and Gentiles*, by R. CLARKE, both published in 1763, and both advocating the larger hope. Other names of authors, favourable to universalism, in this century, are—J. COOKE, London, 1752 ; J. RELLY, 1759 ; Sir G. STONEHOUSE, 1768 ; W. DUDGEON. 1765 ; Rev. C. BERROW, 1772 ; C. CHARNAY, 1784 ; F. LEICESTER, 1786 ; J. WEAVER, 1792 ; J. BROWNE, 1798. About this time ELHANAN WINCHESTER, a follower of JOHN WESLEY, advocated the larger hope in his *Dialogues*; and, indeed, WESLEY himself seems to have finally shared this view, for he published, in 1787, as " one of the *most sensible tracts* he had ever read," a translation from BONNET's *Palingenesie Philosophique*, which seems to advocate universalism, *e.g.*, it teaches : "There will be a perpetual advance of *all the individuals of humanity* towards perfection" (in the other life). There is also a considerable American literature advocating universalism.

In the present century the same steady movement continues, with ever-increasing force, in the direction of the larger hope. The name of ERSKINE, of Linlathen, will be familiar to many. Again, the late Bishop WILBERFORCE is stated on high authority to have finally "leaned to the larger hope," which his son now preaches. Other well-known names may be given as openly teaching, or sympathising with universalism, *e.g.*, TENNYSON, WHITTIER, BRYANT, BROWNING and Mrs. BROWNING, WHITMAN, EDNA LYALL, GEORGE MACDONALD, O. W. HOLMES, Mrs. OLIPHANT, JAMES HINTON, C. BRONTE and her sister EMILY, Gen. GORDON, Miss MULOCK, FREDERICKA BREMER, ELLICE HOPKINS, HESBA STRETTON, FLORENCE NIGHTINGALE, F. SCHLEGEL, DE QUINCEY, EMERSON, LONGFELLOW,

Mrs. BEECHER STOWE. A remarkable fact is the consensus of all the leading poets as well in America as in England in favour of the larger hope, a fact noteworthy if true poetic inspiration be a reality. In theology not a few names may be added, as adopting, or at least in sympathy with, the larger hope, *e.g.*, the late Bishop EWING of Argyll, Canon KINGSLEY, F. D. MAURICE, Dr. COX, BALDWIN BROWN, Bishop WESTCOTT, Dr. LITTLEDALE, the Bishop of Manchester, F. W. ROBERTSON, Sir G. W. COX, A. JUKES, ARCHER GURNEY, PHILLIPS BROOKS, Professor MAYOR, Canon FARRAR, Principal CAIRD, the Bishop of Meath, Dean CHURCH, NEANDER, MARTENSEN, THOLUCK, REUSS, SCHLEIERMACHER, BENGEL, EBERHARD, LAVATER, J. MACLEOD CAMPBELL, the Dean of Wells, Canon WILBERFORCE, Pastor OBERLIN, Bishop KEN, &c.

I do not represent this list as at all exhaustive, yet it is enough to prove that this movement is deep-seated, long continued, and extending itself widely amongst men of the most varied schools of thought. Besides this, we must not forget the very numerous cases in which the traditional creed has been wholly abandoned, for the "conditional immortality" theory, and those cases, also very numerous, in which the larger hope is (practically) held in silence. How vast has been the change in men's minds may be seen in this fact, that in the Church Congress of this year (1890), at least two Bishops—one of them the President, and the most eminent living Anglican theologian—advocate the larger hope.

I do not write these chapters with a view to magnify Patristic authority. My aim is historical. Place, for argument's sake, the Fathers in the lowest rank. They are, at the least, our only possible witnesses to the teaching of christianity in those ages when the language of the New Testament was a living tongue. It is certainly a most important fact in this controversy to find that in an age so little merciful, and when the inducements to silence were so very strong, (p. 83,) the larger hope was so widely held, and based on the authority of Scripture. The higher Patristic theology, in its view of death, of penalty, and of the future state is totally unlike our modern views. If *we* do not, our opponents are wise enough to, see the importance of all this. They are wise enough to see how grievously impaired thereby is their appeal to Scripture, as teaching endless penalty; and how their chance is gone of appealing to that ignorance of history, which calls universalism a modern novelty, or the product of an indifferent and sentimental age.

And here I beg my readers to note that these pages are only a plea for a truly catholic Church, for a genuine, and not a nominal, catholicity. I am pleading that Christ's Holy catholic Church may not be narrowed or dwarfed, but may, with a true catholicity, savingly embrace (sooner or later) every soul for whom its Founder died. I believe this to have been the deepest conviction of many, of very many, of the primitive Saints.

It is possible that in spite of all care and labour, (now extending over several years,) some errors of detail may be found in these chapters; some passages may have been misunderstood. I ask my readers to believe that, if so, I have offended involuntarily. I ask my critics to blame, if they must blame, in a spirit of fairness, not wielding a tomahawk in the service of the God of Love, nor using scorn and taunt in the service of Jesus Christ. But all the main conclusions are, I believe, absolutely true.

The so-called inconsistency of the Fathers has been

frankly faced, and the complete unfairness of the mode of interpretation which is still too common, has been exposed. —see pp. 93-4. When *all the facts* are fairly weighed, pp. 83-94, the evidence for the existence of a great body of universalistic teaching in early times remains clear and wholly unshaken.

Taking a rapid survey of facts, I think we may thus arrange early eschatological teaching. There were at first, probably, three distinct currents. Some held the final annihilation of the wicked; some, especially in North Africa, held their endless punishment; some, perhaps even a majority, taught universalism. By the days of GREGORY of Nyssa the latter view, aided doubtless by the unrivalled learning, genius and piety of ORIGEN had prevailed, and had succeeded in leavening, not the East alone, but much of the West (pp. 148-59). While the doctrine of annihilation has practically disappeared, universalism has established itself, has become the prevailing opinion, even in quarters antagonistic to the school of Alexandria.

But the waning fortunes of the dogma of endless penalty soon revived, and in their turn gained the ascendency. The Church of North Africa, in the person of AUGUSTINE, enters the field. The Greek tongue soon becomes unknown in the West, and the Greek Fathers forgotten. A Latin Christianity, redolent of the soil, developes itself, assuming, in accordance with the Roman bent, a rigid forensic type. On the throne of Him whose name is Love, is now seated a stern Judge (a sort of magnified Roman Governor). The sense of Sin practically dwarfs all else. The Father is lost in the Magistrate.

In the East the decay of the earlier belief was, if less rapid, nearly as complete. Strife within and without the Church, increasing ignorance and corruptions, bitter controversy (and other factors, p. 159) combined to form a soil in which the larger hope of earlier days at length dwindled and almost expired. Indeed, who can wonder that this was so, if he will but reflect how cruel was the age, how narrow is the natural heart of man, how slowly, *even now*, it responds to that which is most divine. The true wonder (to me, at least) is this, viz., the appearance in such an age as that of the later Roman empire of the very idea of universalism—a phenomenon which can, I think, be alone accounted for by the fact that the early Fathers found it, as they tell us, in the New Testament, p. 84.

And so I close this sketch of early universalism, under a deep sense of my personal deficiencies, increased as they are, at once, by the difficulties of limited space (*e.g.*, S. GREGORY of Nyssa alone would furnish extracts enough to fill this volume); and by the no less real difficulty of inducing my readers to view this evidence from the standpoint of the early centuries. Let us take the facts as they then were; let us try to picture a state of society in which the sentiment of mercy was practically unknown; in which all things reeked with vices, too loathsome even to name; add the fear of cruel persecution, often threatening the repose, if not the very existence of the Church; then, under such circumstances, to promise these blood-stained persecutors, these votaries of lust (even though unrepentant in life), a final salvation in the ages to come, must have seemed almost treason to the cause of CHRIST, because only too likely to arrest conversions. And when to this we add the undoubted fact, that the moral principles then current within the Church, explicitly sanctioned dissimulation—thus rendering lawful that concealment (or denial) of universalism which must have seemed so expedient; then it is that we gain some idea of the depth of conviction needed to account for even indirect teaching—for hints even—of the larger hope in the early centuries. And, if so, how much more for an universalism, often, as we have seen, wide enough to assert or imply, the final salvation of every fallen spirit. For in two respects the teaching of this book—let us note the fact—*falls short* of a great body of primitive teaching, (*a*) it states a hope instead of a certainty of restoration, (*b*) it does not extend this TO ALL RATIONAL AND FALLEN SPIRITS; a point which lies beyond my immediate province.

## CHAPTER VI.

## *UNIVERSALISM AND CREATION, &c.*

"Adam which was the Son of God."—S. Luke, iii. 38.

Our next step is an important one, to shew briefly how universalism instead of disturbing the due proportion and harmony of christian doctrine is precisely the element which affirms and establishes both.

We shall find—and the fact is a striking confirmation of the larger hope—that the great verities of our Faith *grow into a living unity* in the light of the great Purpose of Restoration. Creation, Incarnation, Resurrection, Judgment, &c., thus assume their places as parts of one great whole, the 'One thought of the One God,'—*pp.* 207-9. The Bible story opens with Creation, which the New Testament so closely connects with Restoration,—*Col.* i. 16-20. *Heb.* i. 2-3. As all created beings issue out of, so they return unto God—(*p.* 239) all are emphatically pronounced 'Good,' 'Very Good'—*Gen.* i. 4, 10, 12, 18, 21, 25, 31—pregnant words. But man is created in God's very Image and Likeness. What does this involve? It is (1). God's affirmation of universal Fatherhood. (2). God's assumption of the holiest duties towards every man. (3). God's investing every man with inalienable rights.

I contend that such a tie between God and Man can never be broken, that in the Origin of mankind Scripture bids us see their destiny, that God must realise finally that ideal which he traced in Creation. We are told God is not the Father of all men; *He is only their Creator!* What a total misapprehension these words imply of all that is involved in creating man in the likeness of God, in the image of God. Viewed thus, Creation contains the Gospel in germ; it involves universal Fatherhood. "Have we not all one Father," asks the Prophet, why? "Hath not one God *created* us?"—*Mal.* ii. 10. "O Lord, Thou art our Father * * we are all the work of Thy hand." *Is.* lxiv. 8. "The Protevangelium (the earliest gospel) is *Gen.* i. 26. 'Let us make man in Our image, after Our likeness.'"—WESTCOTT *on Heb.* i. 2. Indeed, we may perhaps say of Creation that it is fatherhood extended, it is paternity and something more. For what do we mean by paternity and the obligations it brings? The idea rests essentially on the communication of life to the child by the parent. Now paternity is for us largely blind and instinctive; but Creation is Love acting freely, divinely; knowing all the consequences, assuming all the *responsibility*, involved in the very act of creating a reasonable immortal spirit. "Dieu, dit on, ne doit rien a ses creatures. Le crois qu'il leur doit tout ce qu'il leur promit, en leur donnant l'etre. Or c'est leur promettre un bien, que de leur en donner l'idee, et de leur en faire sentir le besoin."—*Emile.* It seems, then, very strange to seek to escape the consequences of the lesser obligation, by admitting one still greater; to seek, in a word, to evade the results of a divine universal fatherhood, by pleading that God is only the Creator of all. Hence a good Creator, freely creating for a doom of endless sin, freely introducing a dualism, is a profound moral contradiction. Can we even imagine a Good Being of His own free-will calling into existence creatures to hate Him for ever, or certainly creating those who will, *as He knows, hate Him* *for ever, and sin for ever?*\* Thus, in the awful yet tender light of Creation, the traditional creed shrinks and shrivels up—"Seeing then that the spirit comes from God," \* \* says S. JEROME, "it is NOT JUST that they should perish eternally who are sustained by His breath and spirit."— *In Is.* lvii. 6.

I pass to consider the Incarnation. It is the great fact of Christianity. From it flow, and on it depend the Atonement, the Sacraments, the Resurrection; they are, as it were, results of the Incarnation, and extensions of it. Now there are many aspects of this mystery which I do not touch; content to note that one point is quite clearly admitted, that Jesus Christ became Incarnate as the second ADAM. Therefore, to justify such a title, the Incarnation involves the idea of the unity, absolute and organic, of the race of man. "For what purpose is the history of our race traced to its earliest origin \* \* unless its fortunes were regarded *as a whole*, and *it must stand or fall together.*"†— WILBERFORCE *on the Incarnation.* "To that old Creation is opposed the regeneration of man's race, through its new Creation in the second ADAM."—*Ib.* But this logically involves the salvation of the race, "which stands or falls together." It is, to borrow a homely phrase, *all or none*

---

\* "The Church," says NEWMAN, "holds that it were better for the earth to fail and for all the many millions who are upon it to die of starvation in extremest agony, as far as temporal affliction goes, than that one soul, I will not say, should be lost, but should commit ONE VENIAL SIN."—*Angl. difficult.* p. 190. But, if so, how inconceivable does it become that God should freely create millions of beings whose destiny will, to His certain knowledge, be an endless existence in evil hopeless and aggravated, evil *rotting, festering for ever and ever.*

† These statements from the pen of one who teaches that a part of the human race is severed for ever from the second ADAM, are remarkable. They illustrate what has been said (p. 67) of the virtual untruth which runs through our traditional theology.

(p. 71-3). If this were to be stated in the language of science, it would stand thus—ADAM = x, where x represents all humanity. And so Christ, as the last ADAM, sums up all humanity in the spiritual equation. The traditional creed, in fact, constructs an Incarnation of its own, not that of Scripture. Its Incarnate Son may be the Son of God, but is not the Son of Man (of humanity), not the second ADAM. And as the Christ of the traditional creed is not the Christ of Scripture, so its human race is not the true humanity, for it teaches that the race is a collection of atoms, separable, inorganic. But Scripture affirms the reverse: it is quite true that every man bears his own burden of sin and suffering; but there is a truth higher still—the solidarity of the race, in the divine idea and plan. Says WESTCOTT, "Our lives are fragments of some larger life."— *Rev. of the Father*, p. 98. This is the truth, without which the Fall and the Incarnation are unintelligible. In the highest sense Christ does not deal with the units of humanity, for humanity itself is the divine unit in Redemption. Therefore I feel constrained to charge the traditional creed with making void the idea which underlies the Incarnation, the organic unity of mankind.

But a further point must here be noted: as we think of man's Creation in God's Image and Likeness, and all it involves; of the stupendous glory of the Incarnation; of the splendour of the Atonement, there comes of itself a conviction that no anticipations we can form are too magnificent of the destiny of humanity as such, *i.e.*, *as* a whole: no ideals are too lofty. The traditional creed stands self-condemned when confronted with these noble facts; it bears the brand of utter meanness; its message of ruin without remedy, of eternal chaos, and darkness is a denial of the whole purpose and essence of Creation; it is a denial, no less, of the message of the Incarnation to humanity as such, as an organic whole.

I pass to the Atonement. It is an Atonement made by Christ as the last ADAM. Not alone, then, does Christ sooner or later draw to Himself all men, but *He cannot draw less than all men* if He be a new and better ADAM. Therefore, I repeat, the traditional creed, while in words teaching, *in fact* denies the Atonement of the Bible. It asserts an universal salvation—but it really means a salvation that does not save universally—one in which Christ tries to save all, and is defeated. What is this but to dishonour the cross in its very essence: to deny that our Lord is truly the last ADAM, and to treat Him as one who, in the face of assembled creation, in the sight of men and angels, has challenged the powers of evil and has failed?

Long familiarity has blinded us to the significance of the startling provision by which ADAM is linked organically with the whole race in the transmission of guilt. This tie is formed universally, and independently of any volition. To call Christ the second (*i.e.*, last) ADAM is either to dupe men, or it is to assert a tie equally organic and absolute with the *whole human race*. But it is said, that, as men can shake off the heritage of ADAM, so they may the grace of Christ: I reply (I.) so they may, *if* the grace of Christ be only as strong as the sin of ADAM, which S. PAUL clearly denies, *e.g.*, *Rom.* v. 15-21, &c. (II.) Before men can shake off a heritage they must have received it. Hence, unless Christ REPLACES THE RACE IN PARADISE, He has not undone the evil of the Fall (a fact which *is steadily denied, or ignored*, by the traditional creed), and so is not the second ADAM. (III.) It is an illogical process to say that because a partial failure took place (foreseen, and permitted for wise ends), therefore a new dispensation expressly designed to remedy that failure will itself fail. (IV.) In the highest and truest sense God never fails, never can fail.

<blockquote>
And here it is right to point out that two very popular views of the Atonement lead, logically, (their truth I do not discuss) to the larger hope. One theory says that Christ died as the sinner's substitute. But, if so, and if He, as is certain, died for all, then all have a clear *right* to salvation. If the substitute be accepted all *have a right* to go free. Similarly, if Christ's death be the price paid for mankind's redemption, then the acceptance of that price gives mankind a clear *right* to salvation. The substitute being accepted, and the price fully paid for *all*, it is wholly unfair to exact the penalty *twice over*, in any one case, in hell. These obvious conclusions are too often ignored. A few words may be added on a strange view not seldom held. An infinite Atonement pre-supposes, it is said, an infinite guilt, and an infinite penalty. An Infinite Atonement, it may be replied, pre-supposes rather an infinite Love and an infinite Hope; and excludes the chance of failure, possible to a finite Saviour. I have shewn the illogical and unscriptural assumption involved in speaking of human guilt as infinite (p. 47 Note). But, even admitting that the penalty of sin is infinite (for argument's sake), my argument as above is wholly untouched. Be the penalty infinite or no, you cannot equitably exact it twice over.
</blockquote>

Let us pass to the Sacraments. They are an extension of the Incarnation. "The nfluence of the Incarnation extends itself through that sacramental system, which binds *all* men to the head of the race"—WILBERFORCE, p. 14. "As there is a recapitulation of *all*, in heaven and earth in Christ, so there is a recapitulation of all in Christ in the holy sacrament."—Bishop ANDREW, *Sermon of the Nativity*. In the language of theology, the tie formed in Baptism (renewed in Holy Communion) with Christ is so close, that in the famous words of S. LEO, "*Corpus regenerati fit caro Christi.*" "The body of the baptized *becomes the flesh of Jesus Christ.*" But if so, it is impossible to believe that the very flesh of Christ can be sent into an endless hell. Can Jesus Christ cut off, so to speak, His own flesh and sever it from Himself for ever? or rather, to state the case fully, can

Christ assign a portion of Himself to the society of devils for ever? Even Keble seems to feel this. When dwelling on these aspects of Redemption, the cruel theology to which he clings drops off; and rising to true catholicity, he bids us view " Christ's *least* and *worst with hope* to meet above ;" and says, in suggestive words, " *Christ's mark outwears the rankest blot.*" Need I again point out how these words really involve universalism, for our Lord always teaches that those who have been brought nearest to Him and yet disobey, as do impenitent christians, will fare worse in the final judgment than those who have never heard of Him.

Next, let us pursue the Incarnation into another field of thought, and contemplate in its light the Resurrection. The Resurrection is—admitting fully its work for the body—yet *essentially* far more than this. "It is *the new birth of humanity.*"—WESTCOTT, *Gosp. of Res.* It is the crown of Redemption. (I.) It is Life from Christ permeating the whole man, body and spirit. (II.) It is Life permeating the whole of humanity, through the last ADAM. "As in (the) ADAM all die, so in (the) Christ shall be made alive." To a collective death in ADAM is here opposed a collective life in Christ; to a fall, a rising again; to a loss, a gain; and that universal and absolute, one dealing with the race. I say, *a gain, necessarily;* and as involved in the very idea of the Resurrection. For what is the Resurrection? It comes *only* through Christ, Who not merely gives, but Who is the Resurrection and the Life. It is thus the closest union with Christ: it is to share the "kingdom of God:" to bear "the image of the heavenly:" to draw from Christ the gifts of "life," "power," "glory," "incorruption," "immortality," as S. PAUL teaches. And to share all these is, necessarily, to share blessedness; a point I must press. By what imaginable process can death, and blight, and evil be the result of that Resurrection which is Christ? Again, death is in Scripture a name under which are grouped the results of sin. Hence to abolish death, as the Resurrection does, is to abolish sin and its results. But by the Resurrection death is swept away, is, indeed, "swallowed up," and Life in all its fulness of meaning, Life in Christ, Life which is Christ, is communicated.

Meantime, let us notice that this view of the Resurrection seems implied in our Lord's words, *S. Jno.* vi. 39, 40, 54. There the Resurrection is contrasted with loss, and is stated as the result of believing: *cfr. S. Jno.* xi. 25-6: here notice our Lord's rejection of the idea of a Resurrection deferred to the Last Day, as elsewhere He says, "Verily, verily, the hour *now is*, in which they that are in the graves shall hear the voice of the Son of man, and they that hear shall live." —*S. Jno.* v. 25. Here we have to guard against the common error, which destroys the whole force of Christ's words, by severing this present Resurrection from that which is to come. To our Lord, no such division occurs: *nay, to deny any such division* seems His very object, and to teach that the true idea of the Resurrection is of a force essentially spiritual, ever acting; a leaven which, working here and now, shall one day transform and raise the whole man, body, soul, and spirit. Further, the idea of the Resurrection, as a gain from its very nature, seems in harmony with our Lord's words—*S. Matt.* xxii. 30; *Mark* xii. 25; *Luc.* xx. 35-6. The same conception underlies S. PAUL's teaching. "*If* the Spirit of Him, Who raised up Jesus from the dead, dwell in you, He that raised up Jesus from the dead, shall also quicken your mortal bodies."—*Rom.* viii. 11. Here Resurrection is represented as flowing from the indwelling Spirit.

Thus, too, S. PAUL preaches as good news the Resurrection—*Acts* xvii. 18: and connects the Resurrection and light." *ib.* xxvi. 23 (revised version), and significantly *hopes* for the Resurrection of the unjust,—*Acts* xxiv. 15, *i.e.*, hopes that the unjust, shall, with the just, share the benefit of the Resurrection. Doubtless there is (and we are glad to admit it), a Resurrection of judgment.—*S. Jno.* v. 29. For judgment, as we shall see, is itself a part of the great scheme of salvation; and is curative, while, nay rather, *because* it is retributive. To this treatment of the impenitent dead, S. PAUL seems to allude in saying, "But *every man in his own order:* Christ the firstfruits; afterward they that are Christ's;" "Then cometh THE END," *i.e.*, after the time necessary for the subjection to Him of all opposing creatures "when He shall have put down all rule, and all authority and power."—1 *Cor.* xv. 23-4. In other words *all are to be made alive in Christ*, but in due order and succession, vv. 22-3. The reign of Christ is to be prolonged until its aim is attained, v. 25, *i.e.*, the aim just referred too of universal life, v. 22.

Such, broadly speaking, seems to be the view of the Resurrection given in Scripture. Taken narrowly, its statements may seem to conflict. Thus they describe the Resurrection as successive, 1 *Cor.* xv. 23, and *Rev.* xx. 6, and yet simultaneous, 1 *Cor.* xv. 51-2; as present, *S. Jno.* v. 25, and as future (in many passages). All becomes clear if we keep in mind the central idea of the Resurrection as a *spiritual redemptive force* exercised over the whole man—a force present and ever acting (as in the parallel case of judgment); a force which is successive, as it transforms individuals or classes of men; and yet future and simultaneous in some special sense, when the end has come, when the whole of humanity are "risen," when the climax has been by all attained.

I have reserved for the last a more detailed examination of S. PAUL's great argument in 1 *Cor.* xv. Two points of the greatest moment are there taught: (I.) S. PAUL is speaking of the Resurrection of the dead generally, *i.e., of all humanity*. (II.) He asserts in the case of all, the quickening, healing force of the Resurrection; *he knows no other Resurrection than this healing, restoring process.* (I.) That the Apostle is speaking of the Resurrection of *all* seems clear from his words, v. 22-3—"For as in the ADAM ALL die, so in the Christ shall ALL be made alive." Here he plainly describes a process *co-extensive with the race, co-extensive with sin:* again he proceeds to state clearly this universal reference by explaining that life does not reach all at once, but "every man in his own order." He divides the ALL, taking first "they that are Christ's," v. 23, who obtain the Resurrection life at His *parousia*. Thence he passes to the mass of humanity, who are to be gradually "subjected" in the interval before "the end," v. 24. Finally, everything whatsoever and wheresoever is to be subjected to Christ. (On this process, see notes on 1 *Cor.* xv. 25-28; *Eph.* i. 10, i. 22; *Col.* i. 15-20; *Phil.* iii. 21,—Chap. viii.) The final result is summed up in very striking words—"And when all things have been subjected unto Him (Christ) then shall the Son Himself also be subjected unto Him (the Father) that did subject all things unto Him (Christ) in order that God may be ALL IN ALL." Observe the *same* relation subsists *finally* between the whole universe (whatsoever and wheresoever), as that between Christ and the Father—the same original word is used of both. The language of the Apostle admits of no exception at THE END; of no death whatsoever, first or second, for all are made alive in Christ; of no annihilation, for all are restored; of no blot or stain of evil moral or physical. Finally, as the grand result—GOD IS ALL AND IN ALL.

This conception of the Resurrection as a spiritual force, conveying blessedness, we find asserted by many early writers. The first traces of this teaching are perhaps in the works of those Fathers, who seem to teach the extinction of the wicked and to confine the Resurrection to the righteous. See CLEMENS (*Romanus*) *quoted* p. 94. They who contradict the gift of God die "in their wrangling," says S. IGNATIUS. "It would have been better for them to love, so that they might *rise*," *i.e.*, obtain the Resurrection.—*Ad Smyr.* vii. See also *Ad Trall.* ix. "He who raised Christ from the dead, will raise us up also, *if* we do His will," says S. POLYCARP.—*Ad Phil.* ii. So, too, apparently, "*The Teaching of the Apostles*" (p. 94). THEOPHILUS of Antioch teaches that those keeping God's commandments "can be saved, and obtaining the Resurrection, can inherit incorruption."—*Ad Aut.* ii. 27; and IRENÆUS (p. 95) very probably takes the same view. ARNOBIUS asks "what man does not see that, that which is immortal * * cannot be subject to any pain; and that, on the contrary, that cannot be immortal which does suffer pain?"—*Adv. gen.* ii. 14. Passing on from these Fathers, we find abundant early evidence to support the view, which makes the Resurrection a process of restoration from its very nature.—See ATHENAGORAS, p. 108; METHODIUS, p. 111. Again, S. HILARY speaks thus: "When the only begotten Son was about to reconcile to God *all things* in heaven, and on earth * * when death * * should come to an end * * by redeeming man from the law of sin—by making God an object of praise to all, and through all the eternities, by the gift and dignity of our immortality. Now *all* these things the *virtue of the Resurrection accomplished."—In Ps.* lxix., p. 834 (*Paris*, 1652). S. GREGORY of Nyssa abounds with such teaching as the following: "The Resurrection is the *restoration* of our nature to its pristine state."—*De an. et Res.* ii., p. 684. "Therefore, like a potter's vase, man is resolved once more into clay, in order that * * he may *be moulded anew into his original form, by the Resurrection.—Cat. orat.* ch. viii. "Lest sin adhering to us should last for ever, the vessel is, by a kindly providence, dissolved by death for a time, in order that * * mankind should be remoulded; and restored, free from the admixture of sin, to its former life. For that is the Resurrection, namely, the replacing of our nature in its former state."—*In fun. Pulch.* ii. p. 955. S. AMBROSE teaches that: "The Resurrection was given that by death sin should end."—*De bono mort.* ch. iv. "The Resurrection is that by which all the bonds of the enemy are loosed."—*In Ps.* xli. So, too, the AMBROSIASTER. "On the *abolition* of sin, the Resurrection of the dead takes place."—*In Col.* ii. "The Resurrection," says an early author, "is the remoulding of our nature."—*De Sacr.* ii. 6. "Not to sin," says GENNADIUS, "belongs to the immortal and impassible nature."—*In Rom.* vi. 12. In the same tone speaks CLEMENT of Alexandria.—*See Pæd.* iii. ch. 1. The school of Antioch strongly insisted on this view of the Resurrection. DIODORUS has been quoted—p. 137, and THEODORE—p. 142-3. From the latter I add here: "Christ gave the Resurrection in order that, placed in an immortal nature, we should live free from all sin.—*In Rom.* v. 18. "The Apostle proves at length that those who are mortal serve sin, but those who are become immortal are set free from it."

—*ib.* viii. 3. "The Resurrection of the dead (is) the final (greatest) good."—*ib.* xi. In the same spirit THEODORET says—"In the future life the body, when made incorruptible and immortal, cannot admit the filth of sin."—*In Col.* ii. 11. "For after the Resurrection, when our bodies become incorruptible and immortal, grace shall reign in them, *sin having no place left for it.* For when sufferings (passions *pathon*) are put an end to (by the Resurrection), *sin will have no place.*"—*In Rom.* v. 21. Viewed thus, surely a clearer light falls on the Saviour's words, "I am the Resurrection and the Life," words re-echoed in our Creed—"I believe in \* \* the Resurrection of the dead, and the Life everlasting" the Resurrection as bringing to all Life everlasting.

From the Resurrection, let us pass by an easy transition to consider those texts which speak of "death" and "destruction" and "perishing" as the portion of the ungodly. To ascertain the true meaning, let us enquire what is meant by death. There are two answers commonly given. First comes that of the popular creed, which says death in the case of sinners means living for ever in pain and evil. The recoil from such teaching has produced the second view of "death" as meaning "annihilation," now maintained by some. I have already spoken of this view, pp. 8-10; what follows will shew how completely it seems to me to contradict the true Scriptural idea of death.

First, I would ask, in the words of Mr. JUKES, "are any of the varied deaths which Scripture speaks of as incident to man, his non-existence or annihilation? Take as examples the deaths referred to by S. PAUL, in the sixth, seventh, and eighth chapters of the Epistle to the *Romans.* We read (ch. vi., 7), 'He that is dead is free from sin.' Is this 'death' which is freedom from sin, non-existence or annihilation? Again, when the Apostle says (ch. vii. 9), 'I was alive without the law once, but when the commandment came, sin revived, and I died.' Was this 'death,' wrought in him by the law, annihilation? Again, when he says (ch. viii. 6), 'To be carnally minded is death,' is this death non-existence or annihilation? And again, when he says (ch. viii. 38), 'Neither death, nor life, shall separate us,' is the 'death' here referred to annihilation? When ADAM died on the day he sinned (*Gen.* ii. 17), was this annihilation? when his body died, and turned to dust (*Gen.* v. 5), was this annihilation? Is our 'death in trespasses and sins' (*Eph.* ii. 1-2) annihilation? Is our 'death to sin' (*Rom.* vi. 11), annihilation? \* \* Do not these and similar uses of the word prove beyond all question, that whatever else these deaths may be, not one of them is non-existence or annihilation?"

But if death be neither living for ever in pain, nor annihilation, what then is it? Death is, in its narrower aspect, bodily dissolution; it is for man 'a separation from some given form of life which he has lived in;' it is the way out of one state of being into another. Thus understood, how should death shut out hope in any case? Nor is it really opposed to life, in fact it is, when viewed in a truer and higher aspect, a pathway to life; nay, the very condition of life. 'Except a corn of wheat fall into the ground and die, it abideth alone, but, *if it die*, it bringeth forth much fruit.' *S. John* xii. 24. Is there not here a great truth hinted at, of universal application? Is not the connection a very real and vital one between dying and life? and so the Apostle says that 'he that is *dead* is freed from sin,' *Rom.* vi. 7, *i.e.*, is alive to God. Must it not be that this death threatened against the ungodly is, after all, the way, however sharp, to life even for them? as S. PAUL, *Rom.* xi. 15, asks, 'what shall the reconciling of them be but *life from the dead?*' On the view generally held these words, so significant, lose all real force. A tradition, wholly unwarranted, has spread almost universally, which regards death as the close of our training; as assigning a limit beyond which Christ Himself has no power or no will to save the obstinate sinner.

I reply that in both the letter and the spirit, this view contradicts at once the deductions of reason: the teachings of the early church: and the express language of the New Testament. Indeed, to teach truer views of death seems one of the essential objects of the Gospel. Death is, in fact, the crossing from one stage of our journey to another. It is not an end; it is a transit; it is an episode in life, and not its goal. It is not really a terminus, but a starting point. It is "that first breath which our souls draw when we enter Life, which is of all life centre."—*Edwin Arnold.* "Death is the shadow, the dream, and not life, as we hastily judge who measure being by our senses."—WESTCOTT, *Rev. of the Father,* p. 94. The day of death was by a true instinct named in the early church the day of birth. To teach that our training ends at death, is to say that a child's education ends with the nursery.

Therefore, let me ask, on what authority is the common doctrine taught, unknown to antiquity, unknown to Scripture? Who commissioned any to teach, that to die is to pass into a state beyond the reach of Christ's grace? If so, why are we told, so significantly, the story of Christ's evangelising the spirits in prison? Why are those *especially selected* for *evangelisation* who had been in life disobedient, and had so died? Why does the Apostle tell us that the *Gospel was preached even to the dead?*—1 *Pet.* iv. 6, a fact obscured in the authorised version. Why these repeated and exultant questions, "O grave where is thy victory?" "O death where is thy sting?" Why has the New Testament, with such varied illustrations, pressed on us this fact (as of special moment) that Christ has destroyed death, if death is ever to put a stop to His power to save? How could Christ be the Conqueror of death, if death can in *any case* reduce Him to impotence? Can death disarm its victor? So far from this, S. PAUL invokes the analogy of nature, as shewing that death is the condition of life. "Thou fool, that which thou sowest is not quickened, *except it die*,"— in fact

> "There is no gain except by loss,
> There is no life *except by death*"

Who shall limit this truth in its operation? It certainly does hold good in the spiritual order—of that we are assured. S. PAUL, in a passage already quoted, speaks of death as freeing from sin. Let me quote further. "If we be *dead* with Him, we shall live with Him."—2 *Tim.* ii. 11. "We which live are always delivered unto *death* for Jesus' sake, that the *life* also of Jesus might be manifested in us."— 2 *Cor.* iv. 11. And so our Lord declares that "He that loseth His life shall save it."—a statement more than once repeated in the gospels. And the Apostle adds, *Rom.* viii. 13, "if ye mortify the deeds of the body, ye shall live." Thus, too, the Psalmist* strikingly prays, "that the wicked may perish, in order that they may know that God reigns over the earth."—*Ps.* lxxxiii. 17-8. See, too, the verse, "When He slew them then they sought Him."—*Ps.* lxxviii. 34. On these words ORIGEN comments, "He does not say that some sought Him after others had been slain, but He says that the destruction of those who were killed was of such a nature that, when put to death, they sought God."—*De prin.* ii. ch. 5, iii. So, too, Elam is to be first consumed and then restored.—*Jer.* xlix. 37-9. So Canaan is to be destroyed and yet restored.—*Zeph.* ii. 5-7. So is Ammon to be restored after perpetual desolation—*Zeph.* ii. 9 and *Jer.* xlix. 6. So the dead bones are made alive.—*Ez.* xxxvii., and Israel comes up out of her graves.—*ib.* v. 13. *cf.* 1 *Samuel* ii. 6.

---

* True, in the Old Testament the threatenings of "death" and "destruction" are mainly temporal. But the same *principle* underlies God's dealings in both dispensations, and renders the quotations of this chapter strictly revelant.

We thus learn how death becomes the very instrument by which God quickens the sinner, and that in two ways. (I.) By the death of the body, which takes a man out of the present age into a state more fitted to rouse and to save. (II.) By the death of the spirit, *i.e.*, its being searched through and through by God's fiery discipline—by His sharp surgery—till it die to sin and live to righteousness. In all this subject of death, there is an extraordinary narrowness in the views held generally, as though the fact of dying could change God's unchanging purpose; as though His never failing love were extinguished because we pass into a new state of existence; as though the power of Christ's Cross were exhausted in the brief span of our earthly life. So far from this, has not Christ abolished *death?* Is He not Lord of the *dead?* Did He not evangelise the *dead?* Has He not the keys of *death?* On the popular view, what depth of meaning can you possibly assign to these words?

But it may be said, is there not "the second death?" Yes, assuredly. But though it were not the second merely, but the thousandth death, yet it is *but death:* and death *absolutely*, in every degree and power, is destroyed, is blotted out, or there is no real meaning in S. Paul's song of triumph (1 *Cor.* xv. 55). No true victory has been won by Christ if the second death is too strong for Him. Will our opponents explain how "death" can be "SWALLOWED UP" in victory, and yet survive in its most malignant form, *i.e.*, the second death? As Martensen well puts the case, "When S. Paul teaches that death is the last enemy that shall be conquered, evidently in this death he comprehends the second death, else there would still be an enemy to conquer."—*Dogm. Chret.*

A vast body of early opinion affirms that the sinner's

"death" and "destruction" is the Great Artist remoulding* His own work; is the Physician healing, not annihilating. To pulverise the sinner, to destroy, to slay, ALL MEAN REFORMATION. Such is the testimony of a crowd of illustrious names, to most of whom the language of the New Testament was familiar as the language of their every-day life. So CLEMENT asserts that the law in ordering the sinner to be put to death designs his being brought from death to life.—*Strom. lib.* vii. p. 707. ORIGEN has been already quoted. S. METHODIUS asserts that the custom of Scripture is to call destruction that which is only a change for the better.—*Ex.* EPIPHAN. *Adv. hær.* ii. *tom.* i. § 32. IRENÆUS speaks of death as ending sin.—*Adv. hær.* iii. 23-6. S. GREGORY of Nyssa is full of similar teaching. "They who live in the flesh ought, by virtuous conversation, to free themselves from fleshly lusts, lest *after death, they should again need another death, to cleanse away* the remains of fleshly glutinous vice that cling to them."—*De anim. et Res.*, ii. p. 652. This seems to shew the healing agency of even the "second death." "When the Psalmist prays, let sinners and the unrighteous be destroyed, he is (really) praying that sin and unrighteousness may perish."—*De orat. Or.* i. p. 719. The passage continues thus—"And if there be found any such prayer elsewhere (in the Scriptures), it has exactly the same meaning, viz., that of expelling the sin, and not of destroying the man." For S. GREGORY of Nazianzus, see p. 118, and for S. BASIL, p. 120. HILARY has been quoted to the same general effect. So have EUSEBIUS and RUFINUS, MACARIUS MAGNES, TITUS of Bostra, CLEMENT of Alexandria, CHRYSOSTOM, and CYRIL of Alexandria;

---

* So, in heathen mythology the same deity, APOLLO, is the Healer and the Destroyer.

to these I may add MAXIMUS and DIDYMUS: and AMBROSE, pp. 129-30. It would be hardly possible to adduce a stronger chain of testimony. I now turn to S. JEROME (see p. 136). "All God's enemies shall be destroyed, His enemies shall perish and cease to exist, but perish in that wherein they are enemies." S. JEROME even seems to assert the salvation of the "Man of sin," for the passage proceeds thus—"Just as S. PAUL writes to the Thessalonians (of the Man of sin), whom the Lord shall slay with the breath of His mouth. (So) this slaying signifies *not annihilation*, but the *cessation of the evil life*, in which they formerly used to live."—*In Mic.* v. 8. From the AMBROSIASTER I take the following, on the words, "They shall perish." "They perish * * while they are being changed for the better."—*In Heb.* i. 11. And so in the Sibylline Books, the wicked first *perish* and afterwards are saved.—*lib.* ii. vv. 211, 250-340.

And what is true of "death" as threatened against the sinner, is true no less of "judgment," even in its most extreme form. We are not without very distinct teaching in Holy Scripture on this point. "Everywhere," says S. BASIL, "Scripture connects God's justice (righteousness) with His compassions."—*In Ps.* cxvi. 5. Doubtless in a certain sense judgment may be opposed to mercy, and contrasted with it (*S. Jas.* ii. 13), but this is on the surface rather than in essence. As, to take an illustration, death is often contrasted in Scripture with life, and yet is the very pathway to life. (See pp. 185-8). Whenever judgment comes, it comes on Love's errand, if it comes from God. Here is the spiritual watershed between the two theologies. There is the popular theology that says, God loves His enemies, *till they die*. His love then turns into hate and vengeance. His love is, in fact, a question of chronology, or, if one will, of geography, *i.e.*, bounded to this world. And there is the truer theology that teaches with the Bible, that God *is* Love—Love unchanging and eternal in all His ways.

In the first judgment recorded in Scripture, mercy goes hand in hand. If ADAM is to die, mercy follows; the serpent's head is to be bruised. So, too, even the vengeance of eternal fire on Sodom ends in her restoration.—*Jude* vii.; *Ezek.* xvi. 53-5. We thus understand the striking juxtaposition of mercy and judgment in God's revelation of Himself to MOSES.—*Ex.* xxxiv. 6-7 : the same connection we shall find in *Deut.* xxxii. 35 and 39 : *(cfr. Rom.* xii. 19-20.) Thus, too, Israel's Judges were Saviours.—*Judg.* iii. 9: *Obad.* 21. Few more beautiful illustrations of the view I am urging can be found than that afforded by the story of ACHAN, stoned by a terrible judgment with all that he had, in the Valley of Achor—*Josh.* vii. 24-25 : for if we turn to *Hosea* ii. 15 we shall find this promise, " I will give her the Valley of Achor for a door of HOPE," words pregnant with suggestion.

If now we turn to the Psalter, we may note that the fact of God's coming to judgment is a matter of deep joy—*Ps.* lxvii. 4 ; nay, the Psalmist (*Ps.* xcvi. 11-3 ; xcviii. 4-9) bids the sea to roar, the floods to clap their hands, the hills to sing for joy, at the prospect of judgment (as being a part of the great scheme of redemption). And so he hopes in God's judgments (*Ps.* cxix. 43), and comforts himself with them— *ib.* 52-62 (*compare Ps.* xcvii. 8). Of *Ps.* ii. 8-9 I have already spoken. It would be interesting to know how the traditional creed can fairly reconcile Christ's taking the heathen as *His inheritance*, with the terrible judgment inflicted on them, " breaking them in pieces." The more we study the Bible the more clear does the fact become, that *salvation is essen-*

tially linked with the divine judgments. And so, conversely, there is an awfulness even in the divine compassion. There is *mercy* with Thee, *therefore* Thou shalt be *feared*.—Ps. cxxx. 4. And in this spirit we read the suggestive words, "Thou, Lord, art merciful," says the Psalmist, "for Thou renderest to every man according to his work."—*Ps.* lxii. 12. Here is the essence of the question—*retribution is mercy; judgment means salvation.* "The thought," says MAURICE, "of God's ceasing to punish is the real—the unutterable horror. Wrath is not the counteracting force to love, but the attribute of it." So *Ps.* lxvii. 1-4 presents to us the picture of God as judge, in connection with His saving health reaching all nations. So in *Ps.* lxxii. 1, 2, 3-17, judgment leads to a reign of universal righteousness. Again, in *Ps.* xcix. 8, forgiveness and vengeance go together; so *Ps.* ci. 1, combines mercy and judgment, and *Ps.* xxxiii. 5, judgment and loving-kindness. And so we read, "Thy *judgments* are a great deep, O Lord, thou *preservest* man and beast."—*Ps.* xxxvi. 6.

The Prophets are full of similar teaching. Note ISAIAH connecting the words of comfort and pardon to Israel with her having received "double for all her sins."—*Is.* xl. 1-2. So it is said, "Zion shall be *redeemed with judgment.*"—*Is.* i. 27. "When thy *judgments* are in the earth, the inhabitants of the world learn righteousness."—*Is.* xxvi. 9. "Princes shall rule in *judgment*, and a man shall be an hiding place from the wind."—*Is.* xxxii. 1-2. "I will make my *judgment* to rest for a light of the people. \* \* My *salvation* is gone forth."—*Is.* li. 4-5. "Therefore will he be exalted that he may have mercy \* \* for the Lord is a God of *judgment.*"—*Is.* xxx. 18. So again, "He hath filled Zion with *judgment* \* \* and there shall be abundance of *salvation.*"—

*Is.* xxxiii. 5-6. "The Lord is our *Judge* \* \* He will *save* us."—*Is.* xxxiii. 22. We may note how this connection of judgment and salvation runs through the Bible,—see *Is.* xlv. 21-2, where God is described as a *just* God and a *Saviour;* and the passage proceeds to invite all the ends of the earth to look and be saved. Compare with this, *Zech.* ix. 9, "*just* and having *salvation*, and 1 *Jno.* i. 9, "He is \* \* *just* to *forgive* us our sins." So do we read of judgment in connection with the future setting up of God's kingdom of peace and love.—*Is.* ii. 2-4. Nor should we overlook the connection in Christ between God's rule and *salvation*,—*Is.* xl. 10-11; ix. 7, so *Ps.* ciii. 19-22. And let us note the juxta-position of the "helmet" of *salvation*, and "garments of *vengeance*."—*Is.* lix. 17. So the "day of *vengeance*" and the acceptable year are linked together.— *Is.* lxi. 2. And in *Is.* xlii. 1-12 (applied to Christ in the New Testament) we find Him described as setting judgment on the earth (v. 1), but the issue is salvation (v. 7-12). Again, speaking of Christ as the branch, another Prophet tells how "He shall execute *judgment* \* \* in the land. In those days Judah shall be *saved*."—*Jer.* xxxiii. 15. And "I will *betroth thee unto Me* for ever \* \* *in judgment*† and in mercy."—*Hos.* ii. 19. So in *Dan.* vii. 10-14, the universal dominion promised to Christ is closely connected with the Judgment Day. So in *Ezek.* xxiv. 13-4, it is said of Israel, "Thou shalt not be purged of thy filthiness any more, *till I have satisfied My fury upon thee.*"

The passages just quoted (and those that follow) may be compared with those already cited to illustrate the Scriptural meaning of death and destruction. It will also probably

---

†And we may note a remarkable reading in the Septuagint, "I will set judgment unto hope."—*Is.* xxviii. 17.

help our attaining a true view of judgment if we remember that, in a sense most real, judgment is present and continuous. "Les grandes assises de la vallée de Josâphat commencent pour nous chaque soir."—MAD. SWETCHINE. "The world," says EMERSON, "is full of judgment days."—*Spirit. Laws.*

Let us now pass to the New Testament: there we shall find ample proof worthy of our closest study, and shewing the true meaning of judgment, alike here and hereafter, as *conveying salvation.* Take for instance the context, so often overlooked, of our Lord's famous words, *S. John* xii. 32— "Now is the *judgment* of this world, now shall the prince of this world be cast out. And I, if I be lifted up, will draw all men unto Me," *i.e.*, the judgment of the world is the salvation of the world, is the drawing of all men to Christ. Thus, if it be objected that we are told Christ came not to judge, but to save the world,—*S. Jno.* iii. 17, we can point to the above passage, and to the express statement, "*For judgment came I into this world.*"—*S. Jno.* ix. 39. But all difficulty ceases when we remember that *primarily* salvation is Christ's object, but in practice this salvation is attained very often through judgment. Thus note *S. Matt.* xii. 18-21, where the bringing of judgment unto victory is stated as our Lord's object: and again, note the connection of judgment and quickening in *S. Jno.* v. 21-2. Very striking are the words of S. PAUL, which refer to the last Judgment, and seem to shew conclusively that, that great day brings salvation to all who are judged. Turn to *Rom.* xiv. 10—"We must all stand before the judgment seat of Christ," must each render his account to God. But that is far from being the only object of that judgment. Its main and essential purpose is *salvation*. To shew this is easy. For note, that to illustrate the purpose of God in judging, S. PAUL here quotes from *Is.* xlv. 23, which runs thus—"Look unto Me and be ye SAVED, *all ye ends of the earth,* for I am God \* \* I have sworn by Myself that unto Me every knee shall bow. \* \* The word is gone out and shall not return;" it *must* be fulfilled, *i.e.,* God's purpose of salvation must reach effectually the entire race. But this prophetic assertion of an *universal* salvation is here quoted by the Apostle, and is *linked with the Day of Judgment, which, according to him, it describes.* In that Judgment, S. PAUL sees not the final damnation of any man, but the fulfilment of the prophetic promise—a pledge that salvation shall reach every soul of man. Pause, and realise the full significance of this. Beyond the grave, we have S. PAUL looking on to the closing scene; to that Judgment which winds up the great drama of Life, and Sin, and Redemption. And as the Apostle looks he sees in the very Judgment† a process of salvation, he sees a picture bright with hope for every human soul—a picture which he can only describe in terms of the joyful outburst of the prophet, "Look unto Me and *be ye saved, all ye ends of the earth.*"

Bearing all this in mind, a light, clear and distinct, falls on those words of S. PAUL (so unintelligible on the ordinary view), where he declares the gospel to be "the power of God unto salvation, \* \* *for* therein is the wrath of God revealed." Note salvation and wrath linked together; *salvation because the wrath* of God is revealed against all sin —*Rom.* i. 16-8—a connection obscured by the arrangement of the text in our translations. Note, too, the teaching of *Rom.* xii. 19-21, which surely implies that true divine

---

†So the Creed, "He shall come to judge the quick and the dead, Whose kingdom shall have no end." Thus judgment leads to the setting up of Christ's universal empire: and so (suggestively) the Judge sits on a *white* throne (sign of amity).—*Rev.* xx. 11.

vengeance is the overcoming evil by good, by kindness: and *Deut.* xxxii., which is there quoted refers to the healing character of God's vengeance, v. 39. Consider next what S. PAUL says of the case of HYMENÆUS and ALEXANDER— 1 *Tim.* i. 20. They had sinned. He thereupon hands *them over to satan.* You can hardly imagine a more desperate state—thrust by Apostolic authority out of God's Church, and handed over to God's enemy, and that after having made shipwreck of their faith. But what follows? It is that they may *learn* not to blaspheme. As an old Father puts it, "Sinners are handed over to the devil. Wherefore? That they may perish eternally? And where then is the mercy of God? Where is the tender Father? What the Apostle says is this, I have handed over sinners to the devil, that, tormented by him, they may be *converted* to Me."—*In Ps.* cviii. 9 *(in* S. JEROME*).* Another equally striking instance is furnished by the case of the incestuous Corinthian. I have judged already * * to deliver such an one unto satan for the destruction of the flesh, that the spirit may be SAVED."—1 *Cor.* v. 3-5. And so, as it has been well put, this wretched Corinthian was delivered *from* the power of the devil, by being delivered *into* the power of the devil. Few more suggestive passages exist in the New Testament. Here is a man delivered by Apostolic authority —in the name of Jesus Christ—to satan, handed over to satan. But mark the object and the result. It is to end not in death but in life—say rather in life attained by means of God's awful judgment. "O mon ame sois tranquille, et attends en paix le jour des vengeances eternelles, c'est le jour de Christ, et ce sont les vengeances de Christ. C'est donc *un jour de salut, et ce sont des vengeances d'amour.*"—G. MONOD, *Le judgment dernier*, p. 28. In this connection, as shewing how the utmost conceivable severity of the divine judgments is consistent with final salvation, I ask you next to remember how S. PAUL tells of Israel that "wrath is come upon them to the uttermost."—*1 Thess.* ii. 16. The wrath of God to the *uttermost*, and yet the same Apostle tells us that *all Israel shall be saved*. Weigh well these words. It is as though God had exhausted all His vials of anger, and left Himself no more that He could do. And even then does all this wrath mean that hope is at an end, that salvation is impossible? It means the very reverse. Salvation to the uttermost (for ALL ISRAEL shall be saved)— is the end of wrath to the uttermost.

Quite as striking, perhaps even more significant, are S. PETER's words, as he tells the story of the preaching of Christ to the spirits in prison. The spirits are specially described as those of the *disobedient* dead. And mark what follows: "For this cause," he adds, "was the gospel preached even to the *dead*, that they might be *judged* according to men in the flesh, but *live* according to God in the spirit," *i.e.*, in order that even those who had died *in sin* might have the benefit of judgment, and so live to God. Here we have (I.) judgment bringing to the sinner not condemnation, but life (II.) salvation by judgment extended beyond this life (III.) extended to those who neglected, while living, the greatest light then available; and *died impenitent*. All this involves a precise contradiction to the common view of the future of the impenitent dead. The thoughtful reader will note further that the "times of restitution of all things" come when Jesus returns, *Acts* iii. 21, but He returns *to judge* the quick and the dead. Let us finally quote, "I saw another angel, having the everlasting gospel to proclaim * * and he said, fear God and give Him glory, for the hour of

His judgment is come."—*Rev.* xiv. 6-7. Note the *everlasting gospel* proclaimed—how? By *God's judgments.*

This view of Judgment is precisely the teaching of antient catholic Fathers, which I shall here give. Take in proof S. JEROME's striking comment on *Zeph.* iii. 8-10.† There, speaking of the Day of Judgment and its terrors, he says: "The nations, even the multitude of the nations, are gathered to the Judgment, but the kings, *i.e.*, the leaders of perverted dogmas are led up for punishment, in order that on them may be poured out *all the wrath of the fury of the Lord.* And this is not done from any cruelty, as the blood-thirsty Jews fancy, but in *pity*, and with a design to *heal* * * For the nations being assembled for judgment, and the kings for punishment, in order that wrath may be poured out on them: not in part but in whole, and, both *wrath and fury being united* (in order that) whatever is earthy may be consumed in the whole world." The object aimed at (and gained) being that (as the passage proceeds) every one may lay aside his error, and every knee bend in Jesus' name. Need I point out the extreme significance of these words? They are unhesitating in their frank recognition of, nay, in the emphasis laid on "*the wrath of the fury of the Lord,*" "*the whole mass both of wrath and fury.*" But this is a means of salvation. The great Day of Wrath that *is to burn like fire*, and to *consume* the adversaries of God, burns up only what is earthy, bringing to every sinner salvation.

Again, we have S. JEROME commenting on *Rom.* i. 18. "Therein is the wrath of God revealed against all ungodliness," "where wrath is revealed it is *not* inflicted; it does not smite, but it is revealed in order that it may terrify, and

---

† S. JEROME adds that it is possible to understand this passage of Christ's first coming, but he evidently adopts the view above given.

may not be inflicted on the terrified."—*In Hab.* iii. Writing on *Micah* vii. 17, he compares the wicked to serpents, who, as they creep over the earth, drag along with them earthly matter. So the wicked, "shall be troubled *so long as the sinful matter clings to them.*" But when (by the judgment) this has been cleared away, they too shall end by fearing God.

Equally forcible and clear is the teaching of S. GREGORY of Nyssa. "Therefore the divine judgment does not * * bring penalty upon those who have sinned, but * * *works good alone* by separating from evil, and drawing to a share in blessedness." In other words, the penalty is the cure—the unavoidable pain attending the removal of the intruding element of sin.—*De an. et Res.* ii. p. 659. And again: If this (sin) be not cured here, its cure is postponed to a future life. As sharp *remedies* for obstinate cases, so God announces His future judgment *for the cure* of the diseases of the soul, and (*note these words*) that judgment is a threat to the frivolous and vain, "in order that, through fear, * * we may be trained to avoiding evil; *but by those who are more intelligent, it* (the judgment) *is believed to be a medicine,*† a *cure* from God, Who is bringing the creature, which He has formed, back to that state of grace which first existed."—*Cat. orat.* ch. viii.

It will be interesting to compare with them the following from S. BASIL: "Fear edifies the *simpler* sort."—*Deus non est auct. mali,* and from DIDYMUS: "For although the judge at times inflicts tortures and anguish on those who merit them, yet he who *more deeply scans* the reasons of things,

---

† S. GREGORY does not mean to deny the terror of the Judgment Day. Hear his words: "*All creation trembles,* who is without fear? —*In verba Fac. hom. Orat.* ii.

perceiving the purpose of His goodness, Who desires to *amend* the sinner, confesses Him to be good."—*De Sp. Sanc.* ch. 44. Again, S. GREGORY says that the wrath of God, which is to swallow up the sinful, is not wrath at all. "In the case of God, His wrath, though to sinners it seems wrath, and is so called by them, is nothing less than wrath (*i.e., is not wrath at all*), but as though (it were) *wrath* comes to those who, according to God's justice, call it a retribution \* \* (but) *God Himself is not really seen in wrath*."—*In Psalmos* i. p. 359. ORIGEN goes quite as far. "When thou hearest of the wrath of God, believe not that this wrath and indignation are passions of God: they are condescensions of language, designed to convert and improve the child. \* \* So God is described as angry, and says that He is indignant, in order that thou mayest convert and be improved, while in fact He is not angry."—*In Jer. Hom.* xviii. 6. So an old commentator on the Psalms (in S. JEROME) says on *Ps.* vii., that God "awaits the day of vengeance with a *quasi-wrath*, in order that He may correct (amend) by fear the sinner." To the same general effect write S. BASIL, p. 120; S. GREGORY of Nazianzus, p. 118; and CLEMENT, p. 107; and S. HILARY, on *Ps.* lxvii. 3-4, who says that the cause of the nations' *joy* arises from "*the hope of eternal judgment*, and of the nations (Gentiles) directed into the way of life." To bring such teaching home, let us suppose one of our Archbishops were to declare that God's Judgment may terrify *simple* souls, but that the *intelligent see its real end to be the cure of sin;* or imagine a very eminent Bishop asserting that *the eternal fire purifies sinners.*

Again, how shallow is the common view of "fire" as only or chiefly a penal agent. "Fire, in Scripture, is the element of 'life' (*Is.* iv. 5), of 'purification' (*Matt.* iii. 3), of 'atonement'

(*Lev.* xvi. 27), of 'transformation' (2 *Peter* iii. 10), and *never of* 'preservation alive' for purposes of anguish." And the popular view selects precisely this latter use, never found in Scripture, and represents it as the *sole* end of God's fiery judgments! If we take either the teaching of Scripture or of nature, we see that the dominant conception of fire is of a beneficent agent. Nature tells us that fire is a necessary condition of life; its mission is to sustain life; and to purify, even when it dissolves. Extinguish the stores of fire in the universe, and you extinguish all being; universal death reigns. Most strikingly is this connection of fire and life shewn in the facts of nutrition. For we actually burn in order to live; our food is the fuel; our bodies are furnaces; our nutrition is a process of combustion; we are, in fact, "aflame to the very tips of our fingers." And so it is that round the *fireside* life and work gather: when we think of home we speak of the family hearth.

And what Nature teaches, Scripture enforces in no doubtful tone. It is significant to find the Great Source of all life constantly associated with fire in the Bible. Fire is the sign, not of God's wrath, but of *His being*. When God comes to EZEKIEL there is a "fire unfolding itself"—ch. i. 4, 27, and "the appearance of fire"—ch. viii. 2. Christ's eyes are a flame of "fire"—*Rev.* i. 14. And seven lamps of "fire" are the seven Spirits of God.—*ib.* iv. 5. So a fiery stream is said "to go before God," His throne is fiery flame, its wheels are burning fire.—*Dan.* vii. 9, 10. His eyes are lamps of fire—*ib.* 10, 6; He is a wall of fire.—*Zech.* ii. 5. At His touch the mountains smoke.—*Ps.* civ. 32. And God's ministers are a flame of fire—*Ps.* civ. 4; *Heb.* i. 7. It is not meant to deny that the divine fire chastises and destroys. It is meant that purification, not ruin, is the *final* outcome of that fire from above, which consumes—call it, if you please, a paradox—in order that it may save. For if God be love, then by what but by love can His fires be kindled? They are, in fact, the very flame of love; and so we have the key to the words, "Thy God is a *consuming fire*," and "Thy God is a *merciful* God."—*Deut.* iv. 24-31. So God *devours the earth with* fire, in order that finally all may call upon the name of the Lord.—*Zeph.* iii. 8-9 (words full of significance). So ISAIAH tells us of God's *cleansing* the daughters of Zion by * * the spirit of burning (ch. iv. 4) —suggestive words. And, so again, "By *fire* will the Lord plead with *all* flesh."—*Is.* lxvi. 16. And Christ coming to save, comes to purify by "fire."—*Mal.* iii. 2.

Let us note, also, how often "fire" is the sign of a favourable answer from God: when God appears to MOSES at the Bush it is in "fire:" God answers GIDEON by "fire;" and DAVID by "fire."—1 *Chron.* xxi. 26. Again, when He answers ELIJAH on Carmel, it is by "fire;" and in "fire" ELIJAH himself ascends to God. So God sends to ELISHA, for aid, chariots and horses of "fire:" So when the Psalmist calls, God answers by "fire."—*Ps.* xviii. 6-8. And by the pillar of "fire" the Israelites were guided through the wilderness, and in "fire" God gave His law. And in "fire" the great gift of the Holy Ghost descends at Pentecost.

These words bring us to the New Testament. There we find that "fire," like judgment, so far from being the sinner's portion only, is the portion of *all*. Like God's judgment again, it is not future merely, but present; it is "*already kindled,*" *i.e.*, always kindled: its object is not torment, but cleansing. The proof comes from the lips of our Lord Himself. "I am come *to send fire on the earth,*" words that in fact convey all I am seeking to teach, for it is certain that

He came as a Saviour. Thus, coming to *save*, Christ comes *with fire*, nay, with fire already kindled. He comes to baptize with the Holy Ghost, and *with fire*. Therefore, it is that Christ teaches in a solemn passage (usually misunderstood, S. *Mark* ix. 43) that *every one* shall be salted with fire. And so the "fire is to try *every man's* work." He whose work fails is saved (mark the word *saved*), *not damned* "so as by fire," for God's fire, by consuming what is evil, saves and refines. The antient tradition that represents Christ as saying, "He that is near Me is near fire," expresses a vital truth. So MALACHI, already quoted, describes Christ as being in His saving work "like a refiner's fire." And so, echoing *Deut.* iv. 24-31, we are told that "*Our* God is a consuming fire," *i.e.*, God in His closest relation to us: God is love: God is spirit: but "*Our* God is a consuming fire" —a consuming fire, "by which the *whole material substance of sin is* destroyed." When, then, we read—*Ps.* xviii. 12-3 that "coals of fire" go before God, we think of the deeds of love which are "coals of fire" to our enemies.—*Rom.* xii. 20. Thus we who teach hope for all men, do not shrink from but accept, *in their fullest meaning*, these mysterious "fires" of gehenna, of which Christ speaks (kindled for purification), as in a special sense the sinner's doom in the coming ages. But taught by the clearest statements of Scripture (confirmed as they are by many analogies of nature), we see in these "fires" not a denial of, but a mode of fulfilling, the promise—"Behold, I *make all things new*."

Abundant quotations might be made from the Fathers in support of the above view. S. AMBROSE, on *Ps.* i., says: The fiery sword at the gate of Paradise shews "that he who returns to it comes back by fire." ORIGEN says, "As bodily diseases require some nauseous drug * * or actual cautery, how much more is it to be understood that God, our Physician * * should employ (for healing) penal measures of this kind, and even the punishment of fire. * * The *fury of God's vengeance* is profitable for the purgation of souls. That the punishment, which is said to be applied by fire, is *applied with the object of healing*, is taught by *Is.* iv. 4."—*De prin.* ii. x. 6. S. JEROME says: "Fire is God's *last medicine* for the ten tribes, and for heretics, and for *all sinners*," that after God has tried death and destruction, and they have not even then repented, "He may consume them as He did Sodom and Gomorrah; that when consumed, and when the divine fire shall have burned up all that is vilest in them, *they themselves shall be delivered* as a brand snatched from the burning."—*In Amos* iv. 11. "Therefore (*i.e.*, to effect a cure) the world which '*lieth in the evil one*' is burned with divine fire in the Day of Judgment, and the bloody city is laid upon coals of fire."†—*In Ezech.* xxiv. "When they perish in fire * * or are destroyed in the fire of their prince the devil, or certainly are burnt in the fire of which the Lord said, 'I am come to send fire on the earth,' and are (thus) *brought back from their former ways and do penance*, the whole earth shall be full of the glory of the Lord."—*In Hab.* ii. 12. Indeed, S. JEROME is full of this teaching, see, *e.g.*, his remarks on *Mal.* iii. 2-3; *Hos.* iv. 13; *Joel* ii. 1; *Amos* vii. 4, &c., &c. "Finally, after tortures and punishments, the *soul brought forth from the outer darkness, and having paid the very last farthing*, says, I shall behold His righteousness. * * Now he who after God's wrath, says that he sees God's righteousness (justification) promises himself the sight of Christ."—

---

† See *Is.* xlvii. 14-5, quoted by many Fathers, where the Septuagint has a remarkable reading—"Thou hast coals of fire, sit upon them, they will be to thee a help."

*In Micah* vii. 8. So the old commentator (in S. JEROME), speaking of God, says, "He is *fire*, that He may expel the devil's cold."—*In Ps.* clxvii. 18. To the same effect much might be quoted from S. GREGORY of Nyssa. The evil man after death will not become "a sharer in the divine nature, till the cleansing fire shall have removed the stains mingled with the soul."—*Orat. de mort.*, ii. p. 1067. And again, "Thus * * the soul which is united to sin must be set in the fire, so that, that which is unnatural and vile * * may be removed, consumed by the *eternal fire*."—*De an. et Res.* ii. p. 658. Here the *eternal fire* cleanses.

There remains for our consideration a very important class of passages, supposed, erroneously, to favour the popular creed. These passages are those that speak of the "elect," and their fewness; of the "many" called, but the "few" chosen. That God's election is a doctrine clearly revealed in Scripture, no impartial reader can doubt: although unfortunately, around few subjects has the battle of controversy been so furiously waged. One party has, in affirming God's election—which is true, so affirmed it as to make Him into an arbitrary and cruel tyrant—which is false. But the truer and deeper views of God's plan of mercy through Jesus Christ—now in the ascendant I trust—teach us to affirm distinctly the doctrine of the divine election of "the few:" and just because we so affirm it, to connect with it purposes of *universal* mercy. For what is the true end and meaning of God's election? The elect, we reply, are chosen, not for themselves only, but for the sake of others. They are "elect," not merely to be blessed, but to be a source of blessing. It is not merely with the paltry object of saving a few, while the vast majority perish, that God elects; it is with a purpose of mercy to all; it is by "the few" to save "the many;" by the elect to save the world. "If you go to Scripture," says Dr. Cox, "you will find this its constant teaching. Even in those early days when one man, one family, one nation, were successively chosen, to be the depositories of divine truth, when, therefore, if ever we might expect to find the redemptive purpose of God disclosed within narrow and local limitations; when unquestionably it was much fettered and restrained by personal promises, and by national and temporary institutions; the divine purpose is for ever overstepping every limit, every transient localisation and restraint, and claiming as its proper share, all the souls that are and shall be."—*Salvat. Mund.* This admits of easy proof. Take a typical case to shew what God's election really means. Take the case of ABRAHAM, the father and founder of God's elect people. What was the promise to him? 'That in his seed should *all the families of the earth* be blessed.' This was of the essence of God's election. And to this effect S. PAUL speaks with perfect clearness. And thoughtful readers will remark that it is precisely the Apostle who lays most stress on the divine sovereignty, who most clearly teaches universal reconciliation. The promise to ABRAHAM was, S. PAUL tells us, that he should be the heir of the *world, Rom.* iv. 13; words most expressive, and yet without meaning on the common view of election. In other words the Jews, as God's elect, have, as their inheritance, all lands, all peoples. In the same Epistle S. PAUL points out how close the connection is between Israel and the world. Three times over he asserts their very fall to be the riches of the world, and asks if so, what will not the reconciling of Israel be (to the world). In short, on God's elect people hangs the lot and destiny of mankind—see *Gal.* iii. 8, and *Acts* iii. 21-5; the latter passage is very interesting, for S. PETER there asserts the connection between an *universal* restoration, and the promise to ABRAHAM, *i.e.*, his election. A further admirable illustration of this may be given (furnished by Holy Scripture) from its teaching as to the "firstfruits," and as to the "firstborn." Israel, as God's elect, is the "firstfruits"— Israel the "firstborn." But the "firstfruits" imply and pledge the *whole* harvest; the "firstborn" involve and include, in the divine economy, the *whole* family. Hence the promise that "all Israel shall be saved" implies the world's salvation. "The firstborn and firstfruits are the 'few' and the 'little flock;' but these, although 'first delivered from the curse,' have *relation to the whole creation*, which shall be saved in the appointed times by the firstborn seed, that is by Christ and His body."—JUKES. It is thus clear that we, so far from denying the election of the *few*, lay stress on it as *essential* to God's plan of mercy for all. It becomes indeed a corner stone, so to speak, in the edifice of the world's salvation; for His "elect" are the very means by which our Father designs to bless all His children— designs to work out His plan of universal salvation. "The sovereignty by which God reigneth is eternal love."— P. STERRY, *Rise, Race*, &c. "The Lord is King, the earth may be *glad* thereof."—*Ps.* xcvii. 1.

A few closing remarks are needed here, to indicate the principle that is really at stake in these questions. For that principle is vital, and fundamental. It is no less than the Unity of the Godhead; no less than the first article of the Creed, "I believe in *one* God the Father Almighty"—in God Who is ONE, not in nature alone, but in purpose and in will—One and Unchanging. But in place of this God, the popular creed presents us with a Being Who fluctuates between tenderness and wrath,* One Who has ever-changing plans, and a will that is divided, and baffled. For half His creatures His love is in fact momentary, and His vengeance endless. For the other half, His pity is endless, and His wrath transient. "The God we have preached has not been the God Who was manifested in His Son Jesus Christ, but another altogether different Being, in Whom we mingle strangely the Siva and the Vishnu."—F. D. MAURICE. This God is not even Lord in His own house; for the worst and feeblest of His creatures can finally defeat His most cherished plan; can paralyse the Cross of Christ. In such a God I cannot see Him, Who is Almighty and unchanging, Whose property is *always* to have mercy; Whose love, though always punishing sin, never ceases to help the sinner, for "love never faileth;" *never* to all eternity. Against the popular caricature of God, this chapter is thus a special protest—that caricature which represents eternal love as turning to hate, as soon as the sinner dies; which vainly talks of an Eternal Father, Whose judgments mean salvation in one world, and change to damnation in the next; of eternal love, whose fire purifies and refines in time, and then beyond the grave turns to mere (purposeless) torture. What wonder if unbelief abounds, when we invite it by such teaching?

Against this mass of contradiction stands the view here given of "Death," "Judgment," "Fire," "Election." The old truths remain on a basis firmer than before, in harmony and no more in conflict, because they rest ultimately on the Unity of God—unity of essence and unity of purpose. God's essential unity is destroyed when we assign to Him conflicting actions, as though his Love demanded one course

---

* Thoughtful readers may consider how far anger and resentment can be *strictly* predicated of God, Who changes not.

of action, and His Justice another; as though God the Saviour were one person, and God the Judge a wholly different one. Or, again, when we blindly teach that, if His judgments now mean salvation, they at the Great Day mean endless damnation. God, I repeat, in His "judgments," in His "fires," in "death,"* in "election;" God in time and in eternity is ONE and the same God (*Heb.* xiii. 8), and has, and must have to all eternity, but one unchanging purpose —is and must be for ever God our Saviour. The divine Unity is no merely abstract question: it reveals God's essence and character; it is rooted not in the laws of number, but of spirit and will. When ZECHARIAH says, "The Lord shall be king over all the earth," he adds, "in that day shall the Lord be ONE, and His name ONE." And S. PAUL, in declaring that God "will have all men to be saved," bases this not on God's love but on His unity, "for there is ONE GOD," He Who is One in All, and All in One, Who will finally bring back His entire creation to that unity from which it started. Thus, elsewhere, S. PAUL contrasts the unconditional unchanging promises of God in the Gospel with the Law, by laying emphasis on this divine unity—"For God is ONE."—*Gal.* iii. 20. (See LIGHTFOOT *in loco.*) To sever God's action into love and harshness is, says S. GREGORY of Nyssa, but madness, *nay*, "*the madness of babblers!*" At the bare idea that God can be really hard or cruel to His enemies (see note on *S. Luke* vi. 27, ch. viii.), and loving to His friends, he exclaims with a scorn (most rare in his writings)—"Oh, the madness of these babblers! for if God is unmerciful to His foes, He will not be truly kind even to thee His friend."—*De orat.* 1.

---

\* The remarks on death, p. 188, lines 3 and 4, should be compared with what is said, p. 22.

# CHAPTER VII.

## *WHAT THE OLD TESTAMENT TEACHES.*

"From the time at which this great and far-reaching promise or gospel was given to ABRAHAM, the universal scope of the divine Redemption is insisted on with growing emphasis, even in those Hebrew Scriptures, which we too often assume to be animated only by a local and national spirit."—*Salvator Mundi.*

"The whole history of the world is the uninterrupted carrying through of a divine plan of salvation, the primary object of which is His people: in and with them however *also the whole of humanity.*"—*Delitzsch on Ps.* xxxiii. 11.

FROM the Church I turn next to the Old Testament. There we shall find abundant, perhaps to many readers, unexpected confirmation of the larger hope, though I can merely attempt to give an outline of its teaching. True, in the Old Testament, the promises are, it may be said, mainly temporal; but still we have unmistakable evidence of a plan of mercy revealed in its pages, and destined to embrace all men. Nor need this interpretation of the older volume of God's word rest on mere conjecture: let me call as a witness, no less a person than the Apostle S. PETER. The Apostle in one of the very earliest of his addresses, *Acts* iii. 21, takes occasion to explain the real purpose of God in Jesus Christ There is to come, finally, a time of universal restoration, "restitution of *all* things." He adds the significant words that God has promised this "by the mouth of all His holy prophets since the world began;" and, therefore, we who teach this hope are but following in the steps of all God's holy prophets. Thus S. PETER would have us go to the

Old Testament, and weave, as it were, its varied predictions into one concordant whole, till they, with one voice, proclaim the "restitution of all things."

Of the Gospel of Creation I have already spoken: here it is enough to note that, in the divine act which stamps upon man the Image and Likeness of God, we have the Gospel in germ. Thus the opening chapters of Genesis "give to us the largest views of the loving sovereignty of God; and of the divine origin, and destiny of mankind."—WESTCOTT, *Rev. of the Father*. In this great fact, that mankind comes from God, and returns unto (or into) God—*Rom.* xi. 36, and in the divine plan to insure this return, lies the centre of unity of the Bible,—the point to which its "many parts" and "many modes" (*Heb.* i. 1) converge.

Thus we see the true meaning of the Jewish economy—"Its work was for humanity, the idea of Judaism is seen not in the covenant from Sinai, but in the covenant with ABRAHAM."—*ib.*

I have not space to consider minutely the promises of blessing to all men contained in the Old Testament, though they can be traced almost everywhere. At the very moment of the Fall\* is given a promise, that the serpent's head shall be bruised, intimating a complete overthrow. Two points are very significant here. The promise is not of the serpent's wounding only, but of such a wound as involves his destruction; and next the promise is conveyed in close connection with a terrible judgment; it is part of the sentence, it

---

\* Here I may note that even those who take extreme views of future punishment seem to agree in the belief that ADAM and EVE found mercy. But, if so, it may well be asked—shall they who were the authors of the Fall, and all its woe, escape; shall they who, created upright, fall—yet find mercy at the last, while so many involuntary inheritors of a fallen nature are doomed?

is embedded, so to speak, in it. Passing on, we find that with the promise to ABRAHAM was blended an intimation of blessing to the race of man. And this intimation of a world-wide blessing, as has been often pointed out, grows more frequent as the stream of Revelation flows on. We find that in the Law, the Psalms, and the Prophets, are traces, clear and distinct, of universal blessing. Thus of the teaching of the Law a fundamental part rested on the institution of the "firstfruits" and the "firstborn." Elsewhere in this volume has been pointed out the extreme significance of this as bearing on the larger hope, and as fulfilled in Jesus Christ. As the "firstfruits" pledge the whole harvest, and the "firstborn" the whole family, so are the elect people, *i.e.*, God's "firstborn" ("Israel is my son, my firstborn"), a pledge that all are God's, that all are destined to share His blessing (to this the whole story of the Jewish race, when rightly viewed, bears witness; as "firstfruits" they are the channels of blessing to all mankind). Hence it is that we have the repeated promises to ABRAHAM, that "in his seed should all the families of the earth be blessed." Thus the Jewish patriarch becomes in the apostle's striking phrase, "heir of the world," and no less. This principle, by which the elect become a means of blessing to all the rest, is strikingly affirmed in the Jewish law. A sheaf of the "firstfruits" was to be presented to the Lord as pledging and consecrating the whole harvest. (*Lev.* xxiii. 10 and 11.) All the "firstborn" of the herds and flocks were the Lord's (*Deut.* xv. 19), as a pledge that all were His. So were the "firstborn" of their sons. (*Ex.* xxii. 29.) If now we turn to the New Testament, we learn the essential bearing of all this on Christ's kingdom. First the Apostle assures us that if the "firstfruits" be holy, *the* *lump is also holy.* (*Rom.* xi. 16.) Next he asserts that not Israel only, but in a higher sense Christ is the "firstfruits." (1 *Cor.* xv. 23.) And the context implies that Christ conveys, actually imparts, life to *all* as did ADAM death to *all*. And as Israel was the "firstborn" son (*Ex.* iv. 22), so in a sense far higher is Christ the "firstborn" of *every* creature (*Col.* i. 15-20), (the head of *every man,* 1 *Cor.* xi. 3.) Here, too, the context involves the reconciliation through the "first born," Christ, of *every creature* to God. We have thus a double "firstfruits," *i.e.*, Christ, the true "firstfruits," and His people, "a kind of firstfruits." (*James* i. 18.) Christ the "firstborn" (*Col.* i. 18), and again His people (His elect) the "Church of the firstborn." (*Heb.* xii. 23) Now it is very striking to find all this exactly prefigured in the Law; for it speaks of a *double firstfruits;* one which was offered at the Passover, and *on the very day on which Christ rose,* on "the morrow after the Sabbath" (*Lev.* xxiii. 10, 11); the other also distinctly called "firstfruits," (though distinguished by a separate name) which was offered fifty days later at Pentecost.* (*Lev.* xxiii. 17.) Thus does even the Law contain intimations of universal blessing to accrue to all men.

Let us pass on to the Psalter and there also trace this promise of the restitution of all things; for the Psalmists, too, are God's prophets, and are full of the largest forecasts. "When they speak of the coming Messiah, they are at the farthest from claiming the blessings of His reign exclusively for themselves; on the contrary, they say, ' His name shall endure for ever: His name shall be continued as long as the sun; and men shall be blessed in Him; *all* nations shall call Him blessed'" * * "They constantly breathe forth the invitation, 'O praise the Lord *all* ye nations; praise

---

* See for fuller details JUKES' "Restitution of all things," p. 35-37.

Him *all* ye people.'"—*Salv. Mundi.* Other examples of the same address to all nations—to all peoples—bidding them join in God's praise, and surely anticipating that they would one day do so, are frequent in the Psalms. Take, for example, those our Prayer Book has made familiar, *e.g.*, *Cantate Domino.*—*Ps.* xcviii. In it *all* lands are bidden to shew themselves joyful unto the Lord. To the same effect is the familiar clause of the *Jubilate, Ps.* c., "O be joyful in the Lord all *ye* lands." To shew how deeply this idea is embedded in the *Psalter*, let me add a few passages here. "Praise the Lord all ye nations."—*Ps.* cxvii. 1. "Unto Thee shall *all* flesh come."—*Ps.* lxv. 2. "Thou shalt inherit *all* the nations."—*Ps.* lxxxii. 8. "*All* nations shall come and worship Thee."—*Ps.* lxxxvi. 9. "*All* the earth shall worship Thee."—*Ps.* lxvi. 4. "Sing unto the Lord *all the whole earth.*"—*Ps.* xcvi. 1. And so we read, "*All* nations shall do Him service * * *All* the heathen shall praise Him, *All* the earth shall be filled with His Majesty."—*Ps.* lxxii. 11-19. "Let *all* flesh give thanks unto His holy name, for ever and ever."—*Ps.* cxlv. 21. So again, "Praise the Lord ye kings of the earth and *all* people."—*Ps.* cxlviii. 11. "Bless the Lord *all* ye His works."—*Ps.* ciii. 22. "Let *all* the people praise Thee."—*Ps.* lxvii. 3-5. "*All* the ends of the world shall fear Him."—*ib.* 7. "*All* the ends of the world shall remember and turn unto the Lord, and *all* the kindreds of the nations shall worship before Thee."—*Ps.* xxii. 27. This text has a special significance on account of the close connection of this Psalm with the Atonement; as a result of which all the ends of the world shall turn, as it predicts, unto the Lord. Surely all this constitutes a remarkable array of evidence for the complete universality of Christ's kingdom. Can any fair mind accept the traditional creed as a satisfactory explanation of these passages. Here, as ever, men have delighted to narrow the breadth of the divine purpose, and dwarf its proportions. But would these promises, world-wide in their range, be fairly met, by saying that out of all the countless generations of man, only those, yet unborn, shall indeed fully learn to know God? It is impossible so to think; impossible not to see here a foreshadowing of those times of "restitution of *all things*"—which must come if the Bible speaks truly. In this universal hope is to be found the true spirit of the Psalms, in these invitations addressed, not to Israel, but to all nations—nay, to whatsoever exists. Note how, as the Psalter draws to its end, the tone of triumph rises, expands, broadens into the very widest anticipations of universal blessedness (*Ps.* cxlviii.-cl.). In this spirit it closes, "LET EVERYTHING THAT HATH BREATH, praise the Lord."—*Ps.* cl. 6.

Of the greater Prophets the same is true; though I need not speak in detail of them. From amid their varied contents, at times break forth promises of the widest, amplest hope; anticipations of a time of universal bliss and joy; of a world in which all pain and sorrow shall have passed away. But these passages are in the main familiar to you, and I need hardly quote them. They have found their way to the heart of christendom, and have stamped themselves on its literature. "Take, however, only this one sentence from the evangelical prophet, and take it mainly because S. PAUL echoes it back, and interprets it as he echoes it. It is Jehovah Who speaks these words by the mouth of ISAIAH : 'Look unto Me and be ye saved, all ye ends of the earth : for I am God and there is none other : I have sworn by Myself and the word is gone out of My mouth in righteousness and shall not return, that unto Me every knee shall bow and every tongue confess.' Could any words more emphatically declare it to be the divine purpose that the *whole earth*, to the very end of it shall be saved; that every knee shall bend in homage before God, and every tongue take the oath of fealty to Him? Are we not expressly told that this declaration, since it has come from the righteous mouth of God, cannot return unto Him void, but must accomplish its object; that object being the salvation of the human race? S. PAUL echoes this great word (in *Rom.* xiv. 11,) and again in the epistle to the Philippians, and though on his lips it gains definiteness and precision, assuredly it loses no jot or tittle of its breadth: he affirms, *Phil.* ii. 9-11, 'that God hath highly exalted Him, and given Him a name which is above every name, in order that at the name of Jesus every knee shall bow;' not only every knee of man—for now the promise grows incalculably wider—but every knee in heaven and on earth, and under the earth: 'and that every tongue shall confess that Jesus Christ is Lord, to the glory of God the Father.' It is hard to understand ISAIAH as proclaiming less than an universal redemption, but if S. PAUL did not mean to proclaim a redemption as wide as the universe, what use or force is there in words?" —*Salvator Mundi.*

On one passage I must briefly dwell. "He shall see of the travail of his soul, and be SATISFIED."—*Is.* liii. 2. By what ingenuity can hopeless, endless evil be reconciled with these words? How can I accept a creed that asks me to believe that Christ is satisfied, while His own children are given over to endless ruin. Who believes this of Jesus Christ? Who can believe Him "satisfied" with the final and utter ruin of any one soul for whom He died?— "satisfied" that His cross should fail?—"satisfied" with the victory of evil, in so much as a solitary case?

And remember how full are the Prophets, and the Psalms no less, of pictures of the vastness of the divine mercy, of His tenderness that never fails. Even from amid the sadness of the *Lamentations*, we hear a voice assuring us that "the Lord will *not cast off for ever*, but though He cause grief, yet will He have compassion according to the multitude of His mercies."—*Lam.* iii. 31. Or take these words, "I will not contend for ever, neither will I be *always wroth*, for the spirit should fail before Me, and the souls which I have made."—*Is.* lvii. 16. This idea is a favourite one; the contrast between the short duration of God's anger, and the enduring *endless character of His love*. "So in a little wrath I hid My face from thee for a moment; but with *everlasting* kindness will I have mercy on thee, saith the Lord Thy Redeemer."—*Is.* liv. 8. Let us pause here for a moment to dwell on the significance of this fact of the limited duration of the divine anger, so clearly taught in the Old Testament. Take a few instances, "I am merciful, saith the Lord, I will not keep anger for ever."—*Jer.* iii. 12. "His anger endureth but a moment."—*Ps.* xxx. 5. "While His mercy endureth for ever,"—*Ps.* cxxxvi.—a statement repeated no less than twenty-six times in this one Psalm. "He will not always chide, neither keepeth He His anger for ever."— *Ps.* ciii. 9. "He retaineth not His anger for ever, because He delighteth in mercy."—*Mic.* vii. 18. But if this be true, *what becomes of the popular creed?* If God's anger is temporary, how can it be endless? If it endure but a moment, how can it last for ever in even a solitary instance? I would invite our opponents fairly to face these plain and reiterated assertions: and to explain why they feel justified in teaching that God's anger will in many cases last for ever, and that His mercy will not endure for ever.

I may in passing ask attention to two passages in the Book of Daniel. In one, ch. vii. 14, a dominion absolutely universal is promised to the Son of Man, words which may be compared with the numerous passages to the same effect quoted in the next chapter. In the other, ch. ix. 24, a promise is made of a decree to finish transgression, and to *make an end of sins.*

We have spoken of the pictures of universal blessedness that are to be found in the greater prophets, "perhaps," says the author already quoted, "some of you may not be equally familiar with the fact that these same pictures are also to be found in the minor prophets;" (a fact very suggestive) that "every one of these brief poems, or collections of poems, has its tiny Apocalypse. And mark this point well, while each of the minor prophets sees the vision of a whole world redeemed to the love and service of righteousness, this vision of redemption is invariably accompanied by a *vision of judgment*"—(see ch. vi. on judgment.) At least, if not all, yet very many of the minor prophets do predict the coming of a time of universal redemption. So HOSEA xiii. 14, exclaims, "O death, I will be thy plagues. O grave, I will be thy destruction."—(See 1 *Cor.* xv. 55.) So JOEL ii. 28, tells of the spirit as being poured upon *all* flesh. HABAKKUK can look beyond the terrors of judgment and see the "*earth filled with the knowledge of the glory of the Lord, as the waters cover the sea.*"—ch. ii. 14. Is not this wonderful? Can you not enter into S. PETER's words as he stood forth, while yet christianity was scarcely born, to proclaim as its glorious aim and scope, the universal restoration—the paradise of God regained for mankind—all things made new.— *Acts* iii. 21.

But I resume. In ZEPHANIAH we read the same glorious

prospect, the same universal hope. He speaks of God's judgments as being terrible to the nations, in order that "men may worship Him, *every one* from his place, even *all the isles of the heathen.*"—ch. ii. 11. And again, in the same prophet, we are told how God is to send His fiery judgments to purify men, "that they may *all* call upon the name of the Lord to serve Him with one consent" (ch. iii. 8-9). So MALACHI closes the prophetic line with an intimation indeed of judgment—of a refining fire—but together with this is the prospect unfolded, that from the "*rising of the sun unto the going down of the same,* God's name shall be great among the Gentiles, and in *every* place incense and pure offerings shall be offered to Him."—ch. i. 11. The words that introduce this prospect "from the rising up of the sun unto the going down of the same," may well recall the beautiful and suggestive phrase of *Zech.* xiv. 7, "At evening time it shall be light."

Brief as the above survey has been, it has, I trust, served to indicate how, even through all the Old Testament, the thread of *universal* hope runs : how the Law, Prophets and Psalmists of Israel did foreshadow a coming age, when sin should be no more, and sorrow and sighing should flee away for ever. To the New Testament I propose to devote an examination more in detail, as its great importance demands, in the next chapter.

## CHAPTER VIII.

### *WHAT THE NEW TESTAMENT TEACHES.*

"And here I may briefly say, that to my own mind, the language of the New Testament appears *unequivocally to affirm the redemption of all men;* their actual redemption from this evil and diseased state in which we now are; the actual raising up of all to a perfect life. To my mind this *universality* seems to be clearly expressed in Scripture."—HINTON, *The Mystery of Pain.*

WE now turn to an examination of the very many passages in the New Testament which clearly declare, or imply, the salvation of all men: how numerous these are we shall see. The time has fully come for appealing with all boldness on behalf of the larger hope, alike to the letter and the spirit of the New Testament. One thing only I ask, which common fairness and honesty require, that our Lord and His Evangelists and Apostles may be understood to *mean what they say*. Thus, to take a few instances out of many: when they speak of all men I assume them to mean all men, and not some men; when they speak of all things I assume them to mean all things; when they speak of life and salvation as given to the world, I assume them to mean given, and not merely offered; when they speak of the destruction of death, of the devil, of the works of the devil, I assume them to mean that these shall be destroyed and not preserved for ever in hell; when they tell us that the whole of Creation suffers but that it shall be delivered, I assume that they mean an actual deliverance of all created things; when they tell us that Redemption is wider, broader, and stronger than the Fall, I assume that they mean to tell us at least this, that all the evil caused by the Fall shall be swept away; when they describe Christ's empire as extending over all things and all creatures, and tell us that every tongue must join in homage to Him, I assume them to mean what these words convey in their ordinary sense; if I did not, should I not, in fact, be making God a liar?

What does the traditional creed require? It practically requires a MUTILATED BIBLE. And more than this. It bids us expunge precisely that which is noblest and divinest in Holy Scripture. I have no desire to ignore "the Terrors of the Lord"—(see next chapter.) They deserve and shall have full recognition. But I insist, that those teachers misread Holy Scripture who forget, that its essential purpose is to unfold His name, Who is "our Father," and to proclaim His full victory, in the extinction of all evil, and not in its perpetuation in hell. I protest against teaching that "All" means in scriptural phrase absolutely "All" when some evil is foretold, but that "All" means only "some" when spoken of final salvation. So rooted is this most inequitable mode of interpretation, that it has become involuntary. The restitution of all things means, we are told, that only some beings are to be restored, while some are tortured for ever, or annihilated. That God shall be finally "All in All" means that He will shut up many for ever in endless evil, to blaspheme and hate Him eternally, and only save the rest. That His tender mercies are over all His works means, in the ordinary creed, that His tender mercies expire at the gates of hell. Solemn as is the question, there is something almost ludicrous, when we find those who so teach, then turning round to charge us with evading the words of Scripture.

I submit that the entire history of exegesis contains no stranger fact than this persistent ignoring of so large a part of the New Testament. To bring this out clearly, I append the following chain of passages from a long series, clearly and closely linked together, claiming for Christ a saving empire co-extensive with the race, or (perhaps) rather with the whole universe. This connection is clearly marked, for each passage suggests or contains, the same central idea; and thus forms a link in a continuous chain. This chain commences at Creation, when all things were created by Christ, Who, therefore, as S. PAUL implies, reconciles (in fact, re-creates) *all* things unto God.—*Col.* i. 16-20. Hence His work is the restitution of *all* things—*Acts* iii. 21; He is Heir of *all* things—*Heb.* i. 2; in Him *all* nations are to be blessed—*Gal.* iii. 8; for the Father has given Him authority over *all* flesh, to give to *whatsoever* was given to Him eternal life—*S. Jno.* xvii. 2 (see original); and so *all* flesh shall see the salvation of God—*S. Luke* iii. 6. For God, Whose counsel is immutable—*Heb.* vi. 17, Whose attitude towards His enemies is love unchanging—*S. Luke* vi. 27-35, will have *all* men to be saved—1 *Tim.* ii. 4; and *all* to come to repentance—2 *Pet.* iii. 9; and has shut *all* up unto unbelief, in order that He may shew mercy upon *all*—*Rom.* ix. 31; for (out) of Him, as Source, and unto (or into) Him, as End, are all things whatsoever—*Rom.* xi. 36; and He has, therefore, put *all* things in subjection under Christ's feet.—*Eph.* i. 22. And so we are assured that God will gather into one *all* things in Christ—*Eph.* i. 10; and His grace comes upon *all* men unto justification of life—*Rom.* v. 18. So Jesus, knowing that the Father had given *all* things into His hands—*S. Jno.* xiii. 3, promises by His Cross to draw *all* men unto Himself.—*S. Jno.* xii. 32. For having, as stated, received *all* things from the Father—*S. Jno.* iii. 35, *all* that was given comes to Him; and He loses none—*S. Jno.* vi. 37-9; but if any stray, goes after that which is lost *till He find it*—*S. Luke* xv. 4; and so makes *all* things new.—*Rev.* xxi. 5.

And thus He comes in order that *all* men may believe—*S. Jno.* i. 17—that the *world*, through Him, may be saved—*S. Jno.* iii. 17; His grace brings salvation to *all* men—*Tit.* ii. 11; for He takes away the sin of the *world*—*S. Jno.* i. 29; gives His flesh for its life—*S. Jno.* vi. 51; and, because the gifts and callling of God are without repentance (are irrevocable)—*Rom.* ix. 29, He *gives* life to the *world*—*S. Jno.* vi. 33; is the Light of the *world*—*S. Jno.* viii. 12; is the propitiation for the sins of the *whole world*—1 *S. Jno.* ii. 2; is the Saviour of *all* men—1 *Tim.* iv. 10; *destroys* the works of the devil, not some of them only—1 *Jno.* iii. 8; and the devil himself—*Heb.* ii. 14; *abolishes* death—2 *Tim.* i. 10; is manifested to put away sin—*Heb.* ix. 26; and thus subduing *all* things unto Himself—*Phil.* iii. 21; (the context clearly shews this subjugation to be *conformity* to Himself) does not forget the *dead*, but takes the gospel to hades—1 *Pet.* iii. 19; of which He holds the keys—*Rev.* i. 18; for He is the *same* (Saviour) for ever—*Heb.* xiii. 8; thus even the *dead* are evangelised—1 *Pet.* iv. 6; and death and hades destroyed.—*Rev.* xx. 14. Thus *all* are made alive in Him—1 *Cor.* xv. 22; for Christ finishes, completes His work—*S. Jno.* xvii. 4; xix. 30: restores *all* things—*Acts* iii. 21; and there is no more curse—*Rev.* xxii. 2-3; but *every* knee of things in heaven and earth, and under the earth, bends to Him—*Phil.* iii. 10; for the *creation* is delivered from the bondage of corruption—*Rom.* viii. 21; and *every creature* joins in the song of praise—*Rev.* v. 13, and so comes the

END when He delivers up the Kingdom to God, Who is then ALL IN ALL.—1 *Cor.* xv. 24-8.

These passages are, I repeat, not taken at random and piled up anyhow. They are the expression of that Purpose which runs through the Bible, a Purpose first stated in man's creation *in God's image*, a Purpose to be traced in the Law, the Psalms and Prophets, and most clearly in the New Testament. From it we learn, that (I.) Christ came, claiming as His own the entire human race, to the end that He might save and restore *the whole*, and not any fraction of it, however large. (II.) He came with full power "over all flesh," having received "all power in heaven and on earth" over all hearts, all evil, all wills. (III.) He lived and died, and rose again victorious in the fullest sense, "having FINISHED His work," as He expressly claims.

Thus to deny the absolute universality of Christ's redeeming sway,[*] as destined to embrace ALL SOULS AND ALL THINGS WHATSOEVER, seems no less than to withdraw from the New Testament an *essential* and *vital* part of its teaching. For here we are not dealing with some few passages, in which it might be possible to say that "*all*" was used in a lax sense; we have a connected series in which link follows link; a series in which the actual, not the potential, universality of Christ's kingdom is the central and essential thought. Let us now consider a little more in detail, the passages themselves, taking them in their natural and fair meaning, not obscured by any traditional gloss.

"FOR THE SON OF MAN IS COME TO SAVE THAT WHICH WAS LOST."
*S. Matt.* xviii. 11.

Here the question is simply this, will Jesus Christ really do what He has come to do? or will He *fail?*—as the

---

[*] See a tract on Redemption, Its true extent. J. Wright & Co., Bristol, 4d.

traditional creed in spite of all denials indubitably teaches. Will He save *that which was lost* and not *some of the lost merely, a totally different thing?* How can "that which was lost" be saved, if any soul be finally lost?

"IN THE REGENERATION."—(PALINGENESIA)  S. Matt. xix. 28.

This passage, too often passed over, seems certainly to promise that new creation of all things, in which Christ, Who first made, is one day to re-make all things; *cf. Col.* i. 15-20; *Heb.* i. 2. The thoughtful will notice (see context) the connection of restoration and judgment.

"ALL FLESH SHALL SEE THE SALVATION OF GOD."  S. Luke iii. 5.

Quoted from ISAIAH ch. xl. 5, "The seeing is twofold, as appears from the sequel (see ch. lx.). It is (I.) the natural sight of Jehovah's glorious deeds on behalf of His people; and (II.) the spiritual recognition of Jehovah as the Lord." —CHEYNE. Surely, then, these words point in the direction of a salvation which shall be quite universal, "for without holiness no man shall see the Lord."—*Heb.* xii. 14. "The pure in heart shall see God."—*S. Matt.* v. 8.

"BUT I SAY UNTO YOU LOVE YOUR ENEMIES, DO GOOD TO THEM WHICH HATE YOU * * AND YE SHALL BE THE CHILDREN OF THE HIGHEST."  S. Luke vi. 27-35.

"But I say, 'LOVE YOUR ENEMIES.'" Will the advocates of endless penalty frankly tell us how that can be reconciled with the letter, or the spirit, of this text? Will they explain why God commands us to love our enemies, when He consigns His own enemies to an endless hell; and why He bids us to do good to those who hate us, when He means for ever to punish and do evil to those who hate Him?

"BUT WHEN A STRONGER THAN HE SHALL COME UPON HIM AND OVERCOME HIM, HE TAKETH FROM HIM ALL HIS ARMOUR, WHEREIN HE TRUSTED AND DIVIDETH HIS SPOILS."
S. Luke xi. 22; S. Matt. xii. 29.

Here it is asserted (*a*) that Christ is stronger than satan, (*b*) that Christ will overcome satan, (*c*) will take from him all his armour, (*d*) will divide, *i.e.*, take away his spoils. Each of these statements contradicts the popular creed, for that teaches (*a*) that evil is stronger than good, (*b*) that it overcomes good in numberless cases, (*c*) that satan's power for evil is not taken away, but lasts for ever, (*d*) that his spoils —the souls he has captured—are not divided, *i.e.*, taken from him. And observe our Lord's victory over the powers of evil does not consist in shutting up any of their captives in hell, but in liberating all.

"WHAT MAN OF YOU HAVING AN HUNDRED SHEEP * * IF HE LOSE ONE OF THEM, DOTH NOT LEAVE THE NINETY AND NINE * * AND GO AFTER THAT WHICH IS LOST UNTIL HE FIND IT?"
*S. Luke* xv. 4.

Antient commentators follow two main lines, (I.) the hundred sheep are all men ; (II.) are all spiritual creatures : in the former case the wicked are the strayed sheep: in the latter mankind itself, which by the Fall has strayed from the heavenly fold. Both views seem to involve universalism. For in the one all the wicked, in the other all humanity, are sought till they are found. Any narrowing of the "sheep" to the elect, is quite alien from the whole spirit of this parable, which was *specially* addressed to the publican and the sinner. See how broadly Christ bases His argument, "what man of you," He asks, "would not do this?" Observe the immense significance of Christ's teaching. It expressly sanctions the right to argue from those feelings of humanity, shared even by the outcast and sinful, to the divine feelings. (pp. 11, 14-6.) Note, too, the ground taken—*the divine loss.* It is not the man who loses his soul, *it is God Who loses the man ;* (a fact ignored—with much else—in popular teaching.)

> "WHAT WOMAN HAVING TEN PIECES OF SILVER, IF SHE LOSE ONE PIECE, DOTH NOT * * SEEK DILIGENTLY TILL SHE FIND IT?"
> *S. Luke* xv. 8.

Here is precisely the same broad human basis, and the same broad hopeful teaching. Keep steadily in view these facts taught here: (I.)—Our own feelings of love and pity are a safe guide to God's feelings; on these very feelings Christ expressly builds, asking, "what man of you?" (II.)—Every lost soul *is God's loss*, Who, therefore, seeks its recovery; and (III.)—will seek *till He find it*. (IV.)—The whole of the loss is repaired. (V.) If God feel the loss of man, He will *always* feel it. Hence, if sin be endless, the divine Passion must surely be endless too.

> "FOR THE SON OF MAN IS COME TO SEEK AND TO SAVE THAT WHICH WAS LOST." *S. Luke* xix. 10.

If so, I gather from His own parables, and His essential nature, that so long as *anything is lost*, Jesus Christ will go on seeking and saving; for is He not always the same? (*Heb.* xiii. 8.) "The lost" are His charge, and not some of the lost, a very different thing. Or are we to read this verse thus: "He came indeed to save 'the lost'—but those in the fullest sense 'lost' He will never save?"

> "THE SAME CAME * * THAT ALL MEN THROUGH HIM (CHRIST) MIGHT BELIEVE." *S. John* i. 7.

Yes, that *all* men might believe, that is indeed the divine purpose—the purpose of Him Who sent the Baptist. But dare we say, that what God purposes, He will fail to do? I read distinctly of the *immutability* of His counsel (*Heb.* vi. 17). Am I to believe that the immutable purpose of the Almighty and unchanging God shall finally come to nothing?

> "BEHOLD THE LAMB OF GOD, WHICH TAKETH AWAY THE SIN OF THE WORLD." *S. John* i. 29.

Here is the extent of the work of Christ set forth. It is

the world's sin, and not less, that He takes away. But, if it is *taken away*, how can there be an endless hell for its punishment? Is all this playing with words? Are we, then, to assert of Christ, "Behold the Lamb of God Who tries to take away the sin of the world but fails?"

"FOR GOD SENT HIS SON * * THAT THE WORLD THROUGH HIM MIGHT BE SAVED."   *S. John* iii. 17.

Our opponents say, that God's purpose will fail. He, on the contrary, assures us by His Prophet, that His word shall not return unto Him void, but shall accomplish His pleasure.

"THE FATHER LOVETH THE SON, AND HATH GIVEN ALL THINGS INTO HIS HAND."   *S. John* iii. 35.

The relevance of this is obvious, for "*all* that which the Father giveth Me," says Christ, "shall come unto Me," ch. vi. 37. This is one of the large group of passages shewing the absolute universality of Christ's kingdom; compare ch. xiii. 3, and see the connection of the gift of *all things* to Christ and His atoning death. Also see *S. Matt.* xi. 27, where, just before the well-known appeal, "come unto Me," Jesus has been saying that *all things* were delivered unto Him by His Father; a connection surely suggestive. Read, too, *S. Matt.* xxviii. 18, and note the connection between all power given to Christ, and His claim over all nations. So, too, in *Heb.* ii. 8-9, the connection is significant between the gift of *all things* to Jesus Christ, and His tasting death for *every* man. As He creates *all* things (actually) so He redeems and restores *all* things (actually, not potentially); God has given to Him all things; and all things given to Him shall come to Him.

"THE CHRIST, THE SAVIOUR OF THE WORLD."   *S. John* iv. 42.

Christ is here called the Saviour of the *world*. The

larger hope simply pleads, that Christ will, in fact, save the world.

"(HE) WHICH * * GIVETH LIFE UNTO THE WORLD."
S. *John* vi. 33.

The world (*kosmos*) is in Scripture the ungodly mass. It is contrasted with the inner circle of the faithful, the elect. But this world is over and over again claimed by Christ. He gives life to it, and His gifts are "without repentance."

"ALL THAT THE FATHER GIVETH ME SHALL COME TO ME; * * AND THIS IS THE FATHER'S WILL THAT OF ALL WHICH HE HATH GIVEN ME I SHOULD LOSE NOTHING." S. *John* vi. 37-9.

We have seen that God the Father has given to Christ, not some things, but *all* things; and here we have the promise of Jesus Christ, that *all* that has been given to Him shall come to Him, and that nothing shall be lost (S. *Jno.* vi. 12).

"MY FLESH, WHICH I WILL GIVE FOR THE LIFE OF THE WORLD."
S. *John* vi. 51.

Again, it is the *world* for whose life Christ is to give His flesh. Can He give in vain? His gifts are "without repentance," *i.e.*, must be *finally* effective, though they may be resisted.

"THEN SPAKE JESUS * * I AM THE LIGHT OF THE WORLD."
S. *John* viii. 12.

Here, too, the *world* is that of which Christ is the Light as well as the Life.

"AND I, IF I BE LIFTED UP FROM THE EARTH, WILL DRAW ALL MEN UNTO ME." S. *John* xii. 32.

The plainest comment is the best. A partial drawing, *i.e.*, a partial salvation makes His words *untrue*. What our Lord does say is, in the consciousness of power, and using the term applied to the Father's constraining grace, ch. vi. 44, is I will (actually) draw all men. He does not say, or imply,

I will try to draw, and fail. One reads the comments of good men on this passage, with a feeling akin to despair, as they attempt to make Jesus Christ say that which He did not say, and not say that which He did say. What He does say is exactly given in the following lines:—

> So shall I lift up in My pierced hands *
> Beyond the reach of grief and guilt * *
> The whole creation.—*E. B. Browning.*

"FOR I CAME NOT TO JUDGE THE WORLD, BUT TO SAVE THE WORLD." S. *John* xii. 47.

This is as distinct a statement of Christ's purpose as is possible; its force can only be evaded by asserting that Christ would fail to accomplish that very thing which He came to do: and this assertion must be made in the teeth of those explicit passages, which declare the completeness of His triumph.

"JESUS KNOWING THAT THE FATHER HAD GIVEN ALL THINGS INTO HIS HANDS." S. *John* xiii. 3.

These words carry us to the very eve of the Passion. "Knowing that His hour was come," v. 1, Jesus knows, too, that all things have been given into His hands (See ch. iii. 35; xvii. 2; *S. Matt.* xxviii. 18; xi. 27; *Eph.* i. 22). Such knowledge at such an hour is deeply significant. As the Cross draws near, there comes to cheer Him the knowledge that to Him have been given all things, *i.e.*, an assurance of absolute victory.

"AS THOU GAVEST HIM AUTHORITY OVER ALL FLESH, THAT WHATSOEVER THOU HAST GIVEN HIM, TO THEM HE SHOULD GIVE ETERNAL LIFE." S. *John* xvii. 2.

Even the revised version fails to bring out with clearness the central fact, that eternal life has been given to all flesh by Christ. Literally the original runs: "Thou gavest to Him authority over *all* flesh, in order that (as to) ALL which

Thou hast given to Him, to them (*i.e.*, to all), He should give eternal life." The Greek is clear; but our versions fail, in not repeating the emphatic *all* (repeated in the original), which involves the gift (not the offer) of eternal life to ALL by Christ—thus obscuring the meaning. It is necessary to remark, if we would understand S. JOHN's teaching, the emphasis laid on the divine SOVEREIGNTY\* in Redemption, a sovereignty which is love.—(Our recoil from Calvinism has blinded most readers to this truth which pervades all Holy Scripture). Thus the Father disposes all things, and gives all things to Christ, ch. xiii. 3; iii. 35; xvii. 2 (*S. Matt.* xxviii. 18). At the very hour appointed, ch. xvii. 1; ii. 4; xii. 23; xiii. 1: each part of the great work is accomplished.

"IT IS FINISHED."        *S. John* xix. 30; (*cfr.* xvii. 4.)

What is finished? the pain—the Cross? It is inconceivable that such a Speaker, at such an hour, should mean less than this, viz.: ALL is finished in all its extent. The Great End and Goal is now attained—attained in all its length, and breadth, and height. In no respect can that Purpose of salvation fail, which embraces all humanity; for—though the very opposite may seem true—IT IS FINISHED.

"AND HE IS THE PROPITIATION FOR OUR SINS; AND NOT FOR OURS ONLY, BUT ALSO FOR THE SINS OF THE WHOLE WORLD."

1 *S. John* ii. 2.

Notice here the world contrasted with the true disciples; and yet the propitiation is not to be confined to the few, it is for all. S. JOHN's anxiety is to *assert this for all*. Here, as so often, the narrower and wider purposes of salvation are both mentioned: the narrower not excluding, as in the

---

\* It is well to remember this, when we are gravely told that "Omnipotence itself cannot save obstinate sinners." Now in the matter of salvation we have an express assertion that even the camel can go through the needle's eye; for with God "ALL THINGS ARE POSSIBLE."

"HE WAS MANIFESTED TO TAKE AWAY SINS." 1 *S. John* iii. 5.

This should be compared with *S. John* i. 29. There Christ takes away the *sin*—regarded as one vast whole—of all humanity: here the *sins*, *i.e.*, the individual sins of men.

"THE SON OF GOD WAS MANIFESTED THAT HE MIGHT DESTROY THE WORKS OF THE DEVIL." 1 *S. John* iii. 8.

The very purpose of the manifestation of God's Son is here stated to be the sweeping away of satan's works. How then can this *possibly be true*, while pain and sin endure for ever? No ideas can be more exactly opposed than the permanence of evil, and yet the destruction of the works of the devil. Is sin, and all that sin involves, the work of the devil? Yes, or No? You cannot answer in the negative, if you accept the standpoint of Scripture. But, if the affirmative be true, then all hell and sin and sorrow are to be swept away.

"THE FATHER SENT THE SON TO BE THE SAVIOUR OF THE WORLD." 1 *S. John* iv. 14.

Does it not savour of mockery to say that the Father sent the Son to destroy evil, and to save the world, and that the Son is victorious; and yet that neither shall evil be destroyed or the world saved?

"FEAR NOT * * I HAVE THE KEYS OF HELL AND DEATH." *Rev.* i. 18.

Significant words; doubly significant when we remember that Christ had just *used these keys to open the prison doors*, in His Descent into hades. How, if so, can death (the second, or any death) sever from Jesus Christ (*Who holds the keys*)—from His power to save?

"AND EVERY CREATURE WHICH IS IN HEAVEN, AND ON THE EARTH, AND UNDER THE EARTH, * * HEARD I SAYING UNTO HIM THAT SITTETH ON THE THRONE, AND UNTO THE LAMB, BLESSINGS," &c. *Rev.* v. 13.

These words embrace every created thing—on the earth, and under the earth, and in the sea. All are represented as swelling the chorus of praise to God, and to the Lamb. Yes, to such an end we trust and hope that all Creation is indeed coming, because we believe God's distinct promise, that all things shall be made new. How else could *all things* join in this glorious chorus? Compare notes on *Eph.* i. 10; *Phil.* ii. 11.

"DEATH AND HELL WERE CAST INTO THE LAKE OF FIRE."
*Rev.* xx. 14.

"The sense of the whole seems to be that at the final consummation of all things, all evil, physical and moral, will be abolished."—Bishop WARBURTON.

"BEHOLD I MAKE ALL THINGS NEW." *Rev.* xxi. 5.

This is the same glorious hope, not for some, but for *all;* no less than *all things* are to be made new.

"I AM THE ALPHA AND THE OMEGA, THE BEGINNING AND THE END." *Rev.* xxi. 5; (i. 8; xxii. 13).

A thoughtful reader will note that this claims for God a position, which negatives a final dualism: as He was the Source, so He is the Goal of all things. God is the TERMINUS of Creation; the Stream shall return to its Source. The unconscious dualism of current theology is a barrier to any true apprehension of the thought of the Apostle, which seems to be the same as that S. PAUL expresses in *Rom.* xi. 36.

"AND THE LEAVES OF THE TREE WERE FOR THE HEALING OF THE NATIONS. AND THERE SHALL BE NO MORE CURSE."
*Rev.* xxii. 2-3.

Here is a striking hint—as to a future restoration; a hint

that the nations are one day, in a future age, to be healed, for all this is subsequent to the passing away of the present earth, heaven (ch. xxi. 1). And as a result of this healing, there shall be no more curse—no pain—no tears—but *all things* made new.

"THE TIMES OF RESTITUTION OF ALL THINGS." *Acts* iii. 21.

*All things are to be restored;* (*apokatastasis, i.e., complete* restoration), and this is said to be the meaning of the work of Christ, the meaning of the promise to ABRAHAM, of the Jewish covenant (v. 25). This God hath spoken by all "the prophets since the world began," and this is what the larger hope teaches.

"AND HAVE HOPE THAT THERE SHALL BE A RESURRECTION * *
BOTH OF THE JUST AND THE UNJUST." *Acts* xxiv. 15.

Note these words. Could S. PAUL have hoped for a resurrection of the *unjust* if that meant hopeless punishment to them? "Who is *so great a fool*," asks a famous Father, "as to think so great a boon as the Resurrection can be, to those that rise, an occasion of endless torment?"

I may take this opportunity of asking attention to the fact that there runs through Scripture a definite law of *expansion*. First one family is chosen, then this family expands into a nation, then the nation is declared to be the source of blessing to all nations. Side by side with this numerical expansion there is visible a spiritual expansion. The prescribed sacrifices, the elaborate ritual, are pushed aside in favour of a spiritual creed, even in the Old Testament. Passing to the New Testament the law is the same, but more active still. By what, to a hasty judgment seems strange, Christ devotes half His time to the bodies of men, but we see the meaning to be that He cares for the whole man, and this care expands into the noble promise of the

Resurrection. Next comes a most significant expansion. All barriers fall before the march of Redemption. The dead, the *unrepentant* dead, are evangelised; the Cross penetrates hades, 1 *Pet.* iii. 18-20; iv. 6. Nor is this all: there are hints plain enough of a greater expansion still. "All things in heaven," "the Principalities and Powers,"—*Eph.* i. 10; iii. 10, &c.; *Col.* i. 15-20, are drawn within the range of the Atonement. Can any Hope be broader than that here directly suggested by the Bible itself? The question seems rather this:—Are our broadest hopes *broad enough?* Shall there be a corner or nook or abyss, in all the universe of God, finally unlighted by the Cross? Shall there be a sin, or sorrow, or pain unhealed? Is the very Universe, is Creation in all its extent, a field wide enough for the Son of God?

We have seen how numerous are the passages which the writings of *S. Matthew*, *S. Luke* and *S. John* contain, teaching directly or indirectly, the salvation of all men. Let us now consider the epistles of *S. Paul*, *S. Peter*, and that to the *Hebrews*. We shall find in these books the stream of promise still widening—the universality of Redemption indicated with a precision of language and a variety of illustration, which it seems not possible to reconcile with endless evil. *I do not mean* that every passage quoted is in itself conclusive. I do mean that all are relevant, as *links* in that great chain of promise, which enshrines the doctrine of universal restoration. And here an important question arises. How—on the hypothesis of endless evil—can we account for such passages, as naturally and obviously point to the larger hope? That the Bible holds out a hope of universal reconciliation, &c., &c., cannot be denied. And, if this universal restoration is never to take place, *how came this promise to be made?* How came the Bible to raise expectations never destined (as we are told) to be fulfilled, in a matter so unspeakably important? Inspired writers, aware that all things (in the natural sense of the words) will never be restored, and yet asserting positively that they will be restored, present us with a fact, which our opponents may well be invited to account for and explain.

S. PAUL's writings naturally claim special notice here. He is, so to speak, the Statesman-Apostle, whose mind ranges over the whole field of the divine purpose and of human destiny. Two points I must note. (I.) Not merely does S. PAUL assert the divine Sovereignty, but it lies at the centre of his teaching. He sees everywhere a Purpose slowly but surely fulfilling itself, a purpose which may be resisted, but must finally prevail. (II.) In this Apostle the Resurrection is set in striking prominence, as from its essential nature, a spiritual, redemptive force, as indeed the climax of Christ's work for man.

> "THE PROMISE THAT HE SHOULD BE THE HEIR OF THE WORLD * * TO ABRAHAM." *Rom.* iv. 13.

Here remark that the election by God of the Jews really involves *the world's* salvation; for ABRAHAM is "heir of the world," (see on election in ch. vi.) *i.e.*, receives as his inheritance the *whole* world.

> "THEREFORE AS BY THE OFFENCE OF ONE, JUDGMENT CAME UPON ALL MEN TO CONDEMNATION; EVEN SO BY THE RIGHTEOUSNESS OF ONE THE FREE GIFT CAME UPON ALL MEN UNTO JUSTIFICATION OF LIFE." *Rom.* v. 16-8.

I earnestly commend a study of the whole drift and argument of this passage. It is, I think, *absolutely irreconcilable* with a partial salvation. It contains a statement as explicit as words can convey it, of this great truth—God's remedy is CO-EXTENSIVE WITH, AND IS STRONGER, THAN SIN. Wherever, upon whomsoever sin has lighted, there shall

God's grace, through Jesus Christ, come to heal. In the very same sense as "the many" (all men) were made sinners, so "the many" shall have righteousness—not merely offered them—but be made righteous. And here I take my stand on these plain words of Scripture, and maintain that no state of final sin, for any soul, is compatible with them. Will our opponents explain how the grace of God (v. 15) can be *mightier*, in fact, than sin, if there be a hell without end? Will they explain how grace can *much more* abound than the offence—if there be a place of endless evil? Note the great underlying principle, viz., that grace is stronger than sin, always and everywhere stronger (finally).

"BECAUSE THE CREATURE ITSELF ALSO SHALL BE DELIVERED FROM THE BONDAGE OF CORRUPTION INTO THE GLORIOUS LIBERTY OF THE CHILDREN OF GOD. FOR WE KNOW THAT THE WHOLE CREATION GROANETH AND TRAVAILETH IN PAIN TOGETHER UNTIL NOW. \* \* WAITING FOR THE ADOPTION, TO WIT, THE REDEMPTION OF OUR BODY." *Rom.* viii. 21-22-23.

As to the details of S. PAUL's meaning, men may fairly differ; but his central thought seems clear. All created things have been subjected to vanity—to pain and suffering, no account taken of their will—*ouk hekousa*. Yet these are but the travail pains of a new birth; all that suffers shall be delivered from the bondage of corruption. Note how here (alone in the New Testament) are the sufferings of the whole creation alluded to, and how emphatic is the assertion that *every created thing—pasa he ktisis*—is awaiting redemption; and this reaches them by the manifestation of the sons of God, "the firstfruits," or the elect (see ch. vi. on election).

"FOR IF THE CASTING AWAY OF THEM BE THE RECONCILING OF THE WORLD, WHAT SHALL THE RECEIVING OF THEM BE, BUT LIFE FROM THE DEAD? FOR IF THE FIRSTFRUITS BE HOLY, THE LUMP IS ALSO HOLY." *Rom.* xi. 15-16.

The calling of the Jews is linked in God's plan with the

world's salvation (v. 12). They are His people, in the truly divine sense, that by them the world's salvation may be worked out. They, as "firstfruits," represent and pledge the whole world.

"AND SO ALL ISRAEL SHALL BE SAVED." *Rom.* xi. 26.

Here the Apostle's whole argument and the tenor of the context—see particularly v. 7 (and ch. x. 21)—very clearly distinguish "Israel" from the "election" (taken out of Israel), and shew that by Israel *the whole nation* is meant. (Nor does this "election" conflict with the truth that in a wider sense, Israel itself (all Israel) forms the "firstfruits," *i.e.*, the elect people; in fact, as already noticed, there is a double "firstfruits," both in the Law and the Gospel p. 213.) To sum up—(*a*) God's rejection of Israel is apparent only, for His calling is indefeasible, and therefore (*b*) *all* Israel shall be saved—without exception. (*c*) Israel, *i.e.*, the elect, is so closely linked with the world, that their very rejection means the world's salvation—in God's mysterious plan. (*d*) So close is this tie between the elect and the world, that a further promise follows, that Israel's restoration shall be to the world "life *from the dead*"—v. 15—a very suggestive phrase (ch. vi. *on Death*). (*e*) This final salvation of Israel is co-extensive with the whole nation for this further reason, because God's gifts are irrevocable, and were made to all.

"FOR THE GIFTS AND CALLING OF GOD ARE WITHOUT REPENTANCE." *Rom.* xi. 29.

That is, what God gives, He gives effectually. His gifts and His call are IRREVOCABLE; this meaning our versions fail to convey, *cfr. Is.* lv. 11. His word cannot fail of its purpose *finally*. When He calls, men *must hear*—a fact of the deepest significance. Let me ask the advocates of the popular creed, how, if God's call *must be obeyed* (for the whole context seems to shew this to be clearly the apostle's meaning), sooner or later, there is any room for endless disobedience in hell?

"GOD HATH CONCLUDED THEM ALL IN UNBELIEF, THAT HE MIGHT HAVE MERCY UPON ALL." *Rom.* xi. 32.

The original is the widest possible; it is the whole mass of men to whom S. PAUL refers. *The whole* is shut up unto unbelief in order that *the whole* may find mercy; and as the unbelief is actual and absolute, so, if there be a parallelism, must the mercy be equally actual and absolute.

"FOR (OUT) OF HIM AND THROUGH HIM AND UNTO HIM ARE ALL THINGS." *Rom.* xi. 36.

But if so, God is the END of all things, *i.e.*, unto (or perhaps into) Him all things shall return. The original imports that God is at once SOURCE and GOAL; AUTHOR and END of all Creation. No outlook can be more magnificent; no hope more divine, or broader, than this. Naturally, and characteristically, popular teaching practically ignores such a passage. (How different would have been its reception had it contained an anathema.)

"AS I LIVE, SAITH THE LORD, EVERY KNEE SHALL BOW TO ME, AND EVERY TONGUE SHALL CONFESS TO GOD. SO THEN EVERY ONE OF US SHALL GIVE ACCOUNT OF HIMSELF TO GOD." *Rom.* xiv. 11-12.

S. PAUL here quotes the great passage—*Is.* xlv. 22-23, in which *salvation* is promised to the entire human race, and which the apostle connects *with the Judgment*—see p. 195. From the whole context it seems that Christ's empire over *all* is absolute; extends to the dead; implies salvation; and this salvation is linked with His (future) judgment. The word translated "confess" is properly to "offer praise" or "thanksgiving." Thus, S. PAUL's view of the true meaning of the judgment day and its issues, seems in direct conflict with endless ruin.

"AS IN ADAM ALL DIE, EVEN SO IN CHRIST SHALL ALL BE MADE ALIVE." 1 *Cor.* xv. 22.

As ADAM actually brought death, spiritually, to all, so the last ADAM actually gives life, spiritually, to all. No mere offer of life can satisfy the plain language of the text. Nothing less than life really—spiritually imparted to all by the last ADAM—can fairly express S. PAUL's meaning. But it is objected that as death in ADAM is not final in some cases, so life in Christ is not final in some cases. (I.) It would perhaps be enough to answer that the objection misses the mark, for the apostle's thoughts are set simply on one point, on asserting that an universal life succeeds, and *absorbs*, an universal death. But I will reply further, that (II.) the plain words of the text require an *actual communication of life* TO ALL through Christ, else the comparison between ADAM and Christ is NOT TRUE; for it is certain that the link of evil between ADAM and the race is absolute, actual, and universal. And to call Christ the last ADAM, while denying a tie of grace and life equally actual, absolute, and universal, is to dupe men. (III.) The context involves the permanence of this life through Christ, for it claims for Christ a full victory; and requires us to believe that God will be All in All, at the End. (IV.) Life in Christ is thus not alone universal, it is final, v. 24-8.

"FOR HE MUST REIGN, TILL HE HATH PUT ALL ENEMIES UNDER HIS FEET * * THAT GOD MAY BE ALL IN ALL."
1 *Cor.* xv. 25-28.

There is here, at THE END, no place for sin—no trace of evil—no hell—for is not God *All and in All?* His empire is to be unbroken, universal, absolute. And the subjection of all to Him is the same subjection by which He is to be subject to the Father, *i.e.*, harmony and love, and peace; so the context requires. For note, that in summing up the final results of Christ's work, the *same word* is used (in the original) of Christ's own subjection to the Father, and of the subjection of Christ's own enemies to Him. But, obviously, Christ's own subjection can only be love and harmony—hence the *subjection of Christ's enemies cannot mean their endless incarceration in evil and pain.* Such a conception is no less excluded by the assertion that finally God shall be All in All.

"O DEATH, WHERE IS THY STING? O GRAVE, WHERE IS THY VICTORY?" 1 *Cor.* xv. 55.

I ask my readers quietly to think over the whole drift of this chapter and to mark the Apostle's increasing rapture, as his argument expands, and as the prospect opens before him of an universe yet to be, from which every form of death and sin are banished. S. PAUL's words are indeed explicit; and yet is there not more than this? There is surely in S. PAUL a conviction, underlying all beside; a conviction (to which his warmest words give but imperfect expression) of the absolute triumph of Christ, of the flood of glory that is to sweep over all creation, in its widest sense.

"GOD WAS IN CHRIST, RECONCILING THE WORLD UNTO HIMSELF." 2 *Cor.* v. 19.

Is God in earnest in telling us that He reconciles the *world?* Does *He mean what He says*, or does He only mean that He will try to reconcile it, but will be baffled? This question often rises unbidden, as we read these statements of the Bible, and compare them with the popular creed, which turns "all" into "some," when salvation is promised to "all," and turns the "world," when that is said to be saved, into a larger or smaller fraction of men.

"IN THEE SHALL ALL NATIONS BE BLESSED." *Gal.* iii. 8.

The relevance of texts like this lies in the fact that they shew the true meaning of God's election, and are links in that great chain of promise of universal restoration—which S. PETER assures us God spake by the mouth of all His holy prophets, and which he declares to mean the restitution of all things.

"THAT * * HE MIGHT GATHER TOGETHER IN ONE ALL THINGS (ta panta) IN CHRIST, BOTH WHICH ARE IN HEAVEN AND WHICH ARE ON EARTH." *Eph.* i. 10.

The universe in all its extent—the sum total of all existence—is to be brought back to Christ as Head, in unity. Such seems the view of the Apostle. It is the same process as the reconciliation of all things—*Col.* i. 15-20—and the subjection of all things to Christ—1 *Cor.* xv. 27-8—the homage and praise of all things rendered to Christ.—*Phil.* ii. 10-1. But if the universe and its contents are summed up in Christ, where is any possibility of an endless hell, or of a creation permanently divided? The word translated "gather together in one" is found only here, and in *Rom.* xiii. 9, as the law is summed up in one commandment, so is the universe to be summed up in Christ one day.

"GOD PUT ALL THINGS UNDER HIS FEET." *Eph.* i. 22.

The original verb here is the same as that used of the subjection of Christ to the Father.—1 *Cor.* xv. 28, and *Phil.* iii. 21. See note there.

"THAT THE GENTILES SHOULD BE FELLOW HEIRS."

*Eph.* iii. 6.

That is fellow heirs with the Jews. But the promise to

the Jews was that *all* Israel should be saved (see note *Rom.* xi. 26.), and because Jew and Gentile are made *one Eph.* ii. 14,—therefore all Gentiles seem to be included in the promise to all Israel.—*Rom.* xi. 26.

"HE ASCENDED UP FAR ABOVE ALL HEAVENS THAT HE MIGHT FILL ALL THINGS." *Eph.* iv. 10.

But if Christ is to fill all things—the universe—how can evil subsist eternally? This cannot be eluded by asking whether Christ, as God, has not always filled all things; for, to the Apostle, there is some further and *special* sense in which Christ is to fill all things (by the expulsion of evil), as a consequence of His completed work.

"BY HIM TO RECONCILE ALL THINGS UNTO HIMSELF; BY HIM, I SAY, WHETHER THEY BE THINGS IN EARTH, OR THINGS IN HEAVEN." *Col.* i. 15-19-20.

I gladly substitute for my own comments LIGHTFOOT's note on v. 16, "All things must find their meeting point, their reconciliation at length in Him from Whom they took their rise; in the Word as the mediatorial agent, and through the Word in the Father as the primary source. The Word is the final cause as well as the creative agent in the universe. This ultimate goal of the present dispensation in time is similarly stated in several passages. Sometimes it is represented as the birth throe and deliverance of all creation through Christ, as *Rom.* viii. 19. * * Sometimes it is the absolute and final subjection of universal nature to Him as 1 *Cor.* xv. 28. * * Sometimes it is the reconciliation of all things through Him as below, v. 20. Sometimes it is the recapitulation, the gathering up in one head of the universe in Him, as *Eph.* i. 10 * * all alike enunciate the same truth in different terms. The Eternal Word is the Goal of the universe, as He was its starting point. It must end in unity, as it proceeded from unity, and the centre of this unity is Christ." If I venture to add anything it is to protest against explaining away these words. WHATSOEVER has issued from the Eternal Word, returns to Him as its Goal, reconciled, purified, and restored; no other meaning can be fairly extracted from the words quoted.

"THAT IN THE NAME OF JESUS EVERY KNEE SHOULD BOW, OF THINGS IN HEAVEN, AND THINGS IN EARTH, AND THINGS UNDER THE EARTH; AND THAT EVERY TONGUE SHOULD CONFESS THAT JESUS CHRIST IS LORD." *Phil.* ii. 10-11.

This is S. PAUL'S statement of the great vision *(Rev.* v. 13), in which every created thing in heaven and on earth and under the earth unites to sing—Blessing, etc., to God most High. Could a picture more universal be painted—*every* knee, in heaven, on earth, under the earth bending, and every tongue proclaiming God's praise. Such is the force of the original. All things, says LIGHTFOOT, "whatsoever and wheresoever they be. The whole universe, whether animate or inanimate, bends the knee in homage and raises its voice *in praise.*"

"ABLE EVEN TO SUBDUE ALL THINGS UNTO HIMSELF."
*Phil.* iii. 21.

In what sense this subjugation of all things to Christ is to be understood, is clear from the context, "who shall fashion anew the body of our humiliation, that it may be *conformed* to the body of His glory, according to the working whereby He is able even to subdue all things unto Himself." Note the significance of this. No one can doubt that Christ is destined to subdue all things, but this passage shows *decisively* that Christ's subduing all things (in the Scriptural sense) is *making them like unto Himself.* See note on 1 *Cor.* xv. 25.

"GOD OUR SAVIOUR, WHO WILL HAVE ALL MEN TO BE SAVED,
FOR THERE IS ONE GOD." 1 *Tim*. ii. 3-4.

"None can hinder His doing as He wills * * Now His will is that *all* should be saved."—S. JEROME on *Eph*. i. 11. S. PAUL here directs thanksgiving and prayer to be offered for all men on the express ground that God wills the salvation of all. And this divine will S. PAUL grounds on the divine unity—a fact which marks this passage noteworthy—for the One God can have but one eternal (irresistible) purpose. "God is One, the One that is All, that binds up all in one, and one in all, and makes all one."—J. WHITE, *Restoration of all things*. This Divine Oneness is no merely arithmetical proposition. It states a deep spiritual fact, viz., that *Oneness* is of the essence of the divine plan. A Creator who is ONE, and a creation perpetually TWO (*i.e.*, perpetually divided into two classes), is to S. PAUL a thing inconceivable.—See ch. vi. towards the end.

"GOD THE SAVIOUR OF ALL MEN, SPECIALLY OF THOSE THAT
BELIEVE." 1 *Tim*. iv. 10.

Any obscurity in this passage becomes clear the moment we reflect on God's plan by which the elect—those who believe—are first saved, and then become the means, here or in the ages yet to come, of saving all men.

"OUR SAVIOUR JESUS CHRIST, WHO HATH ABOLISHED DEATH."
2 *Tim*. i. 10.

Death is *abolished*, and with death that which it in Scripture implies, sin and evil. For death *abolished*, and yet death in its worst form, the second death, maintained for ever, are plain contradictions. Will those who maintain the doctrine of conditional immortality explain how death can be abolished, and yet swallow up finally all sinners in a sentence of annihilation?

> "FOR THE GRACE OF GOD HATH APPEARED, BRINGING SALVATION TO ALL MEN." *Titus* ii. 11.

Yes, "bringing salvation to all men:" this is precisely the larger hope. But how is "salvation brought to all men" consistent with the damnation of myriads of men—nay, of any man? if, as we are distinctly told, God's gifts are without repentance, *i.e.*, effective and irrevocable.

> "HE ALSO WENT AND PREACHED UNTO THE SPIRITS IN PRISON." 1 *Peter* iii. 19.

These words amount to a complete overthrow of the popular view of the state of the sinful dead; for plainly they assert a process of redemption as *going on after death*. Remark, carefully, who they were to whom Christ took the Gospel, and whom, as the following passage shews, He saved. They were those who had sinned against the greatest light known in their day, and DIED IN THEIR SINS.

> "THE GOSPEL WAS PREACHED EVEN TO THE DEAD, (IN ORDER), THAT THEY MIGHT BE JUDGED * * BUT LIVE IN THE SPIRIT." 1 *Peter* iv. 6.

Notice again here *the connection between judgment and salvation*. Even the (impenitent) dead were evangelised, *in order* that they should have the benefit of judgment, and thus live to God (see on *Judgment*, ch. vi.) Such a text literally cuts up the traditional creed root and branch.

> "THE LORD IS * * NOT WILLING THAT ANY SHOULD PERISH, BUT THAT ALL SHOULD COME TO REPENTANCE." 2 *Peter* iii. 9.

If then any do perish finally, God's will and design must have been finally overthrown: it is obvious that a temporary resistance, permitted for wise ends, differs wholly from a final defiance of God's will.

> "HIS SON, WHOM HE HATH APPOINTED HEIR OF ALL THINGS." *Heb.* i. 2.

It is enough to say that these words express the larger

hope, if fairly and fully understood. They teach the absolute universality of Christ's reign, which the repeated testimony of Scripture shews to be love and peace.

"THOU HAST PUT ALL THINGS IN SUBJECTION UNDER HIS FEET," &c.
*Heb.* ii. 8-10.

Here is an addition to that very large class of passages which speak of Christ's kingdom, as destined to extend over all things, *e.g., Eph.* iv. 10 ; i. 10 ; *Phil.* iii. 9-11 ; *Rev.* v. 13, &c. I have already shewn that subjection to Christ means perfect harmony and peace, in the usage of the New Testament, see notes on *Phil.* iii. 21, and 1 *Cor.* xv. 25. This remarkable passage proceeds to lay stress on Christ's death, as embracing "*every man,*" v. 9 ;—the writer has already strongly asserted the dignity of man, and his vast inheritance, simply *as man*, v. 6-7. This dignity, impaired by the Fall, has been recovered by Christ the Son of Man. And it was right that Christ should suffer in fulfilling the Will of Him (God), for Whom are all things, and through Whom are all things," v. 10, —*all things whatsoever;* words that authorise the widest hope, for God is the Goal of all creation. (See *Rom.* xi. 36.)

"THAT THROUGH DEATH HE MIGHT DESTROY THE DEVIL."
*Heb.* ii. 14.

But the destruction of the devil, as holding the power of death, is quite inconsistent with the continuance of death and evil eternally.

"THE IMMUTABILITY OF HIS COUNSEL." *Heb.* vi. 17.

We admit that a seeming failure there may be of God's purpose: but no real failure is possible. What God's immutable counsel is, we see in 2 *Pet.* iii. 9, where the original word translated "willing" is the same as "counsel" here.

> "HE HATH APPEARED TO PUT AWAY SIN BY THE SACRIFICE OF
> HIMSELF." *Heb.* ix. 26.

Sin has intruded and caused an appearance of failure in God's plan. Christ comes *to sweep sin away.* When will our opponents meet fairly the dilemma, viz., Christ fails, or succeeds in His purpose. If He fails, you contradict Scripture. If He succeeds, you contradict your dogma.

> "JESUS CHRIST, THE SAME YESTERDAY, TO-DAY, AND UNTO THE
> AGES." *Heb.* xiii. 8.

THE SAME throughout "the ages;" words little heeded I fear; and yet which virtually contain the essence of the Gospel—the sum and substance of our hope. For what is it these words teach? not the superficial view that Christ is now a Saviour, and will in future be merely a Judge to condemn; but that, what He was on earth that He is now, and that He will be, through "the ages" (judging ever, but only a Judge that He may by it be a Saviour). They bid us look to a series of ages yet to come, and there see Jesus Christ still working to save; doubtless by penalty, by fiery discipline, in the case of hardened sinners; but still the same Jesus, *i.e.*, Saviour, and destined to continue His work of salvation till the last wanderer shall have been found.

So far from producing every possible passage that teaches the larger hope, I might have easily cited other texts that teach, or imply, the same. Take but two clauses of the Lord's prayer: "Our Father," these two words really involve the whole question—they form a tie, never to be broken, between man and God. "Thy will be done on earth as it is in heaven," But how is His will done in heaven? It is *universally* done. Shall it not then be *universally* done on earth too? Does Christ put into our mouths a petition which He does not design to fulfil, in even larger measure than we can hope? I might have also quoted "God is Love." To this point all His attributes converge. Love is that character, which united they form (love infinite and unchanging). Can this Love consign to endless agony its own children? Can infinite Love ever cease to love?—let the Apostle reply, "Love *never faileth*," is inextinguishable.\*

I would sum up by repeating the three propositions already stated, p. 224. (I.) Christ's Purpose of salvation was deliberately formed to include the whole of our race, and no less. (II.) He received for this end ALL POWER, *i.e.*, power over all wills, all evil, all obstacles, whatsoever and wheresoever. (III.) The Bible claims; the Prophets claim; the Evangelists claim; the Apostles claim; Christ claims absolute success in this task.—*Is.* xlv. 22-3; lv. 11; liii. 11; *S. Jno.* xii. 32; xvii. 4; 1 *Cor.* xv. 22, 27-8; *Rom.* v. 15-21; xi. 29-32; 2 *Tim.* i. 10, &c.

A few words of earnest caution must be added here. I trust it has been made plain in these pages, that in teaching universal salvation, I have not for a moment made light of sin, or advocated the salvation of sinners while they continue such. I earnestly assert the certain punishment of sin (awful it may well be, in its duration and its nature for the hardened offender), but in all cases directed by love and justice to the final extirpation of evil. Nay, I have opposed the popular creed on this very ground, that it in fact teaches

---

\* In the above brief notes I have not attempted an exhaustive comment. It has been my aim to point out the plain natural meaning of the passages cited, in their bearing on the future destiny of man, and to present this meaning in the most simple and straightforward way. Specially have I urged the imperative necessity of truthfulness, of assuming that what the sacred writers say, that they mean, in the ordinary acceptation of their words—that in saying, *e.g.*, "I make all things new," Christ really meant all things and not some things; that in saying, "God is the Saviour of all men," the Apostle meant that God really does save all men.

men to make light of sin, and that in two ways: first, because it sets forth a scheme of retribution so unjust as to make men secretly believe its penalties will never be inflicted; and next, because it in fact asserts that God either will not, or cannot, overcome and destroy evil and sin, but will bear with them for ever and ever. I repeat that not one word has been written in these pages tending to represent God as a merely good-natured Being, Who regards as a light matter the violation of His holy law. Such shallow theology, God forbid that I should teach. Infinite Love is one thing; Infinite Good-nature a totally unlike thing. Love is never feeble, it is (while most tender) most inexorable. In the light of Calvary it is that we are bound to see the guilt of sin. But let us beware, lest, as we stand in thought by the Cross, we virtually dishonour the Atonement by limiting its power to save—by teaching men that Christ is after all vanquished; lest, while in words professing to honour Christ, we, in fact, make *Him a liar*, for He has never said, "I, if I be lifted up, will draw some men," or even "most men," but "I WILL DRAW ALL MEN UNTO ME."

## CHAPTER IX.

### WHAT THE NEW TESTAMENT TEACHES.

"The word 'hell' the sacred writers *never* use in the sense which is generally given to it."—Dr. ERNEST PETAVEL.—*The Struggle for Eternal Life*.

"Nous sommes peutêtre engagés dans quelque erreur énorme, dont le Christianisme un jour nous fera rougir, comme il nous a fait rougir de la torture, de l'esclavage, de la contrainte en matière de religion."—VINET.

WE are often met with the objection, "You look only *at one side of the Bible*." I am determined that, in these pages, no room shall be given for the objection. Most true then it is, that there runs through Holy Scripture a current seeming (to an English reader) to teach the final destruction of the impenitent, and in some few passages their endless punishment. Most fully do I admit all this. I say, *seeming* to teach, advisedly. For the Bible was not written, as vast numbers appear to think, in English, by some Englishman in the 19th century, for his fellow Englishmen. It comes to us from very distant ages; in very many parts; the work of very many minds, but one and all writing from an oriental standpoint, saturated with oriental habits of thought, and in oriental phrase and style. Therefore all depends *on the sense* in which the terms in question are used. Let us go to the Bible itself to decide. Those who turn to the paragragh which follows the note on *S. Matt.* iii. 12 (in this chapter), will see how far from indicating hopeless ruin are the very strongest phrases employed. In the usage of Scripture itself "death" and "destruction" are indeed very often the path to life,—see pp. 9-11, 149, 184-90, &c.

Admitting then these two currents, we at once feel that they are not equal in *quality ;* we feel instinctively the divineness of the one ; it is deeper, diviner, broader, stronger. We feel its kindred with all that is noblest in our nature—I do not mean with what we like best, but with what we recognise as best and most divine, alike in God and in man.

"But the current of terror is louder." No, I do not think so. It may seem so from habit, or because sinners do not readily rise to what is broad and divine. To them vengeance is more credible than love. Yet even were it the louder current, I may point out that God is ever found "in the still small voice." Nor is that which lies on the surface always, or even often, the true meaning of Scripture. Thus, in the predictions of the Messiah, the surface current, which wholly misled the Jews, spoke of a Conqueror, and of splendid earthly triumph. But the true meaning lay underneath the surface, in those fewer, less prominent, but diviner predictions of a suffering Saviour, of His life of toil,—see *Salv. Mund.*

Feeling this, I would face in all frankness all the facts, and entreat an honest and thorough examination. I hope to shew, that while undoubtedly the penalties threatened against sinners are terrible, still they are not *endless.* I believe that *not one passage* can be found anywhere in the Bible that so teaches, when fairly translated and understood. I must ask you, before examining these passages, carefully to bear in mind the following considerations :—(I.) When the horrors of endless sin and pain are so stoutly defended on the (supposed) authority of the Bible, it is well to remember, that slavery was *unanimously* defended for more than fifteen hundred years on exactly similar grounds; so was the infliction of most cruel tortures; so was religious persecution with its indescribable horrors; so was the existence of witches, and the duty of burning them alive. Nay, every theologian in Europe was for centuries persuaded of the truth of actual sexual intercourse between evil spirits and men and women. "Holy men," you say, "everywhere defend endless pain and evil on the authority of Scripture." Holy men, I reply, have with *absolute unanimity* defended, on the authority of Scripture, tenets and practices so abominable that one shudders in attempting to recall them. (II.) A fact of the *deepest significance* is this: that although certain phrases existed, by which the idea of unendingness might have been conveyed, yet none of these is applied by our Lord and His Apostles to the future punishment of the impenitent. Those interested are invited carefully to weigh this very striking fact. (III.) Thus *aiidios* or *ateleutetos* are never used of future punishment in the New Testament. Nor is it anywhere said to be *aneu telous* "without end," nor do we read that it shall go on *pantote*, or *eis to dienekes* "for ever." (IV.) Is it, I ask, conceivable that a sentence so awful as to be absolutely beyond all human thought, should be pronounced against myriads upon myriads of hapless creatures, in language ambiguous, and *admittedly capable of a very different meaning, and habitually so used in the New Testament*, and in the Greek version of the Old Testament, from which Our Lord and the Apostles quote? (V.) It is certainly a strong confirmation of the view which asserts that no unlimited penalty is taught in the New Testament to find so great a body of primitive opinion (and that specially of the Greek speaking Fathers), teaching universalism ON THE AUTHORITY OF THE NEW TESTAMENT.—

See pp. 84, 148, 170. All such teaching obviously contains an implied assertion that the texts, usually relied on, do not teach endless penalty. (VI.) Again, while the texts quoted in favour of the salvation of all men use language clear and explicit, and are a fair rendering of the original in all cases, it is not so in the case of the passages usually alleged to prove endless torment. In those cases where they seem to the English reader so to teach, they are either mistranslated or misinterpreted, or both. Hence we see how inaccurate is the assumption all but universally made, that these terms that seem to teach endless pain and evil *are in the Bible*. They are merely in a certain human and fallible translation of the Bible, a totally different thing. (VI.) It is also to be noted that not a few of the passages usually quoted in support of the traditional creed do not, even if the accuracy of the translation be admitted, contain any assertion of endless pain, though they may seem to teach final destruction (to an ordinary reader.) (VII.) Finally, in addition to all the above, a great difficulty remains in the way of the advocates of the traditional creed. They DARE NOT CARRY OUT THEIR OWN PRINCIPLES. Their principle of interpreting the Bible would compel them to believe what they do not believe, and to teach what no reasonable person could presume to teach. (*a.*) First, it would compel them to believe in the endless torment of the vast majority, at least of all adults (see pp. 4-5). (*b.*) Next it would compel them to believe that this torment goes on for ever and ever IN THE SIGHT OF THE LAMB AND THE HOLY ANGELS (for their satisfaction?)—*Rev.* xiv. 10—and indeed probably in the sight of all the Blessed.—*Is.* lxvi. 24, and *S. Luc.* xvi. 23. But these two things they disbelieve. Nor do they believe the statement that God *creates evil.*—*Is.* xlv. Nor have they any ground, so far as I know, for their disbelief, except that these statements, taken literally, are unworthy of God, *i.e.*, are immoral. Thus, in fact, they stand self-condemned. Nor do they really believe that Israel is to fall *and rise no more.*—*Amos*, v. 2 ; nor do, or can they, take literally the *many* threats of the same kind which Scripture contains.— See paragraph after note on *S. Matt.* iii. 12, in this chapter. (VIII.) As instances of wholly incorrect rendering, take the words translated "hell," "damnation," "everlasting," "eternal," "for ever and ever." "Hell" is, in the New Testament, the rendering of three widely differing Greek words, viz., "Gehenna," "Hades," and "Tartarus," such is the *accuracy* of our translation! "*Gehenna*" occurs eleven times in the New Testament as used by our Lord, and once by S. JAMES. In the original Greek it is taken almost unchanged from the Hebrew *(Ge-hinnom, i.e.*, valley of Hinnom), an example which our translators ought to have followed, and rendered *Gehenna*, as it is, by *Gehenna*. By retaining the term hell with its inevitable associations, they in fact are prejudging the question, and are assuming the part not of translators but of commentators. This valley lay outside Jerusalem : once a pleasant vale, and later a scene of Moloch worship, it had sunk into a common cesspit at last. Into it were flung offal, the carcases of animals, and it would seem, of criminals, and in it were kept fires ever burning (for *purification* be it remembered), while the worms were for ever preying on the decaying matter. The so-called undying worm and flame, of which so much has been made (*a*) were—at least in their literal and primary use—temporal and finite, (*b*) preyed only on the dead body (*c*) and were for purification ; three particulars essential to the due understanding of the passages on which the dogma of endless torments has been so unfairly based. *Hades* is a term, denoting the state or place of spirits, good and bad alike, after death. Our Revisers have, by a tardy justice, struck "hell," as its translation, out of their version. It occurs in the Gospels and Epistles five times, twice in the Acts, and four times in the Revelations. It denotes that intermediate state or place which succeeds death; a state which in our recoil from Romish error we have almost ceased to recognise at all. *Tartarus* occurs once only (in the verbal form) in the New Testament, in 2 *Peter* ii. 4. It also is a classical term, used there most often, although not always, for the place of future punishment of the wicked. Here S. PETER applies it not to human beings, but to the lost angels; and in their case it denotes *no final place of torment*, but a prison in which they are kept *awaiting* their final judgment; hence, to render it by the term "hell" is simply preposterous. "Damnation," "damned,"—both of these terms represent merely two Greek words (and their derivatives), *krino* and *katakrino, i.e.*, to judge and to condemn. Our Revisers have felt how unwarrantable the former translation was, for which there is indeed this excuse, that probably, when the authorised version was made, the meaning of the word "damn" was far milder than it has since become (as was certainly the case with the term "hell.") To import into these words the idea of endless torment is to err against all fairness, for they simply mean\* to "judge," and at most, to "condemn."

Most significant is it that in the original of the New Testament, the horrors of unending agony, which these terms conjure up for so many, vanish when we come to know

---

\* In one passage, 2 *Peter* ii. 3, the word "damnation" represents a different Greek word, "*apoleia*," and is rightly rendered by our Revisers as "destruction" in that place.

that by "damnation" is simply meant "judgment," or at most "condemnation," as our Revisers now fully admit in their version; and by "hell" is only meant, either the place of disembodied souls, *hades*, (as our Revisers now render it) or the Jewish *Gehenna* (see Revised Version), a place of temporary punishment in its literal sense, where the worms fed continually, it is true, and the fire for ever burned; but in both cases purifying, and causing no pain (for the bodies were those of the dead); and where both "undying" worm, and "unquenchable" fire, have long since, in their literal sense, passed away. True it is that Gehenna was by the Jews used, symbolically, of the place of future punishment— a fact to be fully admitted. But the evidence adduced by FARRAR (*Mercy and Judgment*, p. 180-215), by COX, *Salv. Mundi*, p. 70-5, and by an Article in the *XIX. Century*, *August, 1890*, (see, too, PFAFF, quoted p. 80,) seems to make it clear that, *normally*, at least, Gehenna was not believed to involve endless punishment. It was *certainly* a place from which deliverance was possible, and probably one from which deliverance was the rule. Jewish opinion was by no means fixed, but fluctuated much as to the details and the duration of future punishment. Some Rabbis seem to have held (as did certain of the Fathers) the final annihilation of the wicked.

True it is, most true, that while no unending torment is threatened by our Lord, yet His words do convey most solemn warning to the sinner—warning that gains in real weight when its true import is discerned, because the conscience recognises its justice. I accept, then, heartily—in their true natural sense, every warning, however terrible, and every penalty threatened against sinners in Scripture; but that true natural sense is not, as I hope to shew, in any case that of endless evil and torment. My quarrel with the advocates of the popular view (as far as the Scripture is concerned) is that, while assigning to one class of texts a meaning, which they cannot fairly bear, they at the same time wholly put out of view, blot out from the Bible in fact, a very large and weighty class of passages, furnished by the New Testament, in favour of universal salvation. Thus, as so often happens, when men persist in seeing only one side, they fail to apprehend the true meaning, even of that one side, which they present to us as though it were the whole.

Let us next consider the true meaning of the words *aion* and *aionios*.\* These are the originals of the terms rendered by our translators " everlasting," " for ever and ever :" and on this translation, so misleading, a vast portion of the popular dogma of endless torment is built up. I say, without hesitation, misleading and incorrect ; for *aion* means " an age," a limited period, whether long or short, though often of indefinite length ; and the adjective *aionios* means " of the age," " age-long," " æonian," and *never* " everlasting " (of its own proper force), it is true that it may be applied as an epithet to things that are endless, but the idea of endlessness in all such cases comes not from the epithet, but only because it is inherent in the object to which the epithet is

---

\* " The word by itself, whether adjective or substantive, never means endless."—Canon FARRAR. " The conception of eternity, in the Semitic languages, is that of a long duration and series of ages." —Rev. J. S. BLUNT—*Dict. of Theology.* " 'Tis notoriously known," says Bishop RUST, " that the Jews, whether writing in Hebrew or Greek, do by *olam* (the Hebrew word corresponding to *aion*), and *aion* mean any remarkable period and duration, whether it be of life, or dispensation, or polity." " The word *aion* is never used in Scripture, or anywhere else, in the sense of endlessness (vulgarly called eternity), it always meant, both in Scripture and out, a period of time ; else how could it have a plural—how could you talk of the æons and æons of æons as the Scripture does ?"—C. KINGSLEY. So the secular games, celebrated every century were called " eternal " by the Greeks.—See HUET, *Orig.* ii. p. 162.

applied, as in the case of God. Much has been written on the import of the æonian (eternal) life. Altogether to exclude, (with MAURICE) the notion of time seems impracticable, and opposed to the general usage of the New Testament (and of the Septuagint). But while this is so, we may fully recognise that the phrase "eternal life" (æonian life) does at times pass into a region above time, a region wholly moral and spiritual. Thus, in *S. John*, the æonian life (eternal life), of which he speaks, is a life not measured by duration, but a life in the unseen, life in God. Thus, *e.g.*, God's commandment is life eternal.—*S. Jno*. xii. 50. To know Him is life eternal,—*ib*. xvii. 3, and Christ is the eternal life.—1 *S. Jno*. i. 2; v. 20. Admitting, then, the usual reference of *aionios* to time, we note in the word a tendency to rise above this idea, to denote quality, rather than quantity, to indicate the true, the spiritual, in opposition to the unreal, or the earthly. In this sense the eternal is *now* and *here*. Thus "eternal" punishment is one thing, and "everlasting" punishment a very different thing, and so it is that our Revisers have substituted for "everlasting" the word "eternal" in every passage in the New Testament, where *aionios* is the original word. Further, if we take the term strictly, eternal punishment is impossible, for the "eternal" in strictness has no beginning.

Again, a point of great importance is this, that it would have been impossible for the Jews, as it is impossible for us, to accept Christ, except by assigning a limited—nay, a *very limited* duration—to those Mosaic ordinances which were said in the Old Testament to be "for ever," to be "everlasting" (æonian). *Every line of the New Testament, nay, the very existence of Christianity is thus in fact a proof of the limited sense of aionios in Scripture.* Our Baptism in the name of Jesus Christ, our Holy Communion, every prayer uttered in a Christian Church, or in our homes, in the name of the Lord Jesus: our hopes of being "for ever with the Lord"—these contain one and all an affirmation most real, though tacit, of the temporary sense of *aionios*.

As a further illustration of the meaning of *aion* and *aionios*, let me point out that in the Greek version of the Old Testament (the Septuagint)—in common use among the Jews in Our Lord's time, from which He and the Apostles usually quoted, and whose authority, therefore, should be decisive on this point—these terms are *repeatedly* applied to things that have long ceased to exist. Thus the AARONIC priesthood is said to be "everlasting," *Num.* xxv. 13. The land of Canaan is given as an "everlasting" possession, and "for ever," *Gen.* xvii. 8, and xiii. 15. In *Deut.* xxiii. 3, "for ever" is distinctly made an equivalent to "even to the tenth generation." In *Lam.* v. 19, "for ever and ever" is the equivalent of from "generation to generation." The inhabitants of Palestine are to be bondsmen "for ever," *Lev.* xxv. 46. In *Num.* xviii. 19, the heave offerings of the holy things are a covenant "for ever." CALEB obtains his inheritance "for ever," *Josh.* xiv. 9. And DAVID's seed is to endure "for ever," his throne "for ever," his house "for ever;" nay, the passover is to endure "for ever;" and in *Isaiah* xxxii. 14, the forts and towers shall be "dens *for ever, until* the spirit be poured upon us." So in *Jude* vii., Sodom and Gomorrah are said to be suffering the vengeance of eternal (æonian) fire, *i.e.*, their temporal overthrow by fire, for they have a definite promise of final restoration.— *Ez.* xvi. 55.

And Christ's kingdom is to last "for ever," yet we are distinctly told that this very kingdom is to end.—1 *Cor.* xv. 24.

Indeed, quotation might be added to quotation, both from the Bible and from early\* authors, to prove this limited meaning of *aion* and its derivatives; but enough has probably been said to prove that it is wholly impossible, and indeed absurd, to contend that any idea of endless duration is *necessarily or commonly* implied by either *aion* or *aionios*.

Further, if this translation of *aionios* as "eternal," in the sense of endless, be correct, *aion* must mean eternity, *i.e.*, endless duration. But so to render it would reduce Scripture to an absurdity. In the first place, you would have over and over again to talk of the "eternities." We can comprehend what "eternity" is, but what are the "eternities?" You cannot have more than one eternity. The doxology would run thus: "Thine is the kingdom, the power, and the glory, 'unto the eternities.'" In the case of the sin against the Holy Ghost, the translation would then be, "it shall not be forgiven him, neither in this eternity nor in that to come." Our Lord's words, *S. Matt.* xiii. 39, would then run, "the harvest is the end of (the) eternity," *i.e.*, the end of the endless, which is to make our Lord talk nonsense. Again, in *S. Mark* iv. 19, the translation should be, "the cares," not of "this world," but "the cares of this eternity choke the word." In *S. Luke* xvi. 8, "The children of this world," should be "the children of this eternity." *Rom.* xii. 2, should run thus: "Be not conformed to this eternity." In 1 *Cor.* x. 11, the words, "upon whom the ends of the world are come," should be: "the ends of the eternities." Take next, *Gal.* i. 4: "That He might deliver us from this present evil world," should run thus: "from this present evil eternity." In 2 *Tim.* iv. 10, the translation should be: "DEMAS

---

\* Thus JOSEPHUS calls "æonian," the temple of Herod, which was actually destroyed when he wrote. PHILO never uses *aionios* of endless duration.

hath forsaken me, having loved this present eternity." And "Now once at the end of the ages hath He been manifested," should read, on the popular view, "at the end of the eternities." Let me state the dilemma clearly. *Aion* either means endless duration as its necessary, or at least its ordinary significance, or it does not. If it does, the following difficulties at once arise; 1—How, if it mean an endless period, can *aion* have a plural? 2—How came such phrases to be used as those repeatedly occurring in Scripture, where *aion* is added to *aion*, if *aion* is of itself infinite? 3—How come such phrases as for the "*aion*" or *aions* and BEYOND?—*ton aiona kai ep aiona kai eti : eis tous aionas kai eti.*—See (*Sept.*) *Ex.* xv. 18; *Dan.* xii. 3; *Micah* iv. 5. 4—How is it that we repeatedly read of the *end* of the *aion*?—*S. Matt.* xiii. 39-40-49; xxiv. 3; xxviii. 20; 1 *Cor.* x. 11; *Heb.* ix. 26. 5—Finally, if *aion* be infinite, why is it applied over and over to what is strictly finite? *e.g., S. Mark* iv. 19; *Acts* iii. 21; *Rom.* xii. 2; 1 *Cor.* i. 20, ii. 6, iii. 18, x. 11, &c., &c. But if an *aion* be not infinite, what right have we to render the adjective *aionios* (which depends for its meaning on *aion*) by the terms "eternal" (when used as the equivalent of "endless") and "everlasting?"

Indeed our translators have really done further hurt to those who can only read their English Bible. They have, wholly obscured a very important doctrine, that of "the ages." This when fully understood throws a flood of light on the plan of redemption, and the method of the divine working. Take a few instances which show the force and clearness gained, by restoring the true rendering of the words *aion* and *aionios*. Turn to *S. Matt.* xxiv. 3. There our version represents the disciples as asking "what should be the sign of the end of the world." It should be the end of the "age;" the close of the Jewish age marked by the fall of Jerusalem. In *S. Matt.* xiii. 39-40-49, the true rendering is not the end of the "world," but of the "age," an important change. So *S. John* xvii. 3, "this is life eternal," should be "the life of the ages," *i.e.*, peculiar to those ages, in which the scheme of salvation is being worked out. Or take *Heb.* v. 9; ix. 12; xiii. 20, "eternal salvation" should be "æonian" or of the ages; "eternal redemption" is the redemption "of the ages;" the eternal covenant is the "covenant of the ages," the covenant peculiar to the ages of redemption. In *Eph.* iii. 11, "the eternal purpose" is really the purpose of "the ages," *i.e.*, worked out in "the ages." In ch. iii. 21, there occurs a suggestive phrase altogether obscured (as usual, where this word is in question,) by our version, "until all the generations of the age of the ages." Thus it runs in the original, and it is altogether unfair to conceal this elaborate statement by merely rendering "throughout all ages." In 1 *Cor.* x. 11, "the ends of the world" are the "ends of the ages." In ch. ii. 6-7-8, the word *aion* is four times translated "world," it should be "age" or "ages" in all cases. And here it is impossible to avoid asking how—assuming that *aion* does mean "world" in these cases—how it can yield, as an adjective, such a term as "everlasting?" If it mean "world," then the adjective should be "worldly," "of the world." And great force and freshness would be gained in our version by always adhering to the one rendering "age."

Again, in *Heb.* xi. 3, "the worlds were framed," should be "the ages." In *Heb.* ix. 26, "now once in the end of the world" should be, "in the end of the ages." Take, again, the closing words of *S. Jude*, which run literally, "To the only God, be glory, &c., before every age, and now and unto all the ages," *i.e.*, before the ages began, and now, and throughout all the ages yet to come. So *Rev.* i. 6, "glory" is ascribed unto Christ, "unto the ages of the ages," in the original. In 1 *Tim.* i. 17, "the King eternal" should be "the King of ages;" in vi. 17, "charge them that are rich in this world" should be "in this age." 2 *Pet.* ii. 17, "the mist of darkness is reserved for ever" should be "for the age," for a period finite but indefinite. A striking phrase closes this Epistle, ch. iii. 18, obscured in our translation— which renders "to Him be glory both now and for ever," instead of, as the original requires, "unto the day of (the) age," see *v.* 8, which explains the reference. I might easily go on, but enough has been said to shew that Scripture designs teach us the "doctrine of the ages." In these repeated instances there must be some definite purpose in the use of these peculiar terms; and we must deeply regret the unfairness and inconsistency which in the case of *aion* mars and renders unfair our versions. Thus it would be interesting to ask on what principle our Revisers have in one brief epistle employed FIVE different words (or phrases) to translate this one word, *aion*, *e.g.*, *Eph.* i. 21; ii. 2, 7; iii. 11, 21, *e.g.*, "world," "course," "age," "eternal," "for ever." Such are the devious ways of our teachers, and our translators.

Let me state briefly the doctrine of "the ages." "It will, I think, be found, that the adjective—*æonian*—whether applied to 'life,' 'punishment,' 'covenant,' 'times,' or even God Himself, is always connected with remedial labour, and with the idea of ages or periods, in which God is working to meet and correct some awful fall."—JUKES. There is present in the word in fact a certain spiritual force, and a reference to "the ages" in which a redeeming process is going on. It is the more needful to insist on this, because in our recoil from the Roman Catholic teaching about Purgatory, etc., we have gone too far; we have been trained to limit all God's possible dealings with us, to the narrow span of our earthly existence. But this is to shut our eyes to the truer and higher teaching of the Gospel. What does God mean by the repeated reference to these "ages," when He speaks in the New Testament of His redeeming plan? On the popular view these passages go for nothing. Is this fair or reasonable? But by accepting what they plainly teach, we are enabled to harmonize God's threatenings with His clearly expressed purpose to save all men finally. Indeed, in these "ages" is indicated the true scope of redemption, as a vast plan, extending over many periods or ages, of which our present life forms but one, and it may be, a very brief part. Through these "ages" it is clearly taught that Christ's work is to go on, for "Christ *is the same* to-day, and yesterday, and unto 'the ages,'" *Heb*. xiii. 8; and He assures us that He is alive "unto the ages," and has the "keys of death and of hades," *Rev*. i. 18, words significant in this connection. This then, we, taught by Scripture, believe to be the " purpose of the ages," *Eph*. iii. 11. Nay, we are permitted in Holy Scripture a momentary glance beyond that limit— in these glorious words:—"Then," at the expiry it would seem of these ages, " cometh the *End*, " when every enemy vanquished and every wanderer found, " Christ shall have delivered up the kingdom unto God, and God shall be All in All."—1 *Cor*. xv. 28.

"HE SHALL BURN UP THE CHAFF WITH UNQUENCHABLE FIRE."
*S. Matt*. iii. 12, *Luke* iii. 17.

(*a*) Any good lexicon will shew us how little the term translated "unquenchable" really conveys that idea. HOMER often applies it to "glory," "laughter," "shouting," to the brief fire that consumed the Grecian fleet. EUSEBIUS twice says that martyrs were consumed in "unquenchable" fire. *Church Hist.* vi. 41. CYRIL calls the fire, that consumed the burnt offering, unquenchable.—*De ador. lib.* x. It is terrible to think of the agony caused to loving hearts by misleading translations; perhaps most of all by that disgraceful rendering that "never shall be quenched."—*S. Mark* ix. 43-5 (now removed *after* it has worked such evil.) (*b*) Further, if the context be examined, it points to a *present*, and impending judgment, and not a future punishment. (*c*) The whole figure implies not the endless torture of the wicked in a future life, but the destruction by Christ's fiery baptism, already working, of that chaff which surrounds every grain. Nor can any figure express more completely than does burning *chaff*, the idea of evanescence.

And here I earnestly beg my readers to pause and seriously consider, not traditional prejudices, but plain facts. The usage of Scripture shews decisively, that to press words like "unquenchable,"&c., to a narrow literal meaning makes perfect nonsense. Take some typical instances. A fire is kindled against Israel which is to burn for ever—*Jer.* xvii. 4, and yet *all* Israel is to be saved—*Rom.* xi. 26, so is "the whole house of Israel."—*Ez.* xxxix. 25. And again, Israel's hurt is "incurable;" her pain is "incurable"—*Jer.* xxx. 12, 15, but in a moment it is added, "I will heal thee" of the (incurable) wound, v. 17. So, too, HOSEA more than once declares the rejection of Israel by God, and that no more mercy remains for her: and yet in the same breath asserts her final pardon and reconciliation—*Hos.* i. 6-9-10; ii. 4, 10, 14, 15, 19, 23; ix. 15; xiii. 14; xiv. 4; passages well worth our pondering over. In AMOS the same striking teaching occurs. Israel, it is said, shall *no more rise*, ch. v. 2.

Yet God will raise her up.—ch. ix. 11. All fair readers can see the extreme significance of all this; and how very far the principle of interpretation, so plainly involved, really goes. Again, though, as we have seen, an express promise of the restoration of all Israel is given, and repeated in the New Testament—*Rom.* xi. 26, yet an "unquenchable" fire is to burn them up—*Jer.* vii. 20; "everlasting" reproach and "perpetual" shame is to come on them—*Jer.* xxiii. 40; "perpetual" hissing—*Jer.* xviii. 16; and "perpetual" desolations—*Jer.* xxv. 9; "perpetual" backsliding—*Jer.* viii. 5. Surely some righteous indignation is called for against those who construct a sentence of endless damnation against countless millions of God's children (very largely) on the strength of phrases like the above, whose meaning is so completely misapprehended. Let us examine further. Not alone is the sin of Israel "incurable," but so is the wound of Samaria—*Mic.* i. 9. And yet this "incurable" wound is to be cured, for the captivity of Samaria is to be turned again.—*Ezek.* xvi. 53. Nor is this all. Sodom and Gomorrha suffer the vengeance of "eternal fire"—*Jude*, and are to be a "perpetual" desolation—*Zeph.* ii. 9, and yet the "perpetual" desolation is to end in restoration—*Ez.* xvi. 53; and this temporary meaning is constantly that of "perpetual" in Scripture: *e.g.*, *Lev.* iii. 17, xxiv. 9, xxv. 34; *Jer.* xxxiii. 40. So, too, Ammon is to be a "perpetual" desolation—*Zeph.* ii. 9; is to fall and rise no more—*Jer.* xxv. 21, 27; and yet it is to be restored—*Jer.* xlix. 6. And so Elam is to fall and rise no more—*Jer.* xxv. 27, yet in the latter days it is to be restored, ch. xlix. 39. The same is true of Egypt: compare *Jer.* xxv. 19, 27, with *Ezek.* xxix. 13, &c. And Moab is to be destroyed, and yet restored.—*Jer.* xlviii. 4, 47.

Now why is all this? Why in the Prophets do threats

most awful, and hopes most radiant, jostle one against another? Why do Mercy and Terror, Despair and Joy, alternate, as the portion of the *same* persons? Why this seeming chaos? Not because God has conflicting purposes, but precisely because He has no conflicting purposes: threats and hopes are blended because threats and hopes serve the same end. Nay, were the threats of Scripture still more awful than any recorded, were they as clear as they are so often figurative and obscure; and were we stripped of most (or all) of the *direct* promises of universal salvation, still we might have hope, knowing that "God is Love," and that with God "all things are possible."

"WHOSOEVER SHALL SAY, THOU FOOL, SHALL BE IN DANGER OF HELL-FIRE." *S. Matt.* v. 22.

The popular interpretation reduces these words to an absurdity. "It is incredible that to call a man a fool should be so much a worse crime than to call him Raca, that, whereas for the one offence men are to be brought before a court of justice, for the other they are to be damned to an everlasting torment."—*Salv. Mund.* The hell-fire of this passage is the fire of "*Gehenna.*"

"FEAR HIM WHICH IS ABLE TO DESTROY BOTH SOUL AND BODY IN HELL." *S. Matt.* x. 28.

These words point to God's power rather than to His intention. They say God is able to destroy soul and body; they do not say that God will do so. And if they do point to an intention, those who read what has been said above on "death," "destruction," (ch. vi.) will readily perceive how accordant with the usage of Scripture it is to make destruction and death a path to life; see pp. 9-10, 149, 184-90.

"FOR WHAT IS A MAN PROFITED, IF HE SHALL GAIN THE WHOLE WORLD, AND LOSE HIS OWN SOUL?" (LIFE). *S. Matt.* xvi. 26.

This certainly shews that a man by persisting in sin may

lose his soul, a loss greater than that of the whole world. But (I.) how does this loss teach *endless* torment, or *endless* sin? (To be shut out of God's presence for an age would far overbalance the enjoyment of the whole world for a lifetime.) Or how (II.) does it prove anything against a final restitution, against Christ's seeking and finding the lost soul?

"THE DAMNATION OF HELL."          S. *Matt.* xxiii. 33.

No comment is needed here, but to re-instate the true rendering—"the judgment of *Gehenna.*"

"THAT THY WHOLE BODY SHOULD BE CAST INTO HELL."
S. *Matt.* v. 29-30, and xviii. 8-9.

These passages are so similar that they may be considered together, and may be compared with S. *Mark* ix. 43-50, where a full comment is given. The "hell" of the text is "*Gehenna,*" and in ch. xviii. 8, 9, "hell-fire" is the fire of *Gehenna*, and everlasting fire is æonian fire.

"AND THESE SHALL GO AWAY INTO EVERLASTING PUNISHMENT,
BUT THE RIGHTEOUS INTO LIFE ETERNAL."     S. *Matt.* xxv. 46.

This text, if fairly translated, seems to require an interpretation quite distinct from that of the popular theology, and opposed to it. (*a*) "Everlasting" and "eternal" represent *aionios*, and mean "of or belonging to an age"—æonian. (*b*) If a punishment absolutely endless were intended it seems unaccountable that a word should be used which *habitually* does not mean endless, but the opposite. (*c*) The word translated punishment means *pruning, i.e.*, corrective punishment, and should be so rendered. (*d*) So that which is threatened seems *the opposite* of our popular hell; it is a corrective process, "proper to the age"—or "ages." (*e*) And of this beneficent purpose there is a hint, often unnoticed, in the term applied to those on the left hand, it is properly "kids" or "kidlings," a diminutive, implying a certain affection. And so for the paschal offering a kid was eligible (*Ex.* xi. 5) equally with a lamb; and in the Catacombs the Good Shepherd is at times depicted as bearing home on His shoulders A KID, not a lamb, *i.e.*, a GOAT, not a sheep. (*f*) Nor must we forget that, in *Rev.* xx. 11, the throne of judgment is WHITE—the sign of peace and amity. But it is said that the same word is applied to the happiness of the saved and to the punishment of the lost; and that, if it does not mean endless in the latter case, the bliss of the redeemed is rendered uncertain. I reply (I.) even were it so, we are not at liberty to mistranslate, but (II.) in fact it is certainly not so. True, the text does assign an æonian penalty and an æonian reward, but this *leaves perfectly open* the whole question of the precise duration of either.\* For the term æonian is quite indefinite, it does not touch the question of the limit of time; it simply teaches that both reward and penalty go on to a future age or ages. The question what will happen *after* this age or ages is not raised in this passage. (*g*) I have in these comments made two assumptions both very doubtful, and both favourable to the traditional creed. (I.) I have assumed the reference of *aionios* to time, which is not capable of proof; for with perfect fairness it may have here that spiritual, ethical meaning it unquestionably at times has in the New Testament; and the meaning then would be, that just and unjust pass into æonian, *i.e.*, spiritual states of punishment and bliss respectively. (II.) I have

---

\* It must be noted that the endlessness of the happiness of the Redeemed depends, not on any meaning we assign to *aionios*, but on its own intrinsic nature, as resulting from union with Him, Who is endless life; and on texts easily to be found elsewhere, *e.g.*, he that doeth the will of God abideth for ever, 1 *Jno.* ii. 17; Because I live ye shall live also, *S. Jno.* xiv. 19; If a man keep My saying he shall never taste of death.—*S. Jno.* viii. 51, *cf.* v. 35. Compare *Ps.* cii. 28.

assumed the primary reference of this passage to the final Judgment, but that is most improbable; for these words close a *continuous* discourse extending over chapters xxiv-v. (which our division into chapters obscures.) There is no break throughout. And the question of the disciples, in ch. xxiv., is not about the end of the "world," but of the "age." Thus, if we divest ourselves of traditional impressions, and take Scripture itself as our guide, we see that it is not fair to refer to a distant future, that judgment of which Christ Himself says distinctly, (ch. xxiv. 34,) that ALL THE THINGS He is speaking of should be fulfilled before the passing away of the then generation; and which finds a perfectly natural fulfilment in the terrible calamities, consequent on the fall of Jerusalem, and the end of the (Jewish) age (as these events would be described in Eastern metaphor). And indeed our Lord's words, "all the *nations*" v. 32, seem to refer to national judgments, and to indicate, in dramatic form, the principle on which judgment falls on nations; certainly increasing reflection makes this reference seem increasingly probable.

"TO GO INTO HELL, INTO THE UNQUENCHABLE FIRE * * WHERE THEIR WORM DIETH NOT, AND THE FIRE IS NOT QUENCHED. FOR EVERY ONE SHALL BE SALTED WITH FIRE."—*Rev. Vers.*
S. *Mark* ix. 43-50.

(*a*) Note, first, that the revised text *omits* vv. 44 and 46, which lend so much weight to the threats here uttered   (*b*) The whole passage depends on the statement of v. 49—a fact generally overlooked—"*For every one* shall be salted 'with fire.'" These words assign the reason for the preceding clauses, and seem to shew that the true reference in this passage is to some sacrificial or purifying process, which *every one* must undergo; as in 1 *Cor.* iii. 13, "The fire shall try every man's work." If the sacrifice be not made voluntarily, if the eye or the foot be not sacrificed, a sharper sacrifice and a severer penalty will be demanded. (*c*) The word translated hell is Gehenna. (*d*) The phrase, "the fire is not quenched," is quoted from the Old Testament, where it, or a similar phrase, occurs in the Septuagint twelve times, *Lev*. vi. 13; *2 Kings* xxii. 17; *2 Chron.* xxxiv. 25; *Is.* i. 31, xxxiv. 10; *Jer.* vii. 20, xvii. 27; *Ezek.* xx. 47, 48; *Amos* v. 6; *Jer.* xxi. 12. But in *all* these passages the flame is *temporary*. *Is.* lxvi. 24, is the text specially quoted here; and the natural and primary reference is to the worm and to the fire that preyed on the dead bodies of malefactors, cast out into Gehenna. In Eastern metaphor these worms, and this fire are said not to die, and not to be quenched; because the fires were kept always burning to drive away pollution, and the worm was always preying on the corpses and offal. (*e*) In nature both fire and worm purify. (*f*) The (indefensible) translation, "the fire that never shall be quenched," disappears in the Revised Version. The original word is the same occurring in *S. Matt.* iii. 12, and in the note on that text, proved to have been frequently applied to fire, (and to many things,) even of the briefest duration.

"HE THAT SHALL BLASPHEME AGAINST THE HOLY GHOST HATH NEVER FORGIVENESS, BUT IS IN DANGER OF ETERNAL DAMNATION." *S. Mark* iii. 29, *S. Matt.* xii. 32.

On a question involving the interpretation of a phrase, drawn from a language still living in their day, it is most important to note the attitude of most Fathers towards this sin. "The notion," says BINGHAM, "that most of the antients had of the sin against the Holy Ghost, was not that it was absolutely unpardonable, but that men were to be punished for it both in this world and in the next, unless they truly repented of it."—vol. ii. 921. So ATHANASIUS says of this sin, "If they *may obtain pardon*, for there is no sin unpardonable with God to them who truly repent."—*De comm. essent.* So S. CHRYSOSTOM, "We know that this *sin was forgiven to some that repented* of it." \* \* What is then the meaning of it? That it is a sin less capable of forgiveness than all others,—*Hom.* xlii. *in S. Matt.* xii. So VICTOR of Antioch —*Comm. in S. Marc.* iii., S. AMBROSE—*De penit.* ii. 4, &c. And so DIONYSIUS (Syrus), as late as the tenth century, says: "*Many, who did blaspheme against the Holy Ghost, afterwards repented, and obtained pardon,*"—translated from a Syriac MSS. (Dubl. 1762.) Two points are *very noteworthy ;* (I.) that these Fathers did *not* believe any sin to be in itself unpardonable, (II.) that they did *not* believe the phrases *eis ton aiona* or *aionios*, to mean in strictness "never," or "everlasting," as our version renders them. And so nobody will press the similar phrase as to the iniquity of Eli's house not being purged *for ever* —1 *Sam.* iii. 14, to mean that it was literally unpardonable.

I may add that if we retain the authorised text in *S. Mark*, the word rendered "damnation" is merely "judgment." But the true reading is probably *hamartematos*=sin, i.e., is guilty of a sin, whose results last into a future age or ages. The phrase translated "never," is so far from meaning this literally, that it is elsewhere in Scripture followed by "*and beyond*," i.e., and *after*, e.g., *Ex.* xv. 18, *Dan.* xii. 3, &c. In *S. Matt.* the parallel passage is differently worded. "It shall not be forgiven in this world (*i.e., age*) nor in that which is to come." These words imply that there is forgiveness for sin after this life in very many cases—(an awkward fact for the traditional creed,) and therefore repentance *after* death is quite possible. Next, there is no assertion whatever that, *after* this age, and that to come, there may not be forgiveness even for the sin v. the Holy Ghost. A few words may be added. This terrible sin is the sin of the Scribes and Pharisees, *i.e.*, of the hard, narrow religionist, and *not* of the ungodly. The sin itself is very clearly defined, "because they said, He hath an unclean spirit," v. 30. Its essence lies in confounding the works of the Good and Evil Spirits, as, *e.g.*, assigning to God any kind of evil act, p. 37-8. Must it not be a near approximation to this awful sin to assign to God deeds which, like endless torture, our conscience tells us are evil and cruel?

"GOOD WERE IT FOR THAT MAN (JUDAS) IF HE HAD NOT BEEN BORN." *S. Mark* xiv. 21 ; *S. Matt.* xxvi. 24.

Note *carefully* that our Revisers admit that the original

requires a different rendering, viz., "Good were it for Him, if that man had not been born." This obviously alters the meaning completely: it gives an intelligible sense to say that, if there were no JUDAS, it would have been better for the Master, Whom he betrayed. The common rendering *certainly violates* the ordinary rules of Greek syntax. Our opponents must be reminded of this, and also that even if taken in their extremest sense, the words of JUDAS' doom *wholly fail* to prove that he was condemned to endless suffering; for they would be satisfied to the utmost, if JUDAS were annihilated at the Last Day: nay, had he at the moment of betrayal died, "and never suffered one pang more, they would be to the fullest extent true."

But the difficulty, even taking the ordinary rendering, is very great of pressing these words literally. For JUDAS did in some sort repent—*S. Matt.* xxvii. 3. "Four signs of true repentance are present; (I.) his rejection of the wages of iniquity; (II.) his open confession of his guilt; (III.) his public testimony to the innocence of the Man Whom he had betrayed, and (IV.) his profound consciousness that the just wage of such a sin was death."—Cox, *Expos.* i. p. 356. JUDAS, as one of the Twelve, had a special promise of sitting to judge the twelve tribes of Israel. But this was, you will say, *conditional*. Yes, I reply, just so. And may not a threat be as conditional as a promise? And if not, then will any one explain, *why not?* The rich are expressly shut out of the kingdom of heaven. Do our opponents take that literally?

"THE PARABLE OF DIVES." *S. Luke* xvi. 26.

(*a*) DIVES, like JUDAS, is a son of ABRAHAM, who so addresses him, "and *all* Israel shall be saved." (*b*) DIVES was not in hell, but in hades (see Revised Version), *i.e.*, in the intermediate state before the Day of Judgment, for his brethren are alive. (*c*) DIVES is distinctly improved by his chastisement: he has learned to think for others. Can God by His fiery discipline *produce this amendment merely to crush it out in a future state of hopeless pain?* Is this credible? (*a*) It is not said that the gulf shall continue impassable; what is said is, that it is so (was then so). The case is as if a man were imprisoned for a fixed time, and his friends are sternly told "between him and you is a barrier placed which cannot be passed." This would be exactly true, though the barrier were to be removed, when the fixed period of punishment ceased. (*e*) And in any case why may not this gulf be passed by Christ, by Him Who hath the "*keys of death and hell?*" (*f*) Those inclined to doubt what I have just said may be well referred to S. AMBROSE, who, commenting on *Ps.* cxix., says thus: "So then that DIVES in the Gospel, although a sinner, is pressed with penal agonies that he may *escape the sooner*," thus asserting clearly his belief in DIVES' final salvation. And S. JEROME expressly asserts twice over that Christ liberated those souls *who were in this very place*, —*In Zech.* ix. 11; *in Is.* xiv. 7; thus asserting his belief that the great gulf may be crossed. (*g*) Those taking this parable as a literal description of hell and heaven must be reminded of a very serious difficulty which they ignore. The blessed *look on at the torments of the lost.* Is, then, this vision of a ghastly hell and its lost and suffering ones to be really for ever before the eyes of the blessed?—*Rev.* xiv. 10, 11 (to enhance their joy?)

"HE THAT BELIEVETH NOT THE SON SHALL NOT SEE LIFE."
*S. John* iii. 36.

The meaning is clear—the unbeliever, *continuing such*, shall not see life, but if he repent he may obtain peace. If it were not so, all would be lost.

"THE RESURRECTION OF DAMNATION." *S. John* v. 29.

Here it is enough to point to the revised translation, "the resurrection of *judgment*," not even condemnation.

Of the Parables of judgment, let me say that to build awful doctrines on these sacred stories, and their metaphors, is quite unfair. Take perhaps the most stern of all—those in *S. Matt.* xiii., and even in these there is no question of the end of "the world" which is a total mistranslation—it should be "the age" merely; and no hint is given that the "fire" spoken of should go on for ever. Admitting to the fullest the warning they convey, and the stern side of Christ's teaching, yet their true meaning is obscured by adjourning to some remote future the facts asserted; forgetting that the judgment throne is now standing, and that we are now standing before it; and that Christ's "unquenched" fire is now burning; *unquenchable*, thank God, till (as the whole usage of the word in the original imports) it has fully done its work.

And here I add a few notes on certain passages, which escaped notice in former editions. It is said that ESAU "found no place of repentance."—*Heb.* xii. 17. But ESAU, though he lost irrevocably the birthright, was blest. "By faith ISAAC blessed JACOB and ESAU"—*Heb.* xi. 20. S. PAUL speaks of æonian destruction as awaiting sinners.—2 *Thess.* i. 9; and of destruction as their end—*Phil.* iii. 19. I must refer my readers to what has been sufficiently said already on the word "æonian," and on the scriptural use of such terms as "destruction" and "death," pp. 184-90, 258-64.

Some argue from the words, "Behold now is the day of salvation" (2 *Cor.* vi. 2), that salvation is confined to this life only. I might reply in the words of an old Father, "with God *it is always* NOW;" and might ask whether the more reasonable adherents of the traditional creed are prepared in all cases to limit salvation to this present life? But a reference to the original shews here, too, mistranslation and misinterpretation. S. PAUL is quoting *Is.* xlix. 8, which speaks *of Christ* "In a day (not the day) of salvation have I helped thee." It is Christ (*not the sinner*) who is helped, *i.e.*, made strong for the task of saving. In fact S. PAUL is warning the Corinthians not to receive in vain the Gospel, and he supports this plea by a quotation, which reminds them of the grace given to Christ to save in this dispensation. Don't reject, he would urge, an offer accompanied by so much grace. As to a limit of time set, beyond which Christ cannot finally save those who now reject the Gospel, that is not in S. PAUL'S mind here or in ISAIAH'S. I take next *Heb.* vi. 4-6. (*a*) Almost all the Antients explained this of Baptism, *i.e.*, the writer, in their view, simply forbids a repetition of Baptism. Certainly (*b*) few, if any, teachers of to-day would understand this text to deny the power of repentance to any sinner in this life; but why, if so, *so far as this text is concerned*, should the power of repentance be denied after this life? (*c*) The impossibility here spoken of is not *quâ God*, *i.e.*, these words do not bar His grace. (*d*) Thus Christ saves those whose salvation He seems to pronounce impossible, *e.g.*, the rich ZACCHEUS. *Heb.* x. 26-31 presents us with a passage parallel to the above, which asserts that for wilful sin fearful judgment is reserved, and that there is no more sacrifice available. Many Fathers understand this passage merely to teach the impossibility of a second Baptism. The true meaning seems to be that for those continuing in wilful and aggravated sin, only the certain prospect of terrible judgment remains: they need cleansing by fire.—ch. vi. on fire and judgment. The writer is here quoting *Deut.* xxxii., where the divine judgment is viewed rather on its hopeful side, "I kill and *I make alive*, I have wounded and *I heal*, v. 39. I am perfectly aware that this cleansing by fire and judgment will seem strange to some Why? Because a narrow tradition shuts out from their creed a vital doctrine of Scripture. A few words I may add on that saying of our Lord's, "If the salt have lost his savour wherewith shall it be salted?" *S. Luke* xiv. 34; (stated more strongly in *S. Matt.* v. 13; *cf. S. Mark* ix. 50.) It is enough to say though to human power the salt be wholly lost, yet He, who makes the camel to pass through the needle's eye, can assuredly restore the salt; (scientifically speaking, I believe salt never does lose its savour).

We have now considered all the passages of any weight in the New Testament, and supposed to teach the popular creed, except those of the book of *Revelation*. To this let us turn, first protesting against the unfairness of building a definite theory of hell on the imagery of a book of mysterious visions, and full of highly-toned metaphors. Its visions speak the language not of prose but of poetry, the poetry of an Eastern race, far more imaginative and highly wrought than that of the West. To judge these metaphors, as though they spoke the language of scientific theology is worse than unfair, it is even absurd. Take, then, the passages most often quoted to support endless evil and pain, *e.g.*, ch. xiv. 9-11. Terrible as it seems at first sight, it is, I believe, really concerned with the times of NERO—who is the Beast. The worshippers of the Beast who are to be tormented, are his followers; and the reference in the torment is to the terrible earthly calamities actually happening to Rome at that epoch. Who, of whatever school of thought, is there who does not feel a weight rolled away, when he perceives that the true meaning of the worshippers of the Beast being tormented night and day for ever and ever, in *the presence of the Lamb and the holy Angels*—may be fully found in the terrible earthly sufferings which befell Rome, "while the Lamb and the holy Angels are, in human language, represented as cognisant of this punishment?" Even Mr. ELLIOTT, in his *Horæ Apocalypticæ*, explains this passage of merely temporary judgment. I should like our opponents to be frank and to say whether they really believe that the smoke of the torment of the lost goes up *for ever and ever in the sight of the Lamb and of the Holy Angels!* If they do not—as I believe to be the case—will they with equal fairness explain why *on their own principle* they require us elsewhere to take literally similar sayings and similar figures? But—to resume—whether Nero be or be not the Beast, it remains certain that language equally strong is used elsewhere of MERELY TRANSIENT and TEMPORAL judgments. In proof of this, turn to *Isaiah* xxxiv. 9-10, and read the deeply impassioned language in which it describes the temporal calamities of the land of Idumea—its streams are "to be turned into pitch—*its dust into brimstone—its land into burning pitch—it shall not be quenched night nor day—its smoke is to go up for ever.*" Now when we know that these metaphors—sounding so awfully, do yet refer to judgments of a momentary duration, so to speak, we shall the better be able to assign its true meaning to all the figurative and poetical language of this book. Nor do I speak of this book only. The whole Bible is Oriental. Every line breathes the spirit of the East, with its hyperboles and metaphors, and what to us seem utter exaggerations. If such language be taken literally, its whole meaning is lost. When the sacred writers want to describe the dusky redness of a lunar eclipse, they say the moon is "turned into blood." He who perverts Scripture is not the man who reduces this sacred poetry to its true meaning. Nay, that man perverts the Bible who hardens into dogmas the glowing metaphors of Eastern poetry—such conduct LANGE, in his preface to the

Apocalypse calls "a moral scandal." So with Our Lord's words—if I take them literally—I very often pervert their sense. Am I in very deed to *hate* my father and mother because Christ says it is necessary so to do; or to pluck out my right eye literally? Or take a case—well put by Canon FARRAR—Egypt is more than once said, in the Bible, to have been an *iron furnace* to the Jews; and yet their condition there was so far removed from being one of torment that they actually said, "it was well with us there," and positively sighed for its enjoyments. Therefore I maintain that no doctrine of endless pain and evil can be based on Eastern imagery, on metaphors mistranslated very often, and always misinterpreted. Having, then, considered the well-known passage in ch. xiv., I close this chapter by discussing another often quoted passage.

"BUT THE FEARFUL AND UNBELIEVING . . SHALL HAVE THEIR PART IN THE LAKE THAT BURNETH WITH FIRE AND BRIMSTONE; WHICH IS THE SECOND DEATH."  *Revelation* xxi. 8.

(*a*) It will be necessary to consider the entire context of this verse, if we desire to understand its purport. It opens with the vision of the great white throne, ch. xx. 14, and we find that after the judgment of that Great Day, so far from death and hell (Hades) continuing, they are "cast into the lake of fire"—very unlike, nay, contradicting the popular view.

(*b*) Then comes a declaration that God is to dwell with men—not with the saints—but with men as such, and that as a consequence, they shall be *His people, and God shall be with them and be their God.*

(*c*) It is distinctly said, there shall be *no more death, neither sorrow, nor crying, nor any more pain.* Is this not a denial of an endless hell rather than an affirmation of it— nay, an emphatic denial of such a doctrine?

(*d*) Then comes a voice from the throne with a glorious promise, "*Behold I make all things new,*" not some things. Note, too, this promise is remarkably emphasised, it opens with the word "*Behold,*" to draw attention to it: it closes with the command to write it, "for these words are true and faithful." Was there no reason for this? Is there not thus attention drawn to this as the central point of the whole vision, *i.e.*, *all things made new?* But this again is a denial of the popular creed.

(*e*) In close connection with such promises come the highly figurative threats of the lake of fire. It is perhaps possible to argue that this may imply (although I do not think so) the destruction of those cast into it; but it is *wholly impossible to understand it as teaching endless torment* in the face of what has just been promised—(no more crying nor pain, v. 4.) Therefore, I conclude, looking at the repeated promises (see "*c*" and "*d*") of this very passage, which contrast in their *perfect clearness* with the highly figurative language of its threats,* looking at the true meaning of God's judgments and at the whole spirit of Holy Scripture—nay, its express declaration of universal restoration—that what is here taught, is a fire that purifies while it punishes, a fire that is, in God's mysterious way, an agent in making all things new.—On the second death, see ch. vi., p. 188.

We thus see that the Apocalyptic visions lend no support to the dogma of endless torment. That doctrine is not, I

---

*"How little can we build dogmas on such metaphors as the devil being cast with the Beasts (NERO and the Roman world-powers) and the false Prophet—ch. xx. 10-14—into the lake of fire and brimstone * * into which also are to be cast two such abstract entities as 'Death' and 'Hades.' At any rate this lake of fire is on the earth; and immediately *afterwards* we read of that earth being destroyed, and of a *new* heaven and a *new* earth, in which there is to be *no more death or curse.*"—Canon FARRAR.

believe, to be found in a single passage of Scripture if translated accurately and fairly interpreted. And here I would ask those who honestly believe that with this dogma of hell-fire is bound up the sole force able to deter men from sin, to remember that to assert this is to contradict the weight of human experience. For in every age experience has shewn decisively, that it is not the magnitude of the penalty that deters men from sin or crime, it is its reasonableness and the certainty of its infliction, p. 26. On the contrary, few doctrines have done so much to shake the belief in any real punishment of sin hereafter as has that of an endless hell. For, see p. 57, nobody can be found who, *by his acts*, shews that he in fact believes it. Hence, so long as it is taught, the whole subject of future punishment becomes, for the mass of mankind, doubtful and unreal. Thus a tone of secret incredulity is fostered, an incredulity which, beginning at this particular dogma, assuredly does not end there, but affects the whole of revealed religion. It is not merely that those who still teach the popular creed thus furnish the sceptic with the choicest of his weapons, by enlisting the moral forces of our nature on the side of unbelief. They do more than this. They thus, unconsciously I admit, but most effectively, teach men to profess a creed with the lips, to which the spirit and the life render no vital allegiance. By this means the whole Gospel of Jesus Christ is lowered and discredited, for if men see a doctrine of this kind maintained, in words, but in fact denied (because in practice found to be wholly incredible) they will assuredly apply the lesson, so learned, of professed belief and real scepticism, to the whole system of Christian truth.

I have, I trust, not shrunk from the appeal to Scripture; that appeal, I repeat, we court in the interests of the larger hope. But should some doubt still linger, some objections seem to be not wholly answered, then I would remind the wavering that, to ask for mathematical certainty on these points, is to ask for that which they never can obtain. No reasonable person expects mathematical proof of the existence of God. No great theological question exists that is not open to some questionings, more or less plausible, on scriptural grounds. To ask for a demonstration of the larger hope that shall leave no room for any plausible objection is to ask for that, which no reasonable man asks in any similar case.

Before closing, I would dwell on a significant fact which often escapes notice. Even assuming, for argument sake, the accuracy of the interpretation placed by the traditional creed on the passages just discussed, even that wholly fails to prove endless punishment: that might be a reasonable ground for saying, "there are in Scripture two seemingly contradictory sets of passages. I must wait and pray till all becomes clear; and meantime I can formulate no conclusion." But it would furnish no fair ground for saying, "I must expunge from the Bible those passages that teach universal restoration." This is often forgotten, but it is not to be denied. And even this way of putting the case strains many points in favour of the traditional creed. (I.) Because, since all admit God to be Love, and nobody admits that God is cruel, the presumption is wholly in favour of the milder view, turning out the true one. (II.) Because this view is in harmony with the declared will of God to save all men. (III.) Because it is a maxim with theologians, uncontested and uncontestible, that passages of Scripture which teach things unworthy of God are not to be understood literally: on this ground they refuse to believe literally the assertions of Scripture that God hardens the heart, and creates evil.

But, if so, why are we bound to accept literally passages which, on the common interpretation, assign to God acts of terrible cruelty? (IV.) Because the popular view is not only cruel, but is dualistic: while the opposing view rests on this great principle that, good is always, finally, stronger than evil. (V.) Because a promise binds in a sense that a threat does not, for nobody is aggrieved, though a threat remains unfulfilled: take, *e.g.*, the case of Nineveh, where the threat was most precise and distinct. And so I am unable to see, *even on the ground taken by advocates of the traditional creed,* that their conclusions are warranted. And how much less are they warranted, when the interpretations of Scripture on which they rest, are shewn to be untenable?

## CHAPTER X.

### *SUMMARY AND CONCLUSION.*

> "The little Pilgrim listened with an intent face, clasping her hands, and said, 'But it never could be that our Father should be overcome by evil. Is that not known in all the worlds?'"—*The Little Pilgrim.*
>
> "This word is strange and often terrible; but be not afraid, all will come right at last. Rest will conquer Restlessness; Faith will conquer Fear; Order will conquer Disorder; Health will conquer Sickness; Joy will conquer Sorrow; Pleasure will conquer Pain; Life will conquer Death; Right will conquer Wrong. *All will be well at last.*"—*Madame How and Lady Why.*—C. KINGSLEY.

THE question of universalism is usually argued on a basis altogether misleading, *i.e.*, as though the point involved was chiefly, or wholly, man's endless suffering. Odious and repulsive to every moral instinct, as is that dogma, it is not the turning point of this controversy. The vital question is this, that the popular creed by teaching the perpetuity of evil, points to a victorious devil, and to sin as finally triumphant over God. It makes the corrupt, nay, the bestial in our fallen nature to be eternal. It represents what is foulest and most loathsome in man, *i.e.*, the most obstinate sin as being enduring as God Himself. It confers the dignity of immortal life on what is morally abominable. It teaches perpetual Anarchy, and a final Chaos. It enthrones Pandemonium as an eternal fact side by side with Paradise; and, gazing over its fetid and obscene abysses, is not afraid to call this the triumph of Jesus Christ, this the realisation of the promise that God shall be "*All in All.*"

A homely illustration may make my meaning more clear. What should we say of a householder who, prizing purity before all things, and with ample power to gratify his tastes, should sweep into some corner every variety of abomination, there to rot on for ever under his sight? Nor is this all, for it is precisely the least rotten, and offensive, of the mass of moral filth that he removes and cleanses, while permitting the foulest of all (*i.e.*, the most obstinate and the very worst sinners) to rot and putrify for ever. Indeed, according to the current theology, it is exactly because the moral foulness of this mass is so great that it must endure for ever.

I have spoken very plainly, for our opponents do not realise what it is that they have been teaching, and still teach. I have spoken very plainly because of the moral scandal involved in lowering God below the level of humanity; because such teaching justly makes God odious to thousands; because of the manifold and painful evasions of the great moral issues involved, pp. 78-9; because of scepticism justified and increased.

And how instructive is the evident perplexity our opponents feel in reconciling with the triumph of Christ the perpetual duration of that evil, which He expressly came to destroy (1 *John* iii. 8). Thus some (able) men now plead that the resistance of the lost to God will be "passive" only, and their evil "inactive." But passive resistance, if it be not a contradiction in terms, is some form of resistance, and inactive evil is some form of evil, and in both cases Christ's very purpose is defeated. And obviously the worst forms of obstinate sin, for which hell is reserved, are the most active, are essentially active. Therefore, to say that they become inactive is to say that hell exercises a *remedial* influence. And if hell be remedial how near are our opponents to the larger hope? Further, I wish they would frankly tell us how this perpetuity of evil is possible. "Having anchorage in God," says DE QUINCEY, "innumerable entities may possibly be admitted to a participation in the divine *aion*. But what interest in the favor of God can belong to falsehood, to impurity, to malignity? * * Evil would not be evil, if it had that power of self-subsistence which is imparted to it in supposing its æonian life to be co-eternal with that which crowns and glorifies the good."—*Theol. Essays.* And as already noticed, how can a process of degradation be endless?

With all earnestness, I repeat that our choice lies between accepting the victory of Christ or of evil, and *between these alternatives only*. Escape from this dilemma there is none. It avails nothing to diminish, as many now teach, the number of the lost ; or to assert that they will be finally annihilated. All such modifications leave quite *untouched* the central difficulty of the popular creed—the triumph of evil. Sin for ever present with its taint, even in a *single* instance, is sin triumphant. Sin, which God has been unable to remove (and has had no resource but to annihilate the sinner) is sin triumphant and death victorious.

How strange, too, is the delusion, often advocated, viz., that all real objections to the traditional creed are met, if the grosser forms of teaching it are abandoned. This means, I presume, "let us still punish for ever, though all chance of amendment is over. But do not shock the mass of men, do not mention a literal fire : that is to go too far ; retain the agony, but be careful to apply the suffering to the highest part—to the spiritual nature. Rack the spirit with endless woe, and remorse ; hand over to the devil for ever one formed in God's Image, one for whom the Son of

God died; consign man's spirit to endless evil, it lasts only FOR EVER AND EVER! Who can be so *unreasonable* as to murmur?" Men's minds must be deeply drugged by prejudice, and the power of reasoning partly paralysed, when such pleas are advanced; or when they fancy that, by diminishing the area of damnation they elude all objections to endless evil. As though you could solve moral questions by process of arithmetic, or annul the devil's victory by diminishing the number of his victims. So long as one soul for whom Christ died remains in the devil's grip for ever, so long and so far, is the devil victor. Nothing can by a hair's breadth alter that fact.

A further vital point there is; how far Bishop BUTLER designed to teach that "probation" is an adequate description of our moral relationship to God may be uncertain. Yet it is certain that practically his great name is (largely), the authority with those who teach in fact, if not in words, that God is primarily the Judge, or the Moral Governor of His creatures. Against this idea, which is working untold mischief, I earnestly protest. It is the fatal legacy, the *damnosa hereditas*, which the stern and narrowly legal mind of Rome, with a natural bent to cruelty, bequeathed to the Gospel. The God, Who is Love, is thus in practice changed into an Almighty Proconsul, while the Saviour of Men is disguised in the garb of a Roman Governor. Not the mercy-seat, but the seat of judgment is presented to the eye. An inflexible code, and an unbending Judge rule all; on every side is diffused a sense of terror. Love is subordinate, sin becomes the central fact; guilt, not grace, comes first. "Our Father" to all practical purposes, disappears, while the great Taskmaster, or the Moral Governor, or the Accountant-General takes His place. It is not that in so many words the love of God and the divine Fatherhood, are denied, but that they are so often recognised in words only. Shrunken, atrophied, palsied, the doctrine remains, as in some country where the rightful monarch has not been formally dethroned, but has dwindled into a puppet.

Such a system may call itself the Gospel, may point to the support of the greatest names, and be taught in thousands of pulpits (often softened, but the same essentially), yet it is a counterfeit and no true Gospel.

Where has the bright and joyous Christianity vanished which covered the dark recesses of the Catacombs, (p. 105,) with every symbol, that could attest joy and triumph, but gave no place to any dark and painful image, *not even to the Cross?* Why was this? Because to these men the victory of Jesus Christ was a thing really believed in, a fact actually realised, and dominating all else. Because they believed that death, and its sting, was really, truly, universally SWALLOWED UP IN VICTORY. And so they loved to paint Christ radiant with youth and strength, true and absolute Conqueror of death and hell. Perpetual death, moral rottenness for ever festering, what place—such were their thoughts—have such things in a restored creation? Why is the Christ of religious Art now so sad, with anguished features and drooping head—is it because He mourns His approaching defeat? Why have we so very generally banished from our churches the figure of the risen and triumphant Lord—is it because in our heart of hearts we feel in how many cases He fails to triumph? Whither has gone the Vision so noble, so tender, and yet so strong, of the victorious Christ as He descends into Hades, and opening the prison doors brings the disobedient dead back to life?

Yes, "they have taken our Lord away and we know not

where they have laid Him." They have taken "Our Father," too, "the All Father," and we know not where to find Him. For bread they give us a stony creed; judgment without mercy; hell without hope; evil without end; heaven without pity for the lost and the suffering; and a world here, in which to live is truly misery to the thoughtful, as being but the portal and antechamber to endless woe, for so many of their brothers and sisters in Christ, whom they are commanded to love as they love themselves. Catholics (?) indeed we call ourselves, while not one pulpit in a thousand in all England ventures so much as to hint at these glad tidings of the release of the dead from Hades, which Catholic antiquity universally taught, p. 97 Whither, too, has vanished that happier and higher view of death, as a CURE, as the remoulding by the Great Artist of His own Likeness and Image, a view so significant and taught by so many and so famous names? p. 149. By what right have we virtually added to the Antient Creeds the fatal clause, "I believe in an eternity of evil?" p. 147. Why do we never hear the nobler view of the Resurrection as from its very nature a process of restoration? see pp. 122-3, 133, 142-3, 144-5, 178-84. Why has the important fact been steadily ignored, or even denied, of the wide diffusion of universalism in the primitive Church? Why has the Church delighted to accept a cruel and uncatholic Africanism from the Bishop of Hippo, while refusing the nobler and more catholic teaching which the Bishop of Nyssa, p. 121-5, and so many saints freely taught in the Church's greatest age?

I do not mean that there has been a formal acceptance or rejection. I mean that Augustinianism has in fact leavened all Latin christianity, banishing the nobler teachings of true catholicity. Thus, if God is to damn man eternally there is a step certain to be taken (to justify, if possible, such a sentence), viz., the degrading and slandering that nature which man has received from God, and which the Son of God assumed and wears for ever. Thus, too, the Incarnation loses its proper place; the true lesson of Creation is ignored; the fact of the divine Image and Likeness in every man is displaced and forgotten. "Can aught be so *precious* as is the Image of God," asks S. AMBROSE. The very elect are "*lepers covered with dung and mire, ulcers putrified in their father's loins.*"—*Answer to Travers*, § 22. If even HOOKER, the judicious, can so write, how deeply must the fatal leaven have penetrated—indeed its traces are most legible to this day.

To resume, I believe that no doctrine has ever gained so wide a currency, with so little support in Scripture, as has Probation; (and so little support in all the higher Patristic theology). It fact it is not the product of Scripture, it comes from the Philosophers, not from the Prophets, or the Apostles. And any one can notice how it is assumed, and not proved from Scripture, in the books that are current. Doubtless there is an element of probation in education, but, if God is our Father, the fact that dominates all else in our moral relationship to Him, is the education of humanity as His children. Certainly no education can go on without trial, but we are "tried *that we may be educated, and not educated that we may be tried.* \* \* The essential characteristic of a Father's love is that it is *inextinguishable.* \* \* If I am here simply on trial, if I regard God as One Who is keeping a debtor and creditor account with me, I may in word call Him Father, and in word ascribe love to Him, but I cannot really regard Him as Father."—ERSKINE—*The Purpose of God.*

Be it remembered that no reasonable man doubts that God is truly our Governor,* and our Judge. But we deny such a Governor and such a Judge, as the traditional creed depicts; we deny that the Father is ever (practically) lost in the Judge. We are forced to ask, Have these our teachers, learned aright the alphabet of the Gospel? If they had, could they talk as they do? For to say that God is "loving," is in fact to make love an attribute merely, like justice or wrath. God is not loving, for GOD IS LOVE, a distinction which is vital; which affects the whole christian scheme in its essence. Nor is this error all. Our opponents seem not to understand what Love really is; else they could not accuse us of making light of retribution, because we insist that God is Love.

For the very essence of Love is misconceived, when it is confounded with mere good nature; forgetting the awful, inexorable, side of true (divine) love; forgetting, too, that this love is essentially inextinguishable. With a gospel based on errors so cardinal as to substitute for the Father, the almighty Inspector—for His training, the idea of probation merely—with the central fact wrong, what wonder if all the rest is out of gear? Who could expect astronomy to flourish, if men were taught that this earth is the centre, and not the sun? So with the moral universe. If I place Sin at the centre, and not Love—I paralyse every motion, and wholly invert the divine order.

It is a sad fact, that christian teachers should only admit that God is Love, provided no due practical conclusions are drawn from it. It is a sad fact, perhaps the saddest of all

---

* In fact we admit this divine rule far more truly than our opponents. To them God's rule is, in fact, baffled finally and hopelessly by evil, which He never succeeds in extinguishing.

facts to those who try to see fairly, that in so very few, out of the vast number of christian pulpits, is there preached a God, Who is even as good as an average human parent. Those who so preach would themselves loathe the very touch of a human father or mother who should act, as they say God will act towards many (or any, what do numbers matter here?) of His creatures; or as God has in fact acted, when He forced on these unhappy ones the fatal gift of life, and thus in the phrase of the Poet, "cursed them into birth."

How seldom, again, is this question treated as it should be from the *divine standpoint.* Truly we need the profound lesson conveyed by the divine Spirit to an old Prophet, "The battle is *not yours*, BUT GOD'S."—2 *Chron.* xx. 15. This weary, age-long battle with sin is, in its final issue, not ours, *but God's.* It is "the salvation of the Lord," emphatically. —*ib.* v. 17. Now-a-days it is deemed the profoundest theology to forget all this: it is deemed the highest wisdom to hang the final issue of this awful conflict on the sin-stained, frail, ignorant will of a being like man. Instead of a theology they give us an anthropology; instead of a science of God, a science of man. We hear little of God's will, because as it may be conjectured that will points so emphatically to universal salvation.

But the question remains, and will remain till it receives due answer. Is God really Master? or is sin to oust Him from any part of His own house for ever? To reject Calvinism is easy enough, but to reject the divine Sovereignty is to reject holy Scripture, p. 32-3, and may I not add to reject the verdict of reason too?

Again, I entreat my readers to pay no heed to the delusive plea that claims victory for Christ, if He shuts up His enemies in hell, as though the sole victory possible to a divine Being were not the conversion of His enemies; as though the perpetuation of evil in hell were not His defeat. But, in truth, the traditional creed is essentially, if not formally, dualistic. There is a Deity (nominally) supreme, and a rival demi-god, Satan. There are two confronting empires, destined to exactly the same duration. In the middle ages we find actually represented in painting a rival Trinity, a Trinity of Evil.—DIDRON, *Iconog. Chret.* ii. 23. How profound is the revelation thus made of the beliefs ruling the minds of men, still ruling in those who believe that the devil is all but omnipotent, and practically omnipresent.

Let us go to the Bible. Those who have reason to shrink from this appeal are not universalists, but are the advocates of endless sin; of a baffled Saviour; of a victorious devil. It is they who shut their eyes to the teaching of the Bible. It is they who make light of its repeated promises of a restitution of all things. It is they who make Scripture of none effect by their traditions. To the Bible they come drugged by early prejudice; saturated with cruel traditions, to whose horror long familiarity has deadened the mind. And so it is, that many really cannot see the true force of Scripture, when it plainly asserts the restitution of all things. Hence the painful evasions; the halting logic that honestly (for I gladly admit this) but blindly turns the Bible upside down, *i.e.*, teaching that all men drawn to Christ, means half mankind drawn to the devil; all things reconciled through Christ, means the final perdition of half the universe. The notion of the popular creed, *i.e.*, that God is in the Bible detailing the story of His own defeat, how sin has proved too strong for Him, this notion seems wholly unfounded. Assuredly the Bible is not the story of sin, deepening into eternal ruin, of God's Son, worsted in His utmost effort; it is from the opening to the close the story of grace stronger than sin—of life victorious over every form of death—of God triumphing over evil.

Once more I repeat that the larger hope EMPHATICALLY AND FULLY ACCEPTS the doctrine of retribution. Those who picture universalism as some easy-going system, which refuses to face the stern facts of sin and misery and retribution, are hopelessly wrong. *We press on all the impenitent the awful certainty of a wrath to come,* and this with far more chance of acceptance, because taught in a form that does not wound the conscience; because we dare not teach that finite sin shall receive an infinite penalty. Few things have so hindered the spread of the larger hope as the wholly and absolutely groundless notion, that it implies an inadequate sense of sin, and pictures God as a weakly indulgent Being, careless of holiness, provided the happiness of His creatures is secured. In fact it is those who teach the popular creed, and not we, who make light of sin. To teach unending sin in hell, even in a solitary instance, and under any conceivable modification, is to teach the victory of evil. To us this seems at once a libel on God and an untruth—a libel because it imputes to God a final acquiescence in sin; an untruth, because it teaches that His Omnipotence breaks down at the very moment it is most needed, and that His Love and Purity can rest with absolute complacency, while pain and evil riot and rot for ever.

Here we may ask, can any light, however small, be thrown on this awful mystery of sin? For all practical purposes, I reply, there are but two possible views of moral evil. It is endless as God Himself, which is in fact dualism;* or it is

---

*May it not be said a peculiarly evil form of dualism, for in it the Good Spirit freely permits the entrance of evil, which He knows will endure for ever?

temporary, and in God's mysterious plan, permitted only to serve a higher end. Indeed this view of moral evil seems to be substantially that of S. THOMAS AQUINAS; "he makes the elevation of the creature above the original capabilities of his nature, to depend on the introduction of sin."— NEANDER, *Ch. Hist.* viii. 216. Thus it is a stage in the development of the creature, and of this there seems a *hint* conveyed in the story of the first sin. By it man is said to have "BECOME AS ONE OF US," as though the very Fall implied a Rise.* Certainly Scripture asserts that "*God hath shut up all men unto disobedience, in order that He might have mercy upon all?*" Note here the stress boldly laid (I.) on God's agency, and not on man's will. (II). The universality alike of sin and of salvation, both are equally absolute and universal. (III). But sin is permitted *only* as leading up to, as involving salvation. And thus we see not an arrangement by which man starts innocent, free to choose sin or not, but a (virtual) provision for the hereditary transmission of evil; by which innocence *becomes impossible* to all; by which every child of ADAM is, in the divine plan, "*shut up unto (sin) disobedience,*" an arrangement inconceivable on the part of a good and loving Father, except with a settled purpose of mercy to every one. I am not presumptuous enough to fancy that I have a novel solution to offer of this profound mystery, but if the Bible be truly from God, then no solution is possible which refuses (as do almost all interpreters) to treat seriously the following striking passages, on the ground probably that reverence for the Bible is reverence for those parts of the Bible that suit our own views. These passages have been, in fact, completely ostracised.

---

*Does CLEMENT of Alexandria mean this when he speaks of ADAM as " made a man by disobedience."—*Adm. ad gent.*

"I am the Lord; I make peace and CREATE EVIL; I THE LORD DO ALL THESE THINGS."—*Is.* xlv. 7  Note the emphatic repetition, for, true reverence, true honesty, demand a frank recognition of these words. Nor do they stand alone in their general teaching. Take, *e.g.*, the memorable scene when satan appears before God, and receives from Him power over Job, and those passages in which we read of an evil spirit *from the Lord* (1 *Sam.* xvi. 14, xviii. 10 : xix. 9). Again, God is represented as saying to the lying spirit, "Go forth and do so:" and the Lord is said to have "*put a lying spirit*" in the mouth of the prophets (1 *Kings* xxii. 23). So in *Judges* ix. 23, God sends an evil spirit. I advance no theory, but quote Scripture, and protest against explaining it away under the plea of reverence. In addition to all this we have repeated statements that "God hardens" the human heart, "shuts the eyes lest they should see; and the ears lest they should hear."—See *Ex.* iv. 21, vii. 3, ix. 12, x. 1; *Deut.* ii. 30; *Josh.* ix. 20; *Is.* vi. 10, xix. 14, xxix. 10, lxiii. 17; *Jer.* xiii. 13, xx. 7; *Ezek.* xiv. 9, xx. 25; *Am.* iii. 6; *Ps.* cv. 25, &c.  Thus is text heaped upon text, line upon line. It is most strange to find all these brushed away, by the very men who contend for a literal meaning elsewhere? They say, ' It is wrong to press these, *because they are unworthy of God.*" Be it so. But, if so, pray remember that you cannot play fast and loose with a principle. If you brush away a mass of plain texts, because they are unworthy of God, will you explain why I may not brush away texts (quoted to prove endless pain) that are far from plain, crowded with metaphor, ambiguous, and in their cruelty, *as generally interpreted*, unworthy, I will not say of God, but of any decent human being  Observe, that I do not desire to brush them away, but to interpret them rightly ;

yet it is well to shew once more that our opponents do not carry out consistently their own principles, p. 254. Nor is this all. When they brush away texts because unworthy of God, they are again inconsistent, for they thereby affirm the capacity of our moral sense to judge of religious truth and the ways of God, see pp. 14-7, which the traditional creed nearly always in effect, and very often in words, denies.

Nor can we say that in the Old Testament God is represented as doing that which He permits to be done; for the New Testament is emphatic on this point. "Whom He will He HARDENETH."*—*Rom.* ix. 18. "HE HATH SHUT up all men unto unbelief."—*ib.* xi. 32. "GOD GAVE them a spirit of stupor, eyes that they should not see," v. 8. ."*God shall send* them strong delusion, that they should believe a lie."— 2 *Thess.* ii. 11. Such is S. PAUL'S emphatic testimony. S. JOHN, too, echoes and re-affirms (ch. xii. 39-40) ISAIAH'S saying that the Jews COULD NOT believe, BECAUSE *God had blinded their eyes* and *hardened their hearts.* And so our Lord declares that God had "*hid* certain things from the wise,"—*S. Matt.* xi. 25—and that He spoke in parables *in order that* seeing His hearers *might not perceive.*—*S. Mark* iv. 12; *S. Luc.* viii. 10; *cf* 1 *Pet.* ii. 8. The uncompromising, fearless tone of Scripture is remarkable: everywhere it sees the divine hand, and in everything traces a divine Purpose and Will. It seems a false reference for the Bible to explain away all this. Indeed, to a thoughtful mind light comes from calmly facing these hard sayings. And so S. PAUL adds: The law was given *in order* that the "offence might abound."—*Rom.* v. 20 The law "creates transgressions— *ib.* iv. 15; reveals—*ib.* iii. 20—provokes—*ib.* vii. 7-13—

---

*We are not entitled to evade this, because it is sometimes said in Scripture that men harden their own hearts—which is, of course, most true.

multiplies—*ib.* v. 20—sin or transgression."—LIGHTFOOT on *Gal.* iii. 19. This, he adds, is S. PAUL's leading conception of the function of the law.

Here let me sum up briefly and with due reverence (I.) The facts that the law was given "in order that the offence might abound," and that the law was our "tutor" (*Gal.* iii. 24), suggest the *educational* aspect of evil: we seem to understand better the statements of *Gen.* iii. 5, 22. Fresh light falls on the significant words, "GOD HATH SHUT UP all men unto disobedience," and on these, the Creation "was made subject unto vanity," *not willingly*, but by reason of Him who hath subjected the same in hope. (II.) God's sovereignty is everywhere to be traced: the error lies in failing to see that this sovereignty is that of Love. (III.) Again it has been well said that there is no such thing as "pure evil;" "so unrestrained is the inundation of the principle of good into selfishness and sin itself."—EMERSON *on Circles.* "There is a soul of goodness in things evil," says the greatest of Englishmen. (IV.) We have hints in Scripture that by evil permitted *and overcome*, something is gained which, perhaps, could not have been otherwise had, *e.g.*, there is "*more joy* over one repenting sinner, than over ninety-nine just persons who need no repentance." And if there is more joy in heaven, there is more love on earth from the same source, "for to whom little is forgiven the same loveth little." (V.) Sin is very often the result of ignorance; how far this consideration goes I do not decide, but may there not be an element of ignorance* in all sin? (VI.) Nor should we forget that in sinning, if I may say so, the raw

---

*Nor would it be true, in my judgment, to call this ignorance wilful in all cases, so vast is the network of illusions surrounding us.—See 1 *Cor.* ii. 8 (quoted with a little inaccuracy, p. 22). "MOST SINS," says S. GREGORY of Nyssa "are committed from a confusion of judgment as to what is truly good."—*De mort. Or.* ii. p. 1049.

material is very often the same as in the practice of virtue, but turned the wrong way—" there is," says EMERSON, " no moral deformity but is a good passion out of place. I have steadily enforced in these pages the guilt of sin, but it remains true that to sin greatly often demands the same qualities, that rightly used would have been great virtues. (VII.) Whatever the value of the above considerations, the larger hope has nothing to fear from any theory of sin that can be maintained. Take a lenient view of human guilt, and you thereby shut out endless penalty. Take the very sternest view, and the perpetuation of this awful hostility to God becomes inconceivable.

(VIII.) A further consideration remains. As creation is for the Deity to enter into finite relations, and to subject His plans to definite limits, so, perhaps, evil, physical and moral, is in a sense inevitable. And it may be that, by the training and collision, thus involved, a higher type of character is formed than would be otherwise possible, *e.g.*, self sacrifice, self restraint, sympathy, mercy, etc., seem to require a background of evil for their existence; although I believe that certain results of this have not always been thought out by its advocates.* A creation thus advancing to perfection by a certain, if slow, victory over evil, may possibly be a nobler thing than a creation so safe-guarded as to have never fallen. In S. BERNARD's words, " ordinatissimum est minus interdum ordinate fieri aliquid."—*Ep.* xxvi., *ad. Eug.* iii. I shall neither affirm, nor deny, these propositions. But morality and reason require one thing, viz., that creation shall be in fact so advancing; that the victory over evil

---

*Thus, if so, what of heaven? Must evil be present there to elicit virtue? Again, if the highest type of character be the result of conflict with evil, must the Seraphim and Cherubim, &c., have known evil? and so on up to the very throne of God.

shall be a victory indeed, and not a compromise—*i.e.*, they require not partialism *in any form*,* but universalism. Evil in process of extinction, nay, in the divine plan already extinguished—is tolerable. Evil permitted for a time, in order that it may be more completely vanquished, and men thereby trained—that we can understand. But when evil, moral or physical, becomes perpetual; when it ceases to be a means and becomes an end; when it is no merely passing stain, but is wrought into the very tissue of the universe—enduring as God Himself; when God is taught as freely and deliberately permitting the entrance of evil, destined, as He knows, to be an eternal horror in His creation; then we are compelled to refuse assent, compelled by our very reverence for God, by the supreme voice within, which if God anywhere speaks with man, is indeed His voice.

And this prepares us for a very interesting question, viz., whether the evil effects of long continued wilful sin ever wholly pass away. It may be replied, perhaps never in some cases. Some men, if I may for the moment so apply our Lord's striking words, may, in some sense, enter into life halt and maimed. Obstinate persistency in sin may leave on the spirit a wound whose evil effects are permanent. There may be, for I will not attempt to decide, a permanent weakness, though the disease of sin be cured. Two results of this deserve notice. (I.) It furnishes us with a fresh answer to the plausible taunt cast at the larger hope as leading the careless to say, "if this be true I will have my fling, for all will come 'right at last.'" On any view, your fling I reply, will bring on you "the wrath to come"—a retribution terrible†

---

*For annihilation is no victory: it is death triumphant over life.

†An evil result of the traditional creed has been that it, by exaggerated threats, deadens men to any true sense of future penalty. Men grown familiar with endless punishment practically think very

in proportion to the wilfulness of your sin. But, further, your fling *may* involve you in a penalty strictly everlasting. You may, though pardoned, for ever suffer from the numbness and spiritual weakness which your sin leaves behind. (II.) May not this furnish a meeting place for reasonable men on both sides? For final and universal restoration is not opposed to perpetual penalty in a certain sense; because the wilful sinner, though saved, may yet suffer a perpetual loss, *a pœna damni* loss of the highest spiritual blessedness hereafter.

Further, every form of partial salvation is rooted in selfishness. This selfishness is largely unconscious, but not the less real. Most people will have noticed a shocking unwillingness, on the part of the so-called religious world, even to entertain the idea of universalism. The unspoken feeling is often this—"If hell is gone, perhaps my heaven is gone too." And then comes the deduction—What, if so, is to become of ME? We have thus a heaven actually, in some true sense, built on hell; buttressed on endless misery and sin. And this is received as the true Gospel of Jesus Christ. A degrading selfishness is popularised, nay, is sanctified; religion is tainted. Salvation becomes a sort of stampede for life, an universal *sauve qui peut*, a chase, in which the Powers of evil are always catching the hindmost. And most strange of all, this grotesque and tragic scene is gravely asserted to be the victory of Jesus Christ. I do not know whether all this is more strange, or more shocking. For what can be more shocking than that any of the Blessed should be for a moment happy in a heaven literally built

---

lightly of any less penalty, however awful. Thus a critic of this book maintains that the "tragic" element in religion is lost except we retain endless penalty! Is, then 10,000 years (or 100,000) of pain and banishment from God a *comic* thing, and not tragic?

over the anguish and blasphemies of the lost—nay, so long as a solitary mourner sits for ever in hopeless despair? Heaven is likeness to Jesus Christ; and likeness to Jesus Christ is undying sympathy with the lost; is love unquenchable towards His worst enemies. But the heaven which the traditional creed (and every modification of it) offers to us is a thing so hardened, so awful that merely to think of it fills the mind with horror. Deadened sympathies; palsied love; selfishness incarnate; pity for ever withered; such is the heaven too many of the masters of our Israel teach. "It is a mystery," they reply. It is hell, I answer, disguised as heaven. Do they then imagine that we have not wit enough to see that so to answer, where the gravest moral questions are concerned, is a confession that no answer is possible?

"Will ye SPEAK WICKEDLY FOR GOD?" asks the indignant Patriarch. "Woe unto them that call evil good and good evil." Here is the peculiar horror of the traditional creed. In the very Holy of Holies, it places that which revolts and degrades. The God it worships bids us love our enemies, while He consigns to endless perdition His own enemies. Hating sin with an eternal hatred, He provides for it an endless duration, an abiding home. Because it is so very evil, therefore it must go on for ever, for this is the meaning of saying that for the very worst sinners there is after death no hope. Their guilt is so vast, therefore it must endure for ever; it is so very foul, therefore it must defile for ever God's redeemed universe. The Blessed are content to gaze placidly over the abyss of hell, their satisfaction unbroken; their joys undimmed, if not actually heightened, by the torments of the lost (pp. 43-4). And when, finally, the curtain falls on an universe darkened by endless sin, they actually call this the triumph of the Cross; and are content to retire into a heaven of ineffable selfishness, where love is paralysed, and the Spirit of Christ dead; not caring though the wail of the lost for ever rise; the husband grown for ever deaf to the appeal of the wife; the mother unheeding the eternal agony of her child.

DANTE inscribed over the gate of the mediæval hell, "Abandon hope, ye who enter here." Our teachers bid us inscribe over the gate of heaven, words, if possible, more awful, "Abandon love and sympathy: abandon the spirit of Jesus Christ, ye who enter here." They bid us sing—

> "O saints of God, for ever blest,
> In that dear home how sweet your rest."

HOW SWEET YOUR REST, O wives whose husbands for ever burn; O mothers, how sweet your rest, while your children for ever agonise. IN THAT DEAR HOME HOW SWEET YOUR REST!

"You are shocked at reading that the Blessed rejoice over the agonies of hell," pp. 43-4. But have you any reason, nay, any shadow of reason, to be shocked, on your principles? Are you afraid to face the inevitable result of your teaching? MUST not the Blessed acquiesce in, nay be PLEASED with the divine judgments whatever they be? Pray consider this. These judgments, whether healing and finite as we think, or vindictive and endless as you think, are certainly the outcome of the divine Will. They claim your approval as of right. The Bible tells you "The righteous shall REJOICE *when he seeth the vengeance.*"—*Ps.* lviii. 9. Can you escape the conclusion that the shocking passages, pp. 43-4, are justified substantially if your dogma be true?

To resume,—these horrors are taught when, as now, Agnosticism is so threatening; when Science looks on the Gospel with hardly disguised scorn. And too often, an ignorant, if well meaning, clergy are content to cry, "Have faith;" as though God were not the author of reason; as though loyalty to conscience were not the supreme duty of every rational being; and a recognition of its supremacy the very condition by which alone any religion is possible. I am content at the bidding of faith to accept a mystery which transcends my reason; but to prostitute conscience, to dethrone the moral sense, is treason to God; it is "*propter vitam vivendi perdere causam.*"

I do not mean wilful untruth, but I do mean that virtual falsehood stains almost the whole body of our religious literature.* Falsehood is to say one thing, while meaning another. Hence, to assert that the world is saved, while meaning that in fact half the world will be damned; that mankind is rescued, while meaning in fact that many (or few, it matters not which) go to the devil for ever: to do this in a thousand forms, in hymns, in sermons, tracts, treatises, is falsehood; and with such untruth our religious literature is, I repeat, *honey-combed through and through.*

"It is a terrible business to have a falsehood domiciled with truth, and for its possessor, when he is only half convinced or not all convinced of its truth, to take the greatest pains to dress it up like a truth. For the falsehood gets no good from the truth, but the truth gets all maimed by the falsehood. They talk of the love of God, and His mercy, and His pity, and His justice, and His righteousness * * while all the time they are speaking, this hideous companion in their own soul is laughing at all these things. Love of God —what of eternal torture? Righteousness of God—what

---

*"There appears to me in all the English divines a want of believing, or disbelieving, anything because it is true or false. *It is a question which does not seem to occur to them.*"—*Life of* ARNOLD.— *Letter* 152.

U

of eternal evil? Good news, salvation—oh, have done with it all."—STOPFORD BROOKE.

But so long as the popular creed and the Bible are held together, so long must this system of untruth continue. We pray to "our Father," to Whom in the next breath we assign acts towards His own children more cruel than any to which the worst earthly parent would stoop. We thus degrade the Godhead below, FAR BELOW, THE LEVEL OF HUMANITY. What is left for us to worship if the truth be a lie—if love essential be cruelty itself—if God be that, which I dare not write? Nor is this all. Having thus assigned to God acts of infinite cruelty, the popular creed goes on to assure us of His tenderness that *never* wearies—His love that *never* fails. What falsehood, what cruel mockery is this, coming from those who really mean, that this unfailing, eternal Love watches to all eternity, callous and unsympathising, the undying evil, the endless agony of its own children. A merchant who has two contradictory measures is dishonest; but what of the theologian, of whom the same is true, is he less dishonest? It is cruel to torment a cat or a dog for five minutes, but to be callous to all eternity about the endless misery of a wife or a child, is quite right and good. The transient wrongs of a chimney-sweep excite the sincerest pity; but the eternal anguish of the lost human spirit awakes not even a passing gleam of pity in the Blessed. Let a criminal be tortured for an hour by human law, and all the civilised world is roused; but let the same criminal pass to torture without end, and these endless pangs do not disturb for a moment the raptures of the inhabitants of heaven. Vivisection is odious on this earth, but is most just in hell. Is it, then, odious when temporary, and most righteous when endless? *e.g.*, is it most righteous for Eternal Love to vivisect for ever, or at least permit to be vivisected, His own children, in the sight of the Lamb, and the Holy Angels—*Rev* xiv. 10, (for the true meaning of this passage see p. 278-9.)

That Philanthropists (whom we honor) should be unable to bear the sight of the momentary suffering of the outcast here, while they are prepared to accept heaven's joy unmoved by the endless agony of the outcast hereafter, fills the mind with thoughts, for which amazement is too feeble a term.

The apologies offered for the traditional creed are truly worthy of it. Thus many shelter themselves under the phrase, " God will do His best for every man " I can only suppose such an apology meant, not as an argument, but as an ill-timed piece of pleasantry. For what are the admitted facts? An Almighty Being, Who is, on any possible hypothesis, perfectly free to create or not, yet *forces on* myriads of hapless children of His own the fatal gift of existence, knowing that in fact this life of theirs will ripen into endless misery and woe. To call this doing His *best* for them is an abuse of language, could He do worse for them?

Some actually try to defend endless evil by asking, " would the lost be happy if put into heaven." As if the larger hope did not expressly teach the conversion of the lost in the first place.

Another plea for endless evil is made. This I shall state and answer in Mr. Foster's words. " It is usually alleged that there will be an endless continuance of sinning, with probably an endless aggravation, and therefore the punishment must be endless. Is not this like an admission of disproportion between the punishment and the original cause of its infliction? But suppose the case to be so— that is to say, that the punishment is not a retribution *simply* for the guilt of the momentary existence on earth, but a continued punishment of the continued, ever aggravated, guilt in the eternal state: the allegation is of no avail in vindication of the doctrine, because the first consignment to the dreadful state *necessitates a continuance of the criminality*, the doctrine teaching, that it is of the essence, and is an awful aggravation, of the original consignment, that it dooms the condemned to maintain the criminal spirit unchanged for ever. The doom to *sin* as well as to suffer, and, according to the argument, to sin *in order to suffer*, is inflicted as the punishment of the sin committed in the mortal state Virtually, therefore

the eternal punishment is the punishment of the sins of time."—
*Life and Corresp.* vol. i. If, indeed, the sentence on the ungodly
involve a virtual necessity to sin for ever, then the excuse offered is
the deepest accusation possible of the traditional creed: Further,
there is a duplicity in this plea when urged by those who quote texts,
*e.g., S. Matt.* xxv., which state the future punishment to be inflicted
for sins already past.

Few things are more wonderful in this whole question than the reluctance so many feel, to follow out these unhesitating convictions to their *only possible* legitimate conclusion—the rejection of that dogma, which flatly contradicts them. I do not assert, that these convictions are an infallible guide; for indeed of what can it be said that its directions reach us in an infallible form? Can that be said of the Bible itself? Are those who translate it, or who comment on it, infallible? Are those who read it free from error, from prejudice? But no christian, therefore, doubts its divine authority, or fails to see in it a guide practically sufficient, and binding. So in the case of that other, and PRIMARY REVELATION of God to man. We do not claim infallibility for it, yet we do claim that the deliberate verdict of our moral sense represents to us the voice of God speaking for our guidance in daily life, and on which we are absolutely bound to act.

Our opponents will not remember that the moral sense is God's revelation to us; that it is HIS WORD, speaking to us, quite as truly as from the pages of any book. It is pure sophistry to say, "you must yield your ideas to God's revealed will," as though our true moral feelings were not God's revealed will to us.

Let us consider how false it is to say, "We must yield our ideas." Must we? what! our ideas of truth, are they to be yielded? May God say that which we call false, and, if so, does it become truth? But if I must not yield up my idea of Truth, as applied to God, why am I to yield my ideas of Mercy, and Right, and Love? Does God perhaps hate in fact, while professing to love, the righteous? This question is vital. It is bad and terrible to use a cruel plea: it is far worse to use it when you do not, just because you dare not, use it honestly all round. If our human ideas of Right and Wrong are not to be trusted when applied to God, then anything may happen; anything may be right, anything may be wrong; anything may be true, anything may be false. All is Medley, Chaos, Anarchy: hell and heaven may change places. And so, for aught we know, may good and evil—see pp. 11-2 : 15-7. We are in fact Agnostics, for we know nothing really. We may call ourselves anything we please, but (moral) Agnostics we are, and we remain.

This volume has strongly urged the moral degradation due, directly and indirectly, to the doctrine of endless penalty. Here I may state a final instance in an unexpected quarter. It has helped in large measure to promote that immoral casuistry against which at length the human conscience rose in open revolt. This it has effected because that system had its origin in the distinction between mortal and venial sin. Now, as the results of mortal sin were supposed to be so unspeakably awful, if in any way unrepented of, a direct incitement was furnished to narrow, as far as possible, the range of these sins. And thus a perverted ingenuity was set to work in *breaking down* great moral distinctions, and in attenuating systematically the guilt of the graver crimes, in order to stamp them as merely venial offences.—MAINE, *Antient Law*, p. 352.

I have shewn further by abundant evidence, the wide currency, in the early ages, of the broadest universalism, a fact too little known and ignorantly denied. May I again point out that this universalism was essentially based on Scripture, and that it has been re-echoed in later years by the most saintly souls. You may search in vain in all the annals of English religion for a name more saintly than W. LAW, the universalist. Men talk of the "laxity" of universalism. Was it this "laxity" that recommended it to the glowing devotion of LAW, to the sainted MACRINA, (whose death-bed is the most impressive in all primitive annals, p. 121,) to ORIGEN, whose life was one continuous prayer; to a crowd of men like-minded in the early Church? Was the devout ERSKINE of Linlathen drawn by this "laxity" to universalism, or CHARLES GEORGE GORDON, or FLORENCE NIGHTINGALE? Was the holy KEN attracted to a wider hope than that current in his day by this "laxity?" Or was it not that these, like so many of the early saints, had caught more truly the Spirit of Him, the All-Father, Who loving, loves to the end, Who seeks the lost, till He finds them?

Next we have seen (ch. vi.) how close is the connection between Universalism and Creation, Incarnation, Atonement, and Resurrection; and have enquired carefully into the meaning of "Election," "Death," "Judgment," "Fire." I have attempted to shew that the true teaching of Holy Scripture, and of Antiquity, on these points is in absolute harmony with the larger hope, that to insist on one and all is to bring into clearer relief the doctrine of universal salvation.

To attempt to introduce fresh ideas, especially in things religious, into minds saturated with doctrines taught in childhood, and hallowed by so many ties, has been well compared to trying to write on paper already scribbled over. Hence the many compromises, excuses, modifications, now current, on the part of those half convinced that the traditional creed is false. The first shelter that offers is accepted, thus many snatch at Conditional Immortality, not pausing to enquire (even writing volumes without enquiring) whether it so much as fulfils the great primary point of teaching the victory of Jesus Christ, p. 9.

I have steadily sought in these pages, even when necessarily most outspoken, to recognise the perfect sincerity of my opponents; my quarrel, when most earnest, is not with individuals, but with a system. Here I would make a final appeal and ask, if some who read will not try to rise to higher levels, and to see in the larger hope the only view worthy of the All-Father, and of His Justice, which is the handmaid of His Love. Alone this hope explains the wonders of our creation in God's Image; alone it satisfies the majesty of Love and its unquenchable thirst to raise the fallen, and most of all to save finally the most hopeless, the most unrepentant. Alone it really teaches that with God "All things are possible;" alone it sweetens every sorrow, and wipes away every tear. By its light alone are we able to gaze at the very saddest depths of sin, and in its worst discords to hear an undertone of hope. It alone enables us to believe truly in the Eternal Goodness, and its final victory: by it alone do we gain a full and adequate idea of the divine Unity (pp. 209, 245)—One Will, One Love, One Law, One Lord, and "One far-off divine event to which the whole creation moves."

We have carefully considered the all-important question of the teaching of Holy Scripture. We have noted even in the Old Testament, intimations from the very first of a future blessing, designed to embrace all the race of man. These become more distinct as the plan of God is more fully disclosed; and both Psalmists and Prophets unite in their promises of an age yet to come, when the knowledge of the Lord shall cover the earth as the waters cover the sea.

Nor have we forgotten the argument for the larger hope from the tendencies of the Bible, pp. 68, 252, and from the great principles that pervade its teaching, pp. 68, 75, 234-5, 236. I have also tried to shew how completely the traditional creed misapprehends the language and usage of Scripture in its threatenings, pp. 266-8, a subject well worth careful study.

The New Testament received the attention, due to its supreme importance. The passages supposed to teach the popular creed, have been carefully considered, and we have seen reason to conclude that they, one and all, while emphatically warning sinners of the wrath to come, teach nowhere an *endless* punishment.

Lastly, a chapter has been devoted to pointing out how full the New Testament is of passages too often explained away, and yet teaching, or implying, the final salvation of all. So important is this evidence that I here append a brief summary. We have seen how to Christ is assigned a kingdom absolutely without bound or limit; how *all* flesh shall see the salvation He gives. You have read how the Good Shepherd seeks on, till each sheep He has lost is found, and how the Son of Man came to seek and to save, not some of the lost, but simply "that which was lost," or, as it might be rendered, "the destroyed," so little does "destruction" involve final loss. His mission is exactly described as having for its object the salvation of the world, and He is said *to take away* the sin of the whole world. Do these terms represent a partial salvation; are they honestly consistent with it? Again, it is said that *all things* have been given to the Son, and that all that is so given shall come to Him. He is repeatedly described as the Saviour of the world— which yet He does not in fact save on the popular view and as the Light of the world. He is said not to offer, but to *give* life to the world, a totally different thing. He says (no words can be more absolute), speaking of His Cross, that He will draw *all* men unto Himself. He adds, that He came not to judge, but to save the world. Can you, on any fair theory of the meaning of human language, reconcile all this with the horrors of endless evil? If the sin of the *whole world be taken away*, how shall there be a hell for its endless punishment? If *all* things without exception (the original is the widest possible) are given to Christ, and all so given to Him shall come to Him, can you reconcile this with unending misery? pp. 228-9-30. But let us go on: we find language employed by the Evangelists quite as decisive against the popular creed as that just quoted. When, for instance, we read in *S. John* how God's Son was manifested for the very purpose of *destroying the works of the devil*, we are forced to enquire if that is consistent by any possibility with preserving these works in hell for ever? Is there no significance in Christ's telling us that He is "alive unto the ages, and has the *keys* of hell and death?" Or again, what do the promises to make *all* things new, that there shall be no more curse, or pain, mean? If these be not promises of universal restoration, what are they? Lastly, ponder over the vision of the *Apocalypse*, where *every creature* in heaven, on earth, and under the earth (the dead), joins in the song of praise to God; and say if less than an universal salvation can satisfy the plain sense of these words.

To (virtually) evade such words is bad enough; but, having done so, to charge universalists with fearing to appeal to Scripture, is surely not fair. Take next a very large body of fresh passages, teaching the larger hope, from the Epistles of S. PAUL, S. PETER, and that to the *Hebrews*. S. PAUL especially is full of glowing anticipations of the assured triumph of Christ's kingdom over all evil. Thus ABRAHAM is to receive the world, and no less, as His portion, *i.e.*, in the elect, all are to be saved. Whatever sin has done to injure man is to be more than repaired, by the grace of Christ. But is it possible *to undo, in fact, all that sin has done if a single soul\* be left in endless evil?* would not S. PAUL be speaking *untruly* in such a case? Surely a fair answer is due to this enquiry (even though a fair answer seem to lead to universalism). Further, the Apostle says that the *whole creation* shall be delivered into the glorious liberty of God's children. Again, *all* Israel are to be saved (and being the "firstfruits," their salvation involves that of the entire world, pp. 212-3, 238). The Apostle, too, affirms that God's gifts and calling are "without repentance" (irrevocable)—words very significant, for what is the popular creed but an assertion that God's gifts can be set at naught finally? And what S. PAUL asserts is echoed in the Epistle to the *Hebrews*, which assures us of the immutability of God's counsel. Again, if God has shut up *all* in unbelief, it is, S. PAUL says, that He may have mercy upon *all*. Does "*all*" mean "*some*" in the latter clause, and not in the former?

Once more he assures us that if the first ADAM brought death universally, then the last ADAM brings universal life, and that if sin abounds, *much more* shall grace abound. But in saying that the last ADAM has in fact failed in myriads of cases to undo the evil caused by the Fall, you are giving these words a flat contradiction. Then as to Christ's empire,

---

\* "If but one soul were to remain in the power of the devil, death, or hell, to all endless eternity, . . then the devil, death, and hell would have something to boast of against God; . . and thus death would not be entirely swallowed up in victory, but always keep something of his sting, and hell would ever more be able to make a scorn of those who would say, 'O hell, where is thy victory?'"—*The Everlasting Gospel—Paul Siegvolck*, 1753.

we are told that to Him *every* knee shall bow, *i.e.*, "All creation, all things, *whatsoever* and *wheresoever they be*."—(LIGHTFOOT on *Phil.* ii. 10) and *every* tongue confess—the original term means thanksgiving, nay, is *the very term used of our Lord's giving His Father thanks*—*S. Matt.* xi. 25, and that one day—at the End—God shall be *All in All*. It is the Father's good pleasure to sum up all things in Christ; to reconcile all things unto Himself through Christ; are we indeed to believe that anything can be reconciled to God by being consigned to hopeless evil? For it is a virtual, if unconscious, evasion to say that all things are reconciled to God, if, after countless generations have sent their contingents to the devil, some one generation and those succeeding it, shall be fully saved. Further, the Apostle assures us that the living God is the Saviour of *all*, that Jesus Christ has *abolished death*, that the grace of God bringeth salvation to *all* men. Are these statements fairly consistent with a partial salvation?* And why do our opponents never allude to the noble and most inspiring hope, suggested by such a passage as *Rom.* xi. 36? (pp. 239 and 233.)

S. PETER, too, speaks to the same effect. He tells of Christ's preaching the Gospel *to the dead*, who had been disobedient and died so—a story whose significance is the greatest possible, as indicating how behind the veil Christ works on to heal and to save even those who died in sin: and adds, that the Lord is not willing that *any* should perish. Is God's deliberate counsel—such is the original word—to come to nothing? Then in the Epistle to the *Hebrews* we

---

*Further, it is impossible for any thoughtful reader to escape noting how, at times, this Apostle seems on fire, as it were, as he catches sight of a vision of surpassing glory, of a future kingdom to be won by Christ; boundless, limitless, embracing every created thing, whatsoever and wheresover.

have some remarkable testimony, *e.g.*, the assertion that *all things are to be put under Christ*; that His object in dying was to destroy the devil; that once in the end of the age He has appeared to put away, *i.e.*, *abolish sin* by His sacrifice of Himself. Can anyone explain how the abolition of sin can be consistent with maintaining evil in hell for ever? Thus, the traditional creed seems to stand hopelessly opposed to the teaching of Scripture. Does it not almost deny God Himself, because if we are to believe in God at all, there is no room for a *defeated* God? Therefore, either God really wills to save all men in fact, and if so, He will assuredly accomplish this; or He does not so will. The first proposition involves the larger hope, the second is mere Calvinism.\*  I can see no rational alternative.

Such is a brief outline of the teaching of the New Testament, for I have not quoted all its promises of universal salvation. It is no case of building upon Eastern metaphors, of dogma resting upon mistranslations or misconceptions of the original, as in the case of the traditional creed. It is evidence, clear and unambiguous, and repeated. We have, in fact, line upon line, promise upon promise, assertions—reiterated, accumulated—yet amid all their variety closely linked and pointing to this central thought, to the completeness of the triumph of Jesus Christ, to the boundless nature of His saving empire over all; to the assurance of a victory won by His Incarnation, His Death, and His Resurrection over all the powers of evil. "The Father willed through Christ to reconcile the universe once more unto Himself, \* \* and so to restore all things *whatsoever* and *wheresoever they be*."—LIGHTFOOT *on Col.* i. 19, 20.

---

\* And thus, since Calvinism has fallen into universal discredit, there has been a steady movement towards the larger hope on all sides.

This being so, let me next ask, have you, who maintain the traditional creed, ever quietly thought over the terrible slight you unconsciously offer to the whole work of Christ, to His Incarnation and His Passion, by asserting the final loss of countless myriads of our race, or even of any soul for whom He died? He has come, we know, to save the *world*, He, very God of very God, but you proclaim in all your writings, in all your pulpits, that which is, in fact, His defeat. His Apostles announce, in language strong and clear, in words that still throb with life, His victory over death. You announce death's victory over Him, for hell filled to all eternity with its wailing millions is His defeat, nay, His utter defeat. Could you more effectually make light of His Atonement? I read in the Bible that in His death all (actually) died (so vital is the union between Him and all the race of man). Are they, then, to go down to endless evil and woe, those lost ones, *who died with Jesus*—(2 *Cor.* v. 14, *Rev. Ver.*)—these souls of His creating, still wet, so to speak, with His most precious blood, still pursued by His love (for love is unfailing); are these souls to spend an eternity in sin and pain? Is our Lord's Passion to be for these, endless, fruitless, hopeless? Am I to proclaim this as the victory of Jesus Christ, this as the glad tidings of great joy? I do not impugn, I fully recognise, the honesty of my opponents; but it is something more than strange to see thoughtful men teaching that Christ "sees of the travail of His soul and is SATISFIED," while He surveys to all eternity even one immortal spirit for whom He died—one child of His Love in the grip of endless evil, or annihilated.

Permit me further—for I want again to protest against the dishonour done to Scripture by the popular creed—permit me to ask what the meaning is, on the popular view, of the oft-repeated promises of the New Testament assigning to Christ an universal empire? Is IT TRUE, that it is the Father's pleasure that in Christ *all things*, *Eph.* i. 10—the original words are the widest possible—are to be summed up? Is it true that Christ has actually abolished death; nay, that He has been manifested for this very end, that He might destroy *all* the works of the devil? Or is it a mere dream of the Evangelist, when He tells us that God has given to Him all things, and that all things that the Father hath given to Him shall come to Him? But if all this is actually written in Scripture, how can it be truly taught that sin and hell are *endless?* Can sin be everlasting, and yet the sin of the world be truly taken away by the Lamb of God? Can hell for ever prey on the lost, and yet the whole creation be delivered into the glorious liberty of the children of God? Once again, let me say, that a fair answer is due to these questions, and not an answer which is, however honestly meant, in fact an evasion.

Reflect what it is the popular creed is, in fact, teaching—see its inconsistencies—the contradictions of Scripture, to which long usage has deadened its supporters. Christ "holding the keys of hell" and never opening; Christ "making all things new," and yet things and persons innumerable not renewed; the Good Shepherd "seeking till He finds," and yet never finding those precisely who need Him most; "no more pain," and yet pain for evermore; "no more curse," and yet hell echoing for ever with the curses of the lost; "tears wiped from every eye," and yet the lost for ever weeping; every creature which is in "heaven, and on the earth, and under the earth, and such as are on the sea, and all that are in them, saying, 'Blessing and glory and honour to God,'" and yet a number of creatures shut up for ever and ever in misery; "all made alive in Christ," and yet many sunk in hopeless, endless death.

I plead for the acceptance of the larger hope, as taught by so many in primitive days (a fact fully proved); a hope, that it has ever been the purpose of "Our Father" to save all His human children. To believe or to hope for less than this would be, not alone to contradict Scripture, as I have tried to shew, but to mistake its whole scope and purpose. For the Bible is the story of a Restoration, wider, deeper, mightier than the Fall, and therefore bringing to every child of ADAM salvation. It is not, as the popular creed teaches, the self-contradictory story of One Almighty to save, and yet not, in fact, saving those for whom He died. It is the story of infinite Love seeking "till it find;" a Love that never faileth, *never*, though heaven and earth pass away: a Love that is, from its very nature, INEXTINGUISHABLE—being the Love of a divine Father. It is the story of the unchanging purpose of the unchanging Lord God Omnipotent.

Further, by this larger hope, and by it alone, can we accept and harmonise every line and letter of Holy Scripture, its solemn threatenings to the sinner, no less than its repeated promises of life to all. These threatenings I accept implicitly. They are, as we have seen, fully reconciled with the promises of universal salvation the moment we have learned to realize the true meaning of God's judgments and penalties, and have been led by His word to see in "the ages" yet to come His purposes being steadily worked out. Yes, I believe, because the New Testament so teaches, and all reason confirms it, that to this brief life there succeed many ages, and that "through these ages an increasing purpose runs." In these "ages" and during their progress it is that God's threatenings find their complete fulfilment for the ungodly; and the many successive scenes of the drama of Redemption are slowly unfolded, and carried to completion. For God's purpose to save all men once declared must stand firm for ever from His very nature; and to this end it is that His very penalties are inflicted, that in Jesus Christ, one day, all created things may be summed up. And this being so, we who hold the larger hope are prepared fully to believe that there await the sinner in "the ages" yet to come, God's fiery judgments; that æonian disciple protracted till the will of man yield to the will of "our Father," and till, as in the silent prophecy of the familiar words, "that will be done on earth as it is in heaven."

For this I plead, for a HOPE, wide as that which swelled the Saviour's heart, when looking steadily at the Cross He said, "I, if I be lifted up, will draw all men unto Me." I plead for the simple truthfulness of the explicit promise made by all God's holy prophets, "that there shall be a restitution of all things."—*Acts* iii. 21. The issue may be simply stated, *is this promise true* in its fair and natural meaning, or *is it untrue?* The dilemma cannot be avoided —*yes* or *no?*

For my part, in this promise I believe—in the sole true catholicity of the Church of Christ, as destined to embrace all mankind—in the power of His Redemption, as something which no will can resist, to which all things must yield one day in perfect submission, love and harmony. I plead for the acceptance of this central truth as the great Hope of the Gospel, that the victory of Jesus Christ must be final and complete, *i.e.*, that nothing can impair the power of His Cross and Passion to save the entire human race. I believe that He shall see of the travail of His soul, and be satisfied. And I feel assured that less than a world saved, an universe restored, could not satisfy the heart of Jesus Christ, or the love of our Father. I ask all fair and reasonable minds to reject as immoral, and incredible, the picture of a heavenly Parent, Who, being absolutely free and absolute in power and goodness, creates any children of His own, whom He knows to be, in fact, certain to go to endless sin and ruin. Therefore in these pages I have pleaded for the larger hope. Therefore I believe in the vision, glorious, beyond all power of human thought fully to realise, of a " Paradise regained," of an universe from which every stain of sin shall have been swept away, in which every heart shall be full of blessedness, in which "God shall be All and in All."—*Amen.*

THE END.

# ERRATA.

Page 82, line 25, after West insert North Africa excepted; page 89, line 26, for *viii.* read *vii.-8.*; page 91, line 24, after Ps. insert *Tract ii.*; line 25, after ib. insert *i.* Page 92, line 5, instead of *cxl. v.* read *cxlv. 8-9*; page 97, The Gospel of Nicodemus is probably of later date than the 2nd century, and of Gnostic origin; page 107, line 36, omit—*Strom vi.*; page 108, line 25, omit to men; page 109, line 23, for OPSOPOPŒUS read OPSOPŒUS; page 114, line 41, for *39* read *159*; page 115, line 4, the inverted commas should be placed at end of previous line; line 39, after ib. insert 37. Page 123, line 5, after mortality insert literally—stripped of the form which is like the ear of corn; page 129, line 31, omit inverted commas here, and in line 9, page 130; page 140, line 35, for *cxl. 1* read *cxi. 3*; page 154, lines 11 and 14, omit inverted commas; page 160, lines 21-2, omit that of Eustathius, 380, A.D.; line 9, omit from Clement to and. Page 187, lines 25-6, omit from so to *Zeph. ii. 5-7*; page 200, line 10, for *i.* read *Tract ii. ch. xv.*; page 203, line 31, omit inverted commas, insert at beginning of next page; page 222, lines 14-15, omit from in Him to *iii. 8*; line 24, for *ix. 31*, read *xi. 32*; line 28, for will gather read wills to gather; Page 223, line 7, for 17 read 7; line 12, for *ix.* read *xi.*; page 273, line 1, after they insert repent they; page 298, lines 29-30, omit from creates to *ib. iv. 15*; page 320, line 9, for disciple read discipline.

# INDEX.

Africa, North, its School, 128.
Aionios, (and similar words,) do not mean endless, 88-92, 258-65.
Alexandria, its School, 107, 127-8.
Ambrose, S., quoted, 87, 90, 100, 104, 129-132, 172, 183, 203, 273, 275, 291.
Ambrosiaster, quoted, 100, 132-3, 183, 190.
Andrew, of Cæsarea, quoted, 152.
Annihilation, (see Conditional Immortality, Death.)
Anselm, S., quoted, 158.
Antioch, its School, 128, 137, 141, 142, 144, 159.
Apocalypse, of Moses, quoted, 109.
Aquinas, S. Thomas, quoted, 44, 157, 296.
Archelaus, and Manes, Dispute of, quoted, 104.
Arnobius, quoted, 96, 182.
Assemanni, quoted, 137, 152, 154.
Asterius, S., quoted, 102.
Athanasius, S., quoted, 91-99, 113, 272.
Athenagoras, quoted, 108.
Atonement, its bearing on Larger Hope, 14, 70, 176-7, 250, 317.
Augustine, S., view of evil, 104, ignorant of Greek, 82, 129, attests prevalence of universalism, 150.

Barnabas, Epistle of, quoted, 94.
Bar-sudaili, 154.
Basil, S., quoted, 87, 99, 119-21, 190, 199, attests prevalence of universalism, 149.
Basil, of Seleucia (?), quoted, 99.
Bible, see Scripture.
Butler's Analogy, quoted, 35, his influence, 288.
Burnet, Dr. Thomas, quoted, 22, 92.

Cappadocia, its School, 117, 119, 128.
Casaubon, on pious frauds, 85.
Cassian, on pious frauds, 86.
Central Question, The, in this controversy, 21, 285, 287.
Cesarius, of Arles (?), quoted, 101.

Cæsarea, its School, 128.
Christus Patiens, quoted, 100.
Chrysologus, S. Peter, quoted, 103, 146-7.
Chrysostom, S., quoted, 92, 101, 138-141, 273, advocates deceit, 86.
Clement, of Alexandria, quoted, 87, 91, 98, 106-8, 189, 296, absence of terrorism in, 107.
Clemens (Romanus,) quoted, 94, 105.
Clementine, homilies, their teaching, 96.
Common Prayer, Book of, its teaching, 163-5.
Conditional Immortality, discussed, 8-10, 301, (Note) 245, 310-1, taught by a few Fathers, 94-6, 169, 182, (see Death.)
Continuity, Law of, discussed, 21-3.
Corruptions of Christianity, very vile, 78.
Creation, argument from, 18-9, 34-5, 54-5, 172-4, 175, 211, 224, 225, 291.
Creeds, The, their testimony, 147-8, 195 (Note), 207.
Cyril, S., of Alexandria, quoted, 102, 143.

Dallæus, on pious frauds, 85.
Damnation, its true meaning, 256-7.
Danger of teaching Larger Hope discussed, 25-6.
Death, what it is, 184-90, destroys many sources of sin, 22, a cure, not a penalty, 111, 116-7, 130, 132, 133, 140, 145, 149, 189-90, second Death, 188-189, (Gregory of Nyssa) 245.
Defeat of Christ, necessarily involved in Traditional creed, 14, 36, 54, 176, 285, 287, 317, and in Conditional Immortality, 9.
Descent of Christ into hades, universally held in primitive days, 96, illustrated, by quotations, 96-103, argument from, 103, 235, 246, taught in Scripture, 96, 246.

## INDEX—Continued.

Destruction (see Death) is in fact renewal, 109, 112, 114, 120, 126, 129, 136.
Didache, ton Apostolon, quoted, 94, 105.
Didymus, quoted, 99, 125-6, 199.
Diodorus, quoted, 137, alleged condemnation of, 141.
Diognetus, Epistle to, quoted, 105-6.
Dionysius, the Areopagite, 153-4.
Dives, Parable of, 274-5.
Dodwell, on pious frauds, 87.
Domitianus, of Ancyra, quoted, 106, attests early universalism, 151.
Dualism in the traditional creed, (see Unity) 22, 36, 105, 245, 294, 295.

Eastern theology preponderates at first, 82, 127-8.
Edwards, Jonathan, quoted, 44.
Education of Man, lasts beyond the grave, 62-4, 265.
Election, true meaning of, 205-7, 238, 242, 245.
Emerson, on Judgment, 194, on Evil, 299, 300.
Ephrem, S., Syrus, quoted, 99, 117.
Epiphanius, S., quoted, 86, 160.
Erigena, J. S., 153, quoted, 156.
Eternal, not endless, 88-9, 142. 259, (see aionios.)
Eusebius, of Alexandria, quoted, 98.
Eusebius, of Cæsarea, quoted, 90, 98, 99.
Everlasting, (see perpetual and aionios.)
Evil, if permanent, is satan's triumph, 36, 285, 287, 294, 295, (see sin) is transitory, 104, 113, 122-3-4, 126, 130, problem of evil, 295-302.
Expansion, Law of, in Scripture, 234-5.

Facundus, quoted, 151.
Falsehood, pervading religious literature, 67.
Fathers, see Patristic.

Fire, its true meaning, 200-5, Patristic view of, 203-5.
Firstfruits, argument from, in favour of Larger Hope, 207, 212-3 (see Election).
Forgiveness, Christ's Doctrine of, 48-9, 225.
Frauds, Pious, (see Reserve.)
Freewill discussed, 27-34.
Furniss, J. description of hell, 5-6.

Gehenna, its meaning, 255, 257.
Gennadius, quoted, 152, 183.
Gieseler, quoted, 80, 87.
God's character slandered by traditionalists, 18, gifts irrevocable, 238, is End of all Creation, 233, 239, 247, is not loving, but is Love, 77, 191, 249, 292.
Gordon, General, on traditional creed, 17.
Gregory, S., of Nyssa, quoted, 87-91, 104, 121-5, 183, 189, 199, 200, 205, 209, 299.
Gregory, S., of Nazianzus, quoted, 87, 90, 99, 117-9.
Gregory, S., Thaumaturgus, his teaching, 110-11.

Heaven, made to depend on hell, 42, 302, degraded by traditional creed, 43-4, 302-3, 304.
Hell, represents three differing Greek words in New Testament, 255, its popular meaning, 5-7, results of teaching, 3, 25-6, 41, 45.
Heredity, argument from, 74.
Heretics, many, advocate endless punishment, 142.
Hermas, Shepherd of, quoted, 94, 98.
Hierotheus, quoted, 154.
Hilary, S., quoted, 87, 88, 91, 99, 114, 182, 200.
Historical enquiry necessary, 81.
Holmes, O. W., quoted, 45.
Hymns, many teach Larger Hope, 65-6.

Ignatian Epistles, their teaching, 94, 182.

Incarnation, The, contradicts traditional creed, 13-4, 70, 174-6, 177-8, 317.
Irenæus, quoted, 95, 108, 189.
Jerome, S., quoted, 86, 89, 100-1, 125, 132, 133-6, 174, 290, 198, 204, 245, 275, attests prevalence of universalism, 150.
Judas, Case of, 273-4.
Judgment, its true meaning, 190-200, 225, 239-40, 246, Patristic view of, 198-200.
Judging God, 21.
Justice, of God, appealed to by Larger Hope, 2, 311.
Justin, Martyr, quoted, 95.

Keble's teaching, 42, 178.

Latin Christianity, its character, 129, 169, 288, 290-1.
Lecky, on mediæval tortures, 41.
Leo, the Great, 86, 87, 160, 177.
Lightfoot, Bishop, quoted, 12, 209, 243, 244, 299, 315, 316.
Littledale, Dr., quoted, 13, 35.
Lombard, Peter, quoted, 44.
Love, God is, not merely loving, 77, 191, 249, 292, its true nature, 77, 250, 319.

Macarius, Magnes, quoted, 117.
Macrina, S., 119, 121.
Marcellus of Ancyra, quoted, 112, 160.
Martensen, on second death, 188
Maurice, F. D., quoted, 34, 192, 208
Maximus, S., of Turin (?), quoted, 100, 102, 144.
Maximus, of Constantinople, 87, 153, 155.
Methodius, S., quoted, 111-2, 160, 189.
Moral nature, Our, the ultimate foundation of religion, 15, 16, contradicts traditional creed, 11-2, 14-9, 308-9, Christ argues from, 226-7, is a true Revelation, 14, 308.
Morality, its growth, 52-3.
Moral issues, evaded by traditional creed, 78-9.

Munter, on the School of Antioch, 80, 142.

Neander, quoted, 87, 95, 155.
Neo-Platonism, in the Fathers, 115, 131, 133, 153.
Newman, Cardinal, quoted, 127, 174.
Newton, Bishop, on Creation, 34.
Nicodemus, Gospel of, quoted, 97-8.

Œcumenius, quoted, 156-7.
Origen, quoted, 90, 97, 98, 109-10, 200, 203-4, not condemned as an universalist, 159-161, was he ever condemned? 162, writers against, 160, vast influence of, 110.

Pamphilus, S., quoted, 90, 106.
Parables of Judgment, 275-6.
Patristic universalism, at times embraces all fallen spirits, 110, 123, 125, 126, 143, 150, 153-4, 156, 171, very widespread, 80, 127, 148-50, why very important, 83-4, 167-8, alleged inconsistency of, 84, 169, as a rule, unfairly judged, 93, the right standpoint for judging, 83, 170-1, wonderful in such an age, 83-4.
Paulinus, S., quoted, 138.
Pauline, theology, its character, 236.
Perpetual (and similar words), true meaning in Scripture, 266-7.
Petavius, quoted, 118-9.
Periods, three, of early Church history, 82, 158.
Plumptre, Dean, quoted, 123, 126.
Polycarp, S., quoted, 94, 182.
Principles, The great, of Scripture, favour universalism, 68, 75, 234-5.
Probation discussed, 23-4, 288, 291.
Proclus, S., quoted, 87, 103.
Prophets, teach Larger Hope, 215-9.
Psalter, its real teaching, 213-5.

Punishment, its true end, 49-51, three stages of, 50-1, if moderate, most effective, 26, 282, if endless, useless, 49, if endless, unjust, 46-48, if endless, probably impossible, 46-7, 287.

Pusey, Dr., description of hell, 6, inaccuracies of, 88, 124, silence as to Descent into hades, 103.

Reserve, Doctrine of, 85-8, 93-4, in English writers, 92.

Resurrection, stress laid on, by the School of Antioch, 137, 142, 144-5, is restoration, 108, 122-3, 130, 133, 137, 142-3, 144-5, 152, 155, 157, 178-84.

Retribution, enforced by universalism, 3, 19, 27, 77, 249, 257, 295.

Rufinus, quoted, 87, 90, 105, 111, 119, 137-8.

Sacraments, their bearing on universalism, 177-8.

Scepticism, promoted by traditional creed, 2, 17, 36-7, 282.

Scripture, contains two currents of teaching as to future penalty, 251-2, 283-4, has been quoted to support many immoralities, 252-3, appealed to by universalism, 68, 220-4, 294, 311-9, mutilated by traditional creed, 64-5, 221-4, Law of expansion in, 234-5.

Serapion, S , quoted, 112-3.

Sibylline Books, quoted, 90, 109, 190.

Sin, (see Evil,) its guilt not infinite, 47-8 (Note), often flows from ignorance, 22, 299

Slowness of God, argument from, 63-4.

Solidarity of Mankind, 14, 68, 72-4, 174-6.

Sovereignty of God, taught in Scripture, 32-3, 231, 236, 293, 297-8-9.

Spurgeon, C. H., description of hell, 6-7.

Teaching of the Apostles, (see Didache.)

Tertullian, quoted, 87, 97, 128.

Tendencies of the Gospel, argument from, 68.

Testament, The New, its true teaching, 220, 224.

Testimonies of theologians to early universalism, 80, 127, Augustine, Basil, and Jerome, 149-151.

Theodore, of Mopsuestia, quoted, 90, 141-3, 183-4, his alleged heresy, 141-2, 160.

Theodoret, quoted, 91, 95, 102, 144-6, 184.

Theophilus of Alexandria, 160.

Theophilus of Antioch, his teaching, 95, 182.

Theophylact, quoted, 157.

Thomas, S., Acts of, quoted, 98.

Titus of Bostra, quoted, 116-7.

Traditional creed defined, 3-4, propagates scepticism, 2, 17, 36-7, 282, hinders missionary work, 37, argument from its prevalence discussed, 163, 252, is tainted by widespread falsehood, 67, 305-6, is contradicted by popular hymns, 65-6, contradicts the true idea of punishment, 49-51, contradicts God's unity, 207-9, 245,—justice 2,—unchangeableness, 75-6, 227, 248,—slowness, 63,—attitude towards His enemies, 48-9, 225, man's universal instincts, 59, 226-7, man's moral sense, 14-7, 42, 308-9, lowers God below humanity, 35, 39, 293, 306, involves the defeat of Christ, 14, 30, 36, 54, 176, 248, 285, 287-8-9, 293-4, 317, makes His Passion endless, 317, would be a curse to all alike, 55-6, rests on mistranslations and metaphors, 251, 255-7, 258-65, 276, 278-80, really believed by nobody, 56-7, is totally inconsistent, 306-7, if realised would cause madness, 57, involves the loss of those needing Christ most, 40, is an anachronism, 53.

Traditional creed, teaches a lax view of sin, 45, 250, has fostered cruelty, 41, suppresses practically a large part of Scripture, 64-5, 220-4, 258, 294, teaches a cruel God, 53, 303, 306-7, teaches a debased heaven, 43-4, 302-3, 304, fails to account for the promises of Restoration, 235-6, fails to account for the tendencies of the Gospel, 68, makes our Lord's words untrue, 229-30, 250, is unable to carry out its own principles, 254-5, 279, 297-8, blunders as to love, 77, 250, 292, is not warranted even by its own view of Scripture, 283-4, attempted apologies, and modifications of, are unavailing, 4, 5, 7, 18-20, 286, 287, 307-8, banishes "Our Father" practically, 24, 69-70, 288-9, 290, 292, makes men disbelieve retribution, 3, 26, 282, is it possible? 46-7, 79, 287, is unlike primitive christianity, 105, 289-90, slanders human nature, 291, fails to consider the divine standpoint, 293, is dualistic, 22, 36, 105, 294, 295, based on selfishness, 43, 302-3-4, distorts our ideas of penalty, 301 (Note), ineffective practically, 25-6, is unworthy of God, 53, has promoted immoral casuistry, 309, involves rejoicing at hell, 304,

Unchangeableness of God, fatal to traditional creed, 75-6, 248.

Universalism, in harmony with God's slowness, 63-4, appeals to Scripture, 210, 220-4, 294, 311-9, enforces retribution, 3, 19, 27, 77, 249, 257, 295.

Universalism, alone harmonises all Scripture, 319. never condemned by any Council, 162-3, early decay of, explained, 158-9, 170. not opposed to a permanent penalty, 302, is true catholicity, 168, taught in popular hymns, 65-6, existed even in Middle Ages, 157-8, now increasing, 167, 316, reason for adopting as a title, 12, does not mean laxity, 13-4, 310, alleged danger of, 25-6, asserted as our hope, 12, 320, its prevalence in early times, 80, 127, 148-50, 169, Patristic, is based on Scripture, 148, 170, list of authors and others in sympathy with, 165, 167, specially taught where Greek was best known, 82, 148, 168.

Unity of God, argument from, 74, 207-9, 245, 311.

Unpardonable Sin, discussed, 37, 38, 272-3.

Unquenchable, (*asbestos*) its true meaning, 109, 265-6, 272.

Victorinus, M. F., quoted, 87, 99, 115-6.

Victory of Christ, what it is, 222-4, 226, 231, 241-2-3-4, 247, 287, 293-4, 317.

Wesley, John, probably an universalist, 166.

Westcott, Bishop, quoted, 30, 36, 72, 173, 175, 178, 211.

Whittier, on Christ in hades, 104.

Worst, The, claim most sympathy, 40.

Zeno, S., quoted, 87.